1143011396596
54.6206 Reamer, F
eamer, Frederic G.,
n the parole board :

W9-CTI-466

Main

ON THE PAROLE BOARD

FREDERIC G. REAMER

ON THE
PAROLE BOARD

Reflections on Crime, Punishment,
Redemption, and Justice

COLUMBIA UNIVERSITY PRESS
NEW YORK

Columbia University Press
Publishers Since 1893
New York   Chichester, West Sussex
cup.columbia.edu
Copyright © 2017 Columbia University Press
All rights reserved

Library of Congress Cataloging-in-Publication Data

Names: Reamer, Frederic G., 1953– author.
Title: On the parole board : reflections on crime, punishment,
redemption, and justice / Frederic G. Reamer.
Description: New York : Columbia University Press, 2016. |
Includes bibliographical references.
Identifiers: LCCN 2016008167 | ISBN 9780231177320 (cloth : alk. paper) |
ISBN 9780231177337 (pbk. : alk. paper) | ISBN 9780231543323 (e-book)
Subjects: LCSH: Parole. | Punishment. | Retribution. | Justice.
Classification: LCC HV9278 .R394 2016 | DDC 364.6/206—dc23
LC record available at https://lccn.loc.gov/2016008167

Columbia University Press books are printed on permanent
and durable acid-free paper.
Printed in the United States of America

c 10 9 8 7 6 5 4 3 2 1
p 10 9 8 7 6 5 4 3 2 1

Cover design: Jordan Wannemacher
Cover image: © Halfdark / Getty

For Deborah, Emma, and Leah

CONTENTS

PREFACE

I HAVE SPENT much of my life trying to understand crime. My curiosity began when I was six years old. My mother had just died. Soon after, my father began a ritual of escorting me and my nine-year-old brother to the children's section of the Pimlico Branch of the Enoch Pratt Free Library in Baltimore. My brother was becoming quite the bookworm; I was along for the ride.

While my father and brother consulted with a librarian and selected books, I made a habit of surveying book spines on the shelves with no rhyme or reason. I scanned the lower shelves and pulled off books that were within reach of my short arms and whose jackets caught my eye.

I remember the moment vividly, even decades later. During one of our visits I selected a book that had a photo of a prison cell on the jacket. Inside were lots of photos that mesmerized me: inmate reclining on bunk in cell; inmate in the prison yard lifting weights; inmates in handcuffs and leg chains being processed upon admission to the prison to begin serving their sentence; inmates lined up in the food line; the gas chamber.

Week after week, when we visited the library, I headed straight for that book. I sat on the floor cross-legged and stared at the photos. The commentary adjacent to the photos meant nothing to me;

I could barely read. I was transfixed by the images. Why were these men in cages? What did they do that was so bad? Why did they do such bad things? How long do they have to stay there? What's it like to be in prison? My questions were endless, as was my fascination.

To this day I retain both. I served on the Rhode Island Parole Board from 1992 to 2016, nearly a quarter century. I spent years wending my way through the state's prisons, known as High Security, Maximum Security, Medium Security, Minimum Security, Women's, and the Intake Service Center. I have not lost my fascination with the sights and sounds of these astonishingly unnatural, grim, sometimes brutal worlds. I have lost none of my curiosity about why criminals do what they do to land in prison, some for decades, some for life.

During my many years on the Rhode Island Parole Board, I wrestled hard with complicated and daunting questions about the causes of crime, the nature of goodness and evil, the impact of crime on victims, the role of punishment and retribution, the possibilities of redemption and hope, and, especially, justice.

And my work in prisons has affected me in a deeply personal way. This book is not mere intellectual exercise. Beyond the implications of my efforts to sort out the thorny academic and conceptual issues concerning crime and justice, working in prisons has shaped the way I think about my own life. My meetings with inmates and victims have been a mirror for me in so many important ways. Often I try to imagine myself in their shoes. As I sat with sobbing crime victims in anguish as a result of having been assaulted, robbed, scammed, molested, or otherwise violated, I imagined what it must be like to walk through life coping with such horrific trauma. As I sat with inmates in a hearing room a handful of steps away from inmates' cells, I tried to imagine what it must be like to wake up each morning on a rigid schedule of someone else's choosing, share a cell with an inmate who is hostile and threatening, try to block out the pervasive and intrusive sounds of clanging metal doors and strident voices, eat prison food that no one would describe as appealing to the gastronomic senses, cope with the unending monotony of so many prison days, worry about the ever-present risk of assaults and harassment, lie awake at night in my bunk in agony as I think about the slow tick-

tick-tick of the clock moving toward the end of my sentence, cry intensely at the end of a visit with my wife and children as they walk through the opened steel door that leads them back to the prison's main exit, and ruminate obsessively about what the hell has become of my life.

Without fail, in my own nod toward mindfulness, at the end of each parole board hearing day, I walked out the front gate reflecting on the remarkable and glorious fact that I was free. If I chose, I could stop for coffee on the way home or pick up a handful of items at the supermarket. I could stroll with my wife down the bucolic boulevard near our home. I could exercise in the basement of my home in private while listening to National Public Radio. I could open up my refrigerator, grab a piece of fruit, turn on my laptop, and conduct an Internet search for the fascinating history of noble Christians who risked their lives to save Jews during the Holocaust. I could do all this simply because I wanted to. No one would tell me not to or that I need to do something else. My life is my own.

Working in prisons for decades helped me to appreciate freedom—often from moment to moment. What might strike most people as remarkably mundane, routine daily tasks are, for me, compelling reasons to celebrate. On a daily basis I saw how all this could disappear in a flash. One bad moment—driving a car while drunk and slamming into a van filled with kids who are killed on impact, getting into a no-one-saw-this-coming fight and stabbing a fellow bar patron, soliciting a minor for sex, hitting the send button on the computer just once to transfer electronic funds without authorization to cover a large gambling debt—can destroy what would otherwise be a nice life and lead to a five-, ten-, fifteen-year, or life sentence in prison.

This book contains my reflections on these compelling issues, from abstruse puzzles related to crime and justice to the much more personal impact of my work in prisons. I do not claim to have firm and final answers to the enduring questions I raise. In fact, at this stage of my career, I seem to have more questions than answers.

But I know this: Anyone whose job is to decide the fate of prison inmates had better wrestle with these questions, even if we lack certain answers. If we fail to grapple with these relentlessly complex issues, we run the very real risk of becoming arrogant and complacent in the face of decisions that have stunning consequences for both inmates and the public at large.

Few people have the opportunity to see the inside of prisons. Even fewer are charged with the formidable responsibility of deciding whether inmates should be released. In this book I do my best to take you inside this hidden and mysterious world.

Here are my thoughts.

NOTE TO READERS

THIS BOOK includes many examples, including case descriptions, dialogues from parole hearings, police reports, and background reports on inmates. With the exception of the excerpts from the letters of Dave Sempsrott and from newspapers, all are re-creations that use pseudonyms but are based on actual interviews with inmates, victims, and third parties as well as real inmate files and police reports. I have disguised identifying information throughout to protect individuals' privacy, with the exception of information that is a matter of public record or for which I received informed consent to share identifying details.

ON THE PAROLE BOARD

1

GETTING STARTED

*One of the many lessons that one learns in prison is, that things
are what they are and will be what they will be.*

−OSCAR WILDE

J UNE 1983. I walked into the maximum security Missouri State
Penitentiary for the last time, mainly to say good-bye. My senses
were keener than usual, because I knew that when I walked through
the front gate at the end of the day, I would not return. I knew these
final impressions would have to last. I often reflect on how sights and
sounds that are so familiar suddenly take on new, especially intense
meaning when we're about to lose them.

As it turned out, years later my work in that prison with Dave Sempsrott (inmate #34160)—sentenced to serve multiple life sentences for
the gruesome murders he had committed—profoundly influenced
my work in the corrections field and, in particular, my service on the
Rhode Island Parole Board.

My unusual relationship with this multiple murderer has actually
meant much more than that. My relationship with Dave has shaped,
to a great extent, the way I live my life—especially my instincts about
what matters most during this time-limited journey. Dave's circumstances forced me to wrestle with my innermost thoughts and
feelings about criminal behavior, cruelty, culpability, redemption,
and just deserts. I continued to wrestle with these enduring issues,
month in and month out, as I rendered decisions about inmates who
were eligible for parole and release from prison.

The aging paint on the nineteenth-century Missouri State Penitentiary walls seemed especially decrepit as I entered for the last time. The stereophonic din of strident voices and the constant smack of metal against metal were especially harsh.

And the odor. Years later, I still can summon that noxious odor, the pervasive stench made by the bodies of nearly five thousand men who occupied a handful of badly overcrowded buildings on forty-seven acres on the edge of the Missouri River. My wife, Deborah, sometimes joked that I should disrobe at the front door when I returned home from a prison shift. Talk about bringing your work home.

When I passed the threshold into Dave's cell, I felt like I had entered an alternate reality. Here I was, in the six-by-eight-foot cell that served as home for two, and it was not quite fifty square feet—smaller than a standard parking space at the local mall.

Dave's conviction on multiple murders meant he was destined to spend the rest of his life in that prison cell. The two life sentences and the additional fifty-year sentence he received guaranteed that. When I met Dave, he had been in prison for only four of those years. And I think I have troubles?

Dave was sandy-haired, lanky, and, according to the height marker that appears as the backdrop to his prison mug shot, 68 inches tall. He was a chain smoker with stained teeth, in those years a common sight in prisons. Today most prisons prohibit smoking.

Dave sat on the lower bunk of his cramped cell, surprised, I think, to see me standing outside the bars that framed the narrow entrance. He hadn't shown up earlier that day at my farewell banquet thrown by a group of inmates with whom I had worked for nearly two years. I was about to leave my position to move to Rhode Island. I had facilitated weekly sessions for inmates who had been convicted of unusually heinous crimes—murder, aggravated rape, armed robbery, vehicular homicide, and the like. In the group we talked about the inmates' crimes, their efforts to cope with guilt, alienation from family and friends, and the stresses and strains of life in a maximum security penitentiary that had its own interpersonal drama of sexual assaults, drug dealing, and pervasive racial tension. It was intense.

Inmates who attended my group often talked about how the two hours each week provided a temporary escape from the mind-numbing barrage of voices, chaos, and sounds of clashing steel that saturated the prison. For a few precious moments the inmates exercised some modest control over their grim lives.

In an effort to connect with the group, I typically brought some food to share. Given the mundane prison fare, the inmates always appreciated whatever I brought in "from the street." I routinely stopped at the local supermarket to pick up packages of baked goods, cookies (usually the 99-cents-for-a-hundred type), and fruit.

Although the inmates appreciated whatever I brought, I quickly learned that some of what I brought wasn't appreciated by the correctional officer at the control booth at the front gate. In addition to the usual prohibited contraband (drugs, alcohol, weapons), I was not allowed to bring in citrus fruit, gum, or any kind of aerosol can. I learned that citrus doesn't bruise when drugs popular among some inmates are injected into it, thus blocking detection. Gum can be used to jam aged cell locks and to give dining hall dishwashers indigestion. Aerosol cans can be turned into flamethrowers when sprayed in the direction of a BIC lighter that someone is flicking. Truth be known, the correctional officer's inspection of my bags at the control booth was usually so perfunctory that I could have smuggled in just about anything.

I was puzzled that Dave hadn't shown up for my farewell event. But, then, nearly everything about Dave puzzled me. Did he not care that I was leaving my prison position, or did he care so much that he couldn't bear yet another loss in his trauma-filled life?

Dave was extraordinarily hard for me to read. He had faithfully attended our weekly group sessions. No one told him to attend, and he certainly didn't need to impress the Missouri Parole Board; given the multiple life sentences the court had imposed, Dave would never see the board. I could assume only that he attended my group because he got something out of our discussions. But during all those months Dave uttered, at most, three complete sentences. Oh, how I wondered what was going on between his ears. Little did I know how much I would learn about inmates like Dave during the next thirty years.

I quickly glanced around Dave's cell, in part out of nervousness, in part to see if I was disrupting some activity. I was relieved when Dave motioned for me to sit on his small footlocker, the only option available in the cramped space.

"I'm sorry you didn't join us at the banquet," I said. "You missed quite a spread—we had stale bagels with nothing to spread on them, watery orange drink, and some broken oatmeal cookies. How could you resist? Seriously—is everything okay?"

"Yeah," Dave muttered softly.

I knew better than to expect some elaboration. Monosyllables were Dave's trademark. Now what do I say? I thought to myself.

The moment felt like one of those staring contests that nine-year-olds engage in. Who's going to blink first? Fortunately for both of us, Dave's prison-issued, nine-inch, black-and-white television was tuned to the NBC baseball game of the week. The circumstances reminded me of those awkward cocktail party encounters where the participants struggle to find some common ground. Sports. News headlines. The weather. Usually the weather.

"Who's playing?" I asked, staring at the television screen.

"Oakland," Dave said. "I don't know who else."

"Any score?"

"I dunno," Dave replied. "I sort of had it on for some distraction, that's all."

This certainly is taking us far, I thought. Should I mention that this was my last day working at the prison or simply leave it alone? I often talk with my graduate students about how to handle termination sessions with clients, but none of that applied here. This one didn't talk.

The silence and the dead air in that cell block's third-level tier were punctuated by the comfortingly familiar sounds of NBC broadcaster Joe Garagiola's voice as he commented on the baseball game. But again the familiar seemed odd. I instinctively associate the sounds of Major League Baseball telecasts with the friendly confines of my cozy den. Garagiola's soothing voice and the background hum of crowd noise mean it's a sunny summer day. Usually I've just mowed the lawn and am sprawled on the den couch in my official baseball-watching position. It's one of life's lovelier moments.

I could hardly contain my astonishment when I realized that my mind had transported this portion of my world into the harsh, dark cell block of a maximum security penitentiary. I sat on Dave's footlocker trying to take in these incompatible scenes. During seconds that seemed like long minutes, I tried to imagine what it must be like for Dave to watch the outside world on Channel 8 while he was buried in the prison's bowels. Through this electronic window Dave could see fans smiling and laughing in the stands. Eating what they wanted. Dressed however they wished. Leaving for home at will if they became uncomfortable.

He also got to watch the commercials that air while the relief pitcher warms up. Here was a man facing two life sentences, and he was being sold, in turn, a spanking new GM pickup truck, Miller Lite beer, and life insurance. Dave might be thinking he didn't have much use for the truck, but the beer sure would be nice. Yet there is no Miller time in a penitentiary. The life insurance might come in handy, given that Dave had a wife and two children who were likely to survive his death. But of course Dave could not have obtained life insurance in his high-risk setting: the prison had already seen six stabbings that calendar year, and it was only June. Two inmates had died.

I reminded Dave that this would be my last visit. We shook hands, nodded good-bye, and I began walking down the tier in front of the long stretch of cells. A few anonymous faces framed by bars nodded in acknowledgment. At the end of the tier I skipped sure-footed down three flights of narrow stairs. I always hated those stairs. Correctional officers were rarely posted nearby, and I was forever nervous about my unaccompanied treks up and down. I knew that statistically I was probably safer in that cell block than driving my car the thirty-one miles home to Columbia along U.S. 63 from the prison in Missouri's capital, Jefferson City. But I had heard too many stories about incidents on those stairs to be entirely comfortable.

One Tuesday evening my inmate group was meeting as usual in the windowless basement of a building dubbed the All Faiths Chapel that was adjacent to the penitentiary's main yard. I was in a room with eight inmates, none of whom had been sentenced to fewer than twenty-five years. Five, including Dave, had murder convictions, two were serving sentences for rape, and one was a notorious drug dealer with deep ties to organized crime. The group and I were chatting away when the lights in our remote room suddenly went out. Pitch black. For a few agonizingly long moments there was stone silence. We speculated about the power failure and tried to grope our way out of the room toward the darkened stairway that led to the door to the prison yard. I joined the group, trying my best not to display any hint of my inner angst. I began to imagine the headline in the next day's newspaper: "Prison Worker Murdered/Taken Hostage During Penitentiary Power Failure."

The inmates and I found out later that the banks of the nearby Missouri River had overflowed following days of torrential rains in the region. Somehow water had seeped into the prison's power plant and knocked out all electricity in the prison.

We didn't know any of this at the time, of course. For all I knew, I was a pawn in some carefully orchestrated inmate plot to take a hostage and bargain for concessions from prison administrators. I had been meeting with most of the inmates for two years and, for the most part, trusted them. It was the "for the most part" that gave me pause. My sense was that the members of the group respected me and some were genuinely fond of me. I treated them respectfully and earnestly, despite their heinous crimes. I certainly didn't discount or dismiss the seriousness of their crimes; as a social worker I was obligated to treat them professionally and do my best to help them grapple with their misconduct, gain insight, and minimize the likelihood that they would reoffend if they ever left prison. But I also knew from experience that strange, unexpected things happen in prisons, and I was willing to believe my number may have come up in the lottery of unanticipated tragic outcomes.

My heart was beating hard when I heard rapid footsteps rushing toward us as we made our way out of the building to the main yard. To my relief, they belonged to two correctional officers who knew from the prison log that I was in the basement of the building with a group of inmates; they had come to check on my safety and escort me out.

I suppose I had good reason to be fearful, given that just that year inmates had assaulted and severely injured several prison staffers. As we entered and crossed the unlit main yard at twilight, hundreds of other inmates were hooting and hollering as they lingered outside the darkened cell blocks, waiting in the yard for power to be restored and for permission to reenter the buildings. Clearly this was an Event, and as such, everyone's antennae were up. The atmosphere reminded me of the days when I lived on the South Side of Chicago—a walk down certain streets, especially when the sun wasn't out, called for hypervigilance.

The inmates from my group never discussed what they were doing; they simply surrounded me, clearly safeguarding me in case the two correctional officers were outnumbered. I was quite relieved when I made it to the public's side of the front gate. But I felt badly about my momentary lack of faith in the inmates I had come to know in, of all places, the prison's All Faiths Chapel.

IIIIIIIIIIIIIIIIIIIIIIIIIIIIIIIIIIIIIIIIIIIIIIIIIIIIIIIIIIII

My correspondence with Dave had started quite unexpectedly, in January 1983, about six months before my farewell banquet, just before Deborah and I moved to Rhode Island to join the faculty of the Graduate School of Social Work at Rhode Island College in Providence. The month before, just around the holidays, Dave had stopped me in the prison yard one evening as I was about to leave for home. He handed me a brown paper bag and muttered something like, "This is for you for the holidays." To be polite, I opened the bag as we stood in the chilly prison yard, which hummed with inmate activity. I was completely surprised to find that Dave had handcrafted two leather wallets. They were sturdy, western-style wallets, dyed and carefully tooled with my initials.

I was as mystified as I was touched by Dave's thoughtful gesture. True, Dave had attended my group's weekly meetings faithfully for nearly two years. But I had virtually no sense of him. His chronic silence was so ambiguous. I had no way of knowing whether he was shy or passively hostile. Even after all the time we had spent together, we had not engaged in a single conversation. Not one.

As I drove toward Columbia and reflected on Dave's astonishing gesture, it dawned on me that this was Dave's way of reaching out and acknowledging me. For whatever reason, he would not, perhaps could not, reach out with words.

When I arrived home and walked in the front door, Deborah greeted me with her usual and genuinely curious questions about the day's events at the prison. I simply handed her the bag; I watched her take out the wallets and saw her jaw drop. Deborah, a seasoned clinical social worker, is a master at interpreting and understanding meaningful gestures. Her diagnostic acumen often astounds me. All she said was "Wow."

I wrote Dave a rather brief thank-you note. I realized this was my first opportunity to communicate with Dave one on one. After letting him know that I truly appreciated his gift, I told Dave that I had been wondering about him for some time—about his silence, his devotion to our weekly group meetings, his state of mind. I had no idea what his reply would begin to unleash, a steady stream of reflections and insights he would share with me through letters during the next thirty years, until his death in prison at age sixty-five at 8:15 A.M. on July 15, 2013, probably from emphysema (in his last letter he told me he could barely breathe).

> I told you I would be answering your letter in a day or two. Guess I had better do so while I'm not doing anything. I have gotten to the point where it is a big chore just to write a letter anymore. I guess that comes from doing the same thing day in and day out.
>
> I really appreciate your concern about me. Damn, did you ever hear me say so much? Seems like I can express myself better on paper. I would have a helluva time saying this in person.
>
> I am glad you liked my gift. I am happy I was able to give you something to express my appreciation.

To the average reader, this may appear to be an unremarkable, relatively mundane note. To me this was nothing short of amazing, coming from a man who seemed completely devoid of emotion and expressive ability. I had no idea Dave had the ability to construct a coherent sentence, much less convey feeling. What was especially reassuring to me was Dave's insight. He grasped the contrast between his ability to express thoughts on paper and his in-person behavior.

I also found in Dave's brief reply exactly the sort of opening I had hoped for. He seemed to appreciate the chance to open up a bit. He disclosed more than I ever imagined possible: "I have gotten to the point where it is a big chore just to write a letter anymore. I guess that comes from doing the same thing day in and day out." Later in his letter Dave responded directly to my comment about his silence in our group meetings: "You are correct in your observation. I have thoughts I cannot share with anyone, much less the others in our group. I am sure the others are much the same."

I decided to reply to Dave's letter. What a bizarre arrangement, I thought. I see this guy every single week for nearly two years, and the only communication we have is through the mail. During group meetings in the weeks that followed, he never acknowledged our written exchanges. This was certainly one for the textbooks: thera-mail. But all those letters from Dave over thirty years had a profound influence on my approach to the decisions I made as a member of the Rhode Island Parole Board.

|||||||||||||||||||||||||||||||||||||||||||||||||||||||||||||

I never set out to be appointed to the board. It happened. By statute the Rhode Island Parole Board is required to include a law enforcement official; lawyer; psychiatrist, neurologist, or psychologist; and a professional with experience in the field of corrections or social work. My background in corrections and social work fit the bill. Toward the end of 1991 the then-director of the Rhode Island Department of Corrections invited me to his office to discuss the possibility that I might serve on the board. I actually don't know how I came to the attention of the state's governor, who held the authority to appoint parole board members; all I know is that he had sought the director's opinion about appointing me. I passed muster and began serving on the board in January 1992.

Before that I had spent several years working in prisons as a social worker, in a federal prison in Illinois and in the Missouri State Penitentiary; in Rhode Island I worked part time for two years in the state's forensic unit, part of the state psychiatric hospital, with patients who were incompetent to stand trial or had been found not guilty by reason of mental defect. With the benefit of hindsight, I now understand that my relationship with Dave Sempsrott shaped much about the way I think about crime, cruelty, goodness, tragedy, and hope—and I brought all this to my parole board decisions.

For nearly a quarter century on the parole board I did my best to make sound decisions about which inmates should be released from prison and which should not. It's not an exact science by any stretch. In fact, the decisions my parole board colleagues and I made came out of a complicated stew of life's most graphic dramas, filled with intrigue, poignant testimony, indescribable anguish and rage, triumphs, pathos, and lots and lots of hope. Hope held by inmates that we would open our prisons' front gates and let them out. Hope held by victims that we would throw away the proverbial key. Hope held by parole board members that our decisions would have good, not disastrous, outcomes.

No parole board member, anywhere, wants to turn on the nightly news and hear the anchor intone: "Paroled criminal arrested and charged with armed robbery." Yet it has happened to me, just as it happens to parole board members everywhere. The truth is, making parole decisions has much in common with meteorology. Parole boards everywhere examine mounds of shifting, sometimes elusive, data. They use historic patterns to forecast a future that will be shaped by many complex variables. They deal with odds and probability, not certainty. Just as the brightest meteorologists in the world are sometimes caught by surprise when a storm system no one predicted appears suddenly, parole board members can do only their best in light of human beings' notoriously unpredictable behavioral tendencies. No one on this planet, no matter how smart and prescient, can forecast with complete accuracy how convicted felons are going to behave long after their release from prison, whether on parole or at the last possible moment of their sentence.

Given all that uncertainty, the only surefire way to ensure that incarcerated inmates never commit another crime outside prison is to keep all of them locked up—forever. And no sensible person pushes for that public policy. For one thing, its expense would tear every public budget asunder. For another, the concept of universal life sentences for all offenders denies the possibility of yet another form of hope, the hope that people who make horrible mistakes have the capacity to change their life course and redeem themselves.

I continue to hold fast to that hope, even though I know, deep down, that some inmates I voted to parole were all too likely to commit new crimes, some serious. When I walked out of my state's prisons at the end of parole board hearing days, I typically reflected on my decisions, especially the hard ones. I always revisited that hope that I had made good judgments and that the citizens who surrounded me outside those prisons, including my family and close friends, would not be worse off because of my choices.

Before each parole board hearing day I spent hours and hours poring over the records contained in my Rhode Island Department of Corrections laptop. Police records. Prison counselors' reports. Correspondence from inmates, who usually pleaded to be released, and from victims, who usually begged the parole board to deny the inmates' petition for release. Psychological and substance abuse assessments. Summaries of the inmates' rehabilitation and educational programs. Letters from potential employers and inmates' relatives. Court records. Prison disciplinary reports.

On hearing days the board met with every victim who wished to meet with us. We scheduled these meetings in half-hour increments; sometimes we ran over, especially when victims' heart-wrenching testimony simply took longer to relate. Nearly always victims shared their anguish as they relived the domestic violence, home invasion, armed robbery, vicious assault, molestation, rape, theft, arson, or embezzlement. Some victims hobbled into the hearing room because of the severe injuries they had suffered at the hands of the perpetrators. In one case we met with a victim who entered the room using a walker. The inmate, whose blood alcohol level was three times the legal limit the night of the crime, had slammed into the victim's car while driving southbound in the northbound lane on I-95; the victim's passenger was killed in the crash. Victims sometimes lifted their shirts to show board members scars from stabbings.

Some of the victims were victims only indirectly; they met with us to talk about their relative who had been murdered by the inmate. By the end of a typical hearing session, the board had heard victim after victim heave and sob, even years after the crime. We kept an ample supply of tissues on hand; on occasion I grabbed one for myself.

Immediately after our meetings with victims, which we held in an administrative building some distance from the prisons to avoid subjecting already traumatized victims to having to enter the prisons, we relocated to whichever institutions housed the inmates whose parole petitions were before us. Often the immediacy of this sequence—victims' anguished testimony followed only hours later by the inmates' hearings—was breathtaking.

The board's protocol was routine. Correctional officers summoned inmates whose parole board hearings were on the day's calendar. The inmates sat in a closely supervised group outside the hearing room. One by one staffers escorted each inmate into the hearing room. Depending on the prison, male inmates in Rhode Island who were in general population wore khaki uniforms or blue jumpsuits. Female inmates wore green. If a male inmate was wearing orange, we knew he had been disciplined for violating prison rules and had been placed in segregation, where he might spend three or four weeks—but sometimes a shorter stint for lesser infractions—in a stripped-down cell for twenty-three hours each day.[1] In extreme cases, when an inmate has assaulted and severely injured a correctional officer, for example, the term in segregation may run six months or a year.

Once an inmate was brought into the hearing room, the chair of the parole board introduced the board and usually asked the inmate to comment on their crime. The vast majority of inmates admitted their guilt. That surprises many people who are not familiar with prison culture. Over the years many friends of mine looked at me skeptically when I told them it was rare for me to hear an inmate claim to be innocent. Occasionally an inmate would tell me he was guilty of most or all the crimes with which he had been charged over the years but not the one for which he was serving the current sentence. Typically these inmates would say they had agreed to plead guilty to a crime they did not commit to avoid the possibility of a longer sentence had they gone to trial and been convicted. Veteran criminal court defendants know quite well that pleading guilty to a crime and negotiating a sentence with the prosecutor is likely to result in a shorter sentence than a judge would impose if the case goes to trial and the defendant is found guilty. That is, defendants often pay a steep price if they roll the dice and insist on a full trial. The criminal justice system provides incentives to plead guilty and conserve the court system's limited resources.

> I swear I didn't do that armed robbery. I wasn't even around that house. Yeah, I pled guilty, but my lawyer told me that if I went to trial I'd be looking at eight to ten years. I couldn't take that chance, not with my

record. I took the deal when they agreed to drop the charge to breaking and entering and give me two years. I just couldn't take the chance.

DARNELL, SENTENCED TO TWO YEARS FOR BREAKING AND ENTERING

Some inmates are represented at parole hearings by attorneys, at the inmates' expense, but most go it alone. The provision in the Sixth Amendment to the U.S. Constitution guaranteeing criminal defendants a right to legal counsel does not extend to parole board hearings.

After inmates shared their version of the crime, parole board members asked questions. During the hearing each board member had an opportunity to broach any subject germane to an inmate's case and potential parole. Most questions concerned the facts of the case, victim impact, the inmate's insight into the circumstances that led to the crime, the inmate's sense of remorse and restitution plans, participation in prison-based rehabilitation and education programs, criminal record, previous experiences on parole, mental health and substance abuse challenges, family and other community supports, gang affiliations, immigration status, and housing and job plans.

QUESTION: I see here that you robbed the convenience store nearly five years after you were released from prison the last time. One report says you were doing real well for several years before the robbery. What happened? How did things fall apart?

ANSWER: It's true. I was doing great. When I left here the last time, I did what you folks told me to do. I went to the mental health center. I took my meds and kept my appointments. I went to my NA [Narcotics Anonymous] meetings. Things was going good, you know what I'm sayin'? Me and my baby mama got back together. And then it fell apart. My woman left me for another man. I got real depressed and stopped going to meetings. I started to mess up at work and got fired. I just plain gave up and relapsed on heroin. When I couldn't afford it no more, I got desperate and hit [robbed] the convenience store. I messed up is what I did.

FRANK, SENTENCED TO SEVEN YEARS FOR ARMED ROBBERY

QUESTION: I see here that you embezzled about $37,000 from your employer. You'd never been in any kind of trouble before. As far as I can tell, you were leading a rather charmed life: husband, two children, a house, a good job at the bank. Was this gambling related? ANSWER: Yes, that's exactly what happened. I was leading a double life. My family had no idea that I was in such deep trouble. My husband knew I went to the casino a few times a month; he thought I went with my best friend. I lied to him. The truth is that I had become a compulsive gambler and usually went by myself. I even called in sick at work and went to the casino. I kept fooling myself, the way so many problem gamblers do; I somehow convinced myself that it was just a matter of time before my luck would turn around and I'd start winning again. Well, it didn't quite work out that way. When I realized I was in real deep and had lost most of my family's savings, I got desperate. As an assistant bank manager, I was familiar with how deposits are processed. I figured out a way to divert several wealthy customers' funds. I always planned to pay the money back. Obviously that didn't happen. I can't believe I let things spin out of control so badly. I'm so ashamed. I can't believe my husband is sticking with me.

MARTHA, SENTENCED TO FOUR YEARS FOR EMBEZZLEMENT

On a typical day the parole board conducted about twenty-five hearings. Some were relatively short. Stefan was serving a nine-year sentence for home invasion and assault with a deadly weapon. He and his codefendant had broken into the home of someone they thought was a drug dealer. Their plan was to rob the dealer, who was known to keep large amounts of cash on hand. Their plan went awry when they broke into a neighbor's apartment by mistake. The startled homeowner confronted the pair and grabbed a knife to protect himself. According to the police report, Stefan wrestled the knife out of the victim's hand and stabbed him, causing serious wounds to the victim's abdomen and shoulder. By law Stefan was eligible for his first parole board hearing after serving one-third of his sentence, three years.

Two weeks before his scheduled hearing, Stefan assaulted another inmate; they had been members of rival gangs when they were on the street. Ordinarily prison staffers who learn that new inmates have an enemy elsewhere in the prison system place them in different institutions to minimize the likelihood of mayhem; somehow Stefan and his old rival had been housed in the same institution, perhaps because neither disclosed the issue at the time of their incarceration. When the pair encountered each other one morning in the prison dining hall, they exchanged words, which led to a fight. A nearby correctional officer immediately called a "Code Blue," which quickly summoned assistance from colleagues. In prison parlance a Code Blue signals an emergency. Several nearby correctional officers hastened to the dining hall and subdued the inmates. Stefan was so out of control that an officer had to spray him with OC (oleoresin capsicum), commonly known as pepper spray. OC is a chemical compound that irritates the eyes and causes tears, pain, and temporary blindness.

As a result of the fight Stefan was placed in a segregation cell for thirty days. Because he was in a secure segregation unit and confined to his cell for twenty-three hours each day, Stefan could not be escorted to the parole board's hearing room in another section of the prison. The board had to go to him.

We held segregation unit hearings at the end of the hearing day. To reach the segregation unit, the board, escorted by a correctional officer, had to enter what can only be described as a prison within a prison. After we left our usual hearing room in the center of the sprawling prison complex, we had to pass through a solid metal door and walk about forty yards, again accompanied by a corrections officer, through the open-air yard in the middle of the prison complex. Typically, when the weather was decent, hundreds of inmates were milling about, chatting, lifting weights, and playing basketball. When the parole board walked through the prison yard toward the metal door labeled Segregation Unit, hundreds of heads and pairs of eyes turned toward us. The stares were more curious than menacing. Occasionally a familiar inmate came over to greet us and give the peripatetic board a brief update on his parole-related circumstances, usually details about how he has been spending his time since his last parole hearing. Every once in a while we would hear a snide comment. Our small huddle of parole board officials, dressed in civilian clothes and cradling our laptops, certainly stood out in this sea of khaki inmate uniforms.

To meet with Stefan in the segregation unit, we passed through yet another secure electronic door. Stefan was brought handcuffed to the board's hearing room in the segregation unit; he was wearing the orange uniform of a segregation inmate.

His cell was one of several that surrounded a secure, bulletproof control center staffed by correctional officers. Adjacent to the segregation cells is a small outdoor recreation area that contains several cages—with fencing on all four sides and above—that allow inmates some fresh air during the very brief periods they are allowed out of their cells. Inmates can walk around the small cage and exercise if they wish but cannot do much else. The best comparison is an archaic zoo that houses animals in small, bare cages. That's not hyperbole.

The segregation unit was remarkably stark and barren. On the day we met with Stefan, I glanced at the various cell doors and noticed several inmates were staring at me through the small windows. There wasn't much else for them to do, so the board's arrival provided some much-needed distraction, if only for a moment.

The parole board's meeting with Stefan was brief. We reminded him of the board's policy that inmates must have at least six months without disciplinary action in order to be seriously considered for parole. We told him we would schedule a hearing approximately six months from the day he was placed in segregation. Stefan tried to convince us that he did not start the fight in the dining hall and was only defending himself. We explained that we knew it was frustrating to be in this predicament, but the board was not in a position to ignore or overrule the judgment of the prison officials who had concluded that he had instigated the fight. We reminded Stefan that prison staffers had reviewed video footage of the fight, which was standard practice, and he had the right to appeal the disciplinary ruling. Stefan nodded and turned away, waiting to be escorted back to his segregation cell by the correctional officer who lingered in the doorway. Even though Stefan was deeply disappointed, I suspect he appreciated having had this opportunity to be out of his tiny, bare segregation cell for ten minutes.

In contrast to the relatively brief parole board hearings we conducted in the prison's segregation unit, the board often spent considerable time with an inmate to get a progress report and explore the inmate's reflections on the crime, insights, remorse, rehabilitation program participation, disciplinary record, and long-term plans. We did this even when an inmate was not a serious candidate for parole, perhaps because of the length of their sentence, the seriousness of the crime, the inmate's prison disciplinary record, or lack of participation in relevant treatment programs.

The longest parole board hearings tended to be for inmates whose unique circumstances warranted serious consideration. These included inmates who had clearly worked hard to address the issues in their lives, as evidenced by their impressive insight and earnest participation in mental health counseling and treatment programs for substance abuse, domestic violence, or sex offenders. These hearings were the heart and soul of the parole board's work, requiring us to weigh and balance recognition of the inmate's progress with the gravity of the offense and, often, victims' intense opposition to parole.

And then there were the daunting cases of inmates who had been convicted of serious crimes and for some reason had not participated in rigorous rehabilitation programs or demonstrated genuine insight. In some instances these inmates simply had not taken the initiative to get help, which, of course, was a bad omen. In other instances inmates had waited for many months for a spot to open up in one or more treatment programs; because of budget constraints some inmates—particularly those serving sentences of modest length—approached the end of incarceration without receiving all the help they wanted and needed. When this occurred, the parole board had to decide the probable effect on public safety if we released these inmates to highly structured residential treatment programs while under the board's jurisdiction. Such decisions to release were not motivated by a sense of leniency, despite any outward appearance; rather they reflected the parole board's wish to avoid releasing a high-risk inmate from prison without strict supervision and treatment. For some inmates, release on parole to a residential or outpatient mental health or addictions treatment program allows them access to much-needed services that would not be available to them otherwise.

|||||||||||||||||||||||||||||||||||||||||||||||||||||||||

The concept of parole dates to the Middle Ages. The term *parole*, which is French for "speech" or "word," was used when prisoners gave their word upon their release. Alexander Maconochie, a Scottish geographer and captain in the Royal Navy, introduced the modern idea of parole in the mid-1800s when he was appointed superintendent of the British penal colonies on Norfolk Island, off the coast of Australia. In the United States, Zebulon Brockway introduced parole when he became superintendent of Elmira Reformatory in Elmira, New York, in 1876.[2]

Every state has its own laws stipulating when inmates are eligible for parole and the release criteria the parole board should follow. State laws have many similarities and noteworthy differences. Several states have abolished parole altogether as part of a get-tough-on-crime agenda. Among states that offer parole, some require inmates to serve a minimum number of years before becoming eligible for parole; the minimum can vary depending on the nature of the crime (for example, violent, sex, property, drug). Other states require inmates to serve a minimum percentage of their sentence before becoming eligible for parole (usually one-third, one-half, or two-thirds), and these percentages can vary for different categories of crime. In Rhode Island, inmates are required to serve one-third of their sentence for most offenses before becoming eligible for parole. When I first joined the parole board in 1992, inmates serving a life sentence were required to serve ten years before becoming eligible for parole. Several years later the state legislature added five years to the minimum time served on a life sentence. Current state law requires inmates sentenced to life imprisonment to serve twenty years before becoming eligible for parole.

According to state law (Rhode Island General Laws, Title 13-8-14), the parole board is required to consider various criteria before releasing an inmate:

1. That the prisoner has substantially observed the rules of the institution in which confined, as evidenced by reports submitted to the board by the director of the department of corrections, or his or her designated representatives, in a form to be prescribed by the director;

2. That release would not depreciate the seriousness of the prisoner's offense or promote disrespect for the law;

3. That there is a reasonable probability that the prisoner, if released, would live and remain at liberty without violating the law;

4. That the prisoner can properly assume a role in the city or town in which he or she is to reside. In assessing the prisoner's role in the community the board shall consider:

    i. Whether or not the prisoner has employment;

    ii. The location of his or her residence and place of employment; and

    iii. The needs of the prisoner for special services, including but not limited to, specialized medical care and rehabilitative services; and

5. That any and all restitution imposed pursuant to § 12-19-32 has been paid in full, or satisfactory arrangements have been made with the court if the person has the ability to pay. Any agreement shall be in writing and it is the burden of the person seeking parole to satisfy the parole board that this requirement has been met. Any person subject to the provisions of this section may request an ability to pay hearing, by filing the request with the court which imposed the original sentence.

The board also spent considerable time with inmates accused of violating their parole. In these cases the board explored the circumstances surrounding the offenders' rearrest and decided whether to detain them or release them to the community. All parole board members were on call to issue detention warrants if police and/or parole officers had reason to believe that a parolee had violated conditions of parole. I dreaded those occasional middle-of-the-night telephone calls from a parole officer asking me to sign and fax a warrant authorizing detention of a parolee.

If the parolee accused of violating parole had not been charged with a new offense but apparently had violated parole nonetheless (for example, by missing mandated counseling appointments or violating home confinement restrictions), the board had the option of re-releasing the inmate with additional, usually stricter, conditions. For instance, when a parolee had difficulty complying with his schedule, the board could have required him to wear a GPS bracelet so that his parole officer could monitor the parolee's whereabouts. If a parolee was living on his own and violated parole by using drugs, we might have released him to a residential substance abuse treatment program, assuming he was complying with all other parole conditions.

At the conclusion of each hearing board members formally voted on whether to grant or deny parole. The majority prevailed, except in the case of inmates serving a life sentence. Those inmates needed the unanimous vote of the board to win parole. Sometimes we agreed that we would deny parole and simply disagreed about when to schedule the inmate's next parole hearing. Some board members, for example, might have wanted to see an inmate in one year, while others preferred an eighteen-month review, so we would compromise on fifteen months.

Inmates usually received written notice of the parole board's decision the day after the hearing. Some inmates won so-called immediate parole (which, practically speaking, means the following month because of the time required for staffers to verify the inmate's release plan), and sometimes their release was set for a more distant date. At times the board voted to release an inmate six, nine, or twelve months later to allow time for the inmate to complete a prison-based treatment program, to extend the time the inmate served in prison because of public safety concerns, or to incarcerate the inmate as long as possible but with enough time remaining on the sentence to allow completion of a strict residential program (typically a community-based residential drug abuse treatment facility) while the inmate was still under the parole board's supervision.

|||||||||||||||||||||||||||||||||||||||||||||||||||||||||||

Dave Sempsrott was born on February 1, 1948, in McLeansboro, Illinois, located in the rural, southern end of the state. The Rand McNally map uses its smallest print for the town. Dave was one of ten children, three of whom, including Dave, were placed in foster care following their parents' separation and their mother's hospitalization for psychiatric treatment.

> I remember very little about my mother during those days and nothing about my father. I've been told my father worked for an oil company;

my mother had babies. From the talks I have had with my brothers and sisters, my mother was very bitter about the state taking us from her. I remember she never gave up trying to locate us after we were adopted.

I can only remember a couple of things from those years. Before we were adopted my older brother and I were living with some people and my younger brother was living with another family. I remember my brother and I were smoking cigarette butts from an ashtray and getting our butts spanked for doing so. Up to age 11 or 12 I had a bed-wetting problem. My foster dad used to make me stand on a stool with my nose in a circle when I wet the bed.

I think his wife got tired of washing sheets and so my brother and I were sent to another home. From what I remember this new family was nice. I can only remember being scolded by them—no whippings. One day my brother and I were throwing rocks at this man's cows. He told us at supper that the cows had told on us and not to do it anymore. From then on we did not let the cows see who was throwing rocks at them.

In several subsequent letters to me, Dave wrote about how he was eventually adopted and started engaging in some adolescent mischief. He described running away from his adoptive home, spending about a year in a residential program in Ohio after using his adoptive father's car without permission, being sexually abused by a staff member at this program, and enlisting in the army. After his army discharge Dave worked a series of jobs as a stock clerk in a warehouse, gas station attendant, sandwich deliveryman, and tow truck driver. During this period, Dave said, he met a woman he later married (after she became pregnant with their daughter), and he began experimenting with drugs, a destructive pattern that eventually led to the crimes for which he was serving multiple life sentences.

‖‖

I have often wondered what drew me to Dave, a man who, over time and with no intent on his part, shaped much about the way I think about crime, criminals, and parole. I am horrified when I stop to consider the crimes that led to his life sentences. In one important sense it seems that no such person, and I use the term loosely, deserves

considerate attention in any form. Intellectually I know I am supposed to feel about Dave the way people feel about notorious murderers such as Charles Manson, Ted Bundy, Jeffrey Dahmer, David
Berkowitz, and John Wayne Gacy. The events and outcomes are unspeakable. One should simply acknowledge and reflect on the horror
and then move on.

But I can't. As I write these words, I recall reading the British play-
wright Peter Shaffer's preface to his play *Equus*, about the life and
psyche of a seventeen-year-old stable boy who plunged a steel spike
into the eyes of six horses:

> One weekend over two years ago, I was driving with a friend through
> bleak countryside. We passed a stable. Suddenly he was reminded by
> it of an alarming crime which he had heard about recently at a dinner
> party in London. He knew only one horrible detail, and his complete
> mention of it could barely have lasted a minute—but it was enough to
> arouse in me an intense fascination.

Sometimes true horror and puzzlement combine to compel a
search for some satisfactory answer. That's certainly the feeling I got
month after month as I reviewed inmates' files to prepare for parole
board hearings and then met with them and their victims. What I
found with some criminals I met is that it was hard for me to get past
the revulsion, in part because their crimes and prison-based conduct
were so ugly. Some inmates—fortunately a distinct minority, in my
experience—displayed no remorse and showed a hard-edged callous-
ness that was disconcerting and quite alienating. My sophisticated
professional education and experience told me complex and compelling reasons are behind their misconduct and arrogance—the abusive early years, perhaps, or their contemporary anxiety and trauma
that led them to be defensive, full of bravado, and project their inner
turmoil. I admit that at times I was just unable to rise above my disgust. Fortunately that was relatively rare.

This is what made my relationship with Dave so perplexing to me.
I know I was moved in part by his consistently gentle persona whenever I spent time with him. I wanted Dave to feel anguish about his
crimes, and he did. The torment he knew was real. It tortured him

daily—and nightly—in a way I find unimaginable. What must it be like, I have often wondered, to fall asleep to those horrific memories?

I wasn't saying I don't ever think about that night. I do, but I usually try to push it out again as quickly as possible. It is painful for me to think about it. I hate myself for that night. I am certainly not proud of what I did. I've felt nothing but shame since it happened. I cannot look someone in the eye—not even you—and discuss that night.

When I first read this passage from one of Dave's letters to me, I realized that this may have finally revealed why we had developed no in-person relationship, despite our weekly contact for nearly two years. The subject of his crime was simply too horrifying for him to relive in conversation, directly or indirectly. Better to not unleash the demon.

My curiosity was aroused, of course. At that point all I knew was that Dave had been convicted of murder. I also knew that Dave had no record of violence before these murders. I decided I should not ask Dave for details. Instead, I chose to contact the prominent St. Louis, Missouri, newspapers at the time, the *St. Louis Globe-Democrat* and *St. Louis Post-Dispatch,* to see whether their archives contained articles about Dave's crimes. I was hardly prepared for the package I received from the now-defunct *Globe-Democrat*:

St. Charles Man Is Charged in Triple Slaying in County

Jan. 29–30, 1977. A St. Charles man has been charged in warrants with capital murder in connection with the slaying earlier this month of a 22-year-old man, a 23-year-old woman and her 4-year-old daughter in a Northwest St. Louis County apartment.

St. Louis County Detectives Lester Rinehardt and William Crosswhite said the man charged, David Lee Sempsrott, 29, of the 500 block of Houston St., St. Charles, has admitted the triple slaying to police but told them [he] has no idea why he committed the crime.

The bodies of Mrs. Mary Blair, her daughter, Angela, and Donald (Donnie) Chronister were found by police, Tuesday, Jan. 11, in the apartment Chronister and Mrs. Blair had been sharing for about the last two years at 10510 Cinnamon Dr., authorities said.

Sempsrott, who police said had no record of violence, was charged with three counts of capital murder in warrants issued Friday by St. Louis County Magistrate Leonard F. Martin.

No bond was set in the case, which will be presented to the county grand jury, authorities said.

Rinehardt and Crosswhite questioned Sempsrott in connection with the slayings Jan. 13, but he left the state for nine days when they attempted to question him further, authorities said.

He returned to Missouri Thursday morning, and the detectives talked to him by phone, authorities said. They made an appointment to interview Sempsrott at 2 P.M. Thursday, but he did not appear at that time, police said.

However, Thursday night St. Charles police received a call from a man they said they believed to be Sempsrott's brother-in-law who told them the suspect would meet officers at a restaurant and surrender there, authorities said.

Sempsrott, who met Chronister about seven years ago, accompanied police Friday to the scene of the slayings where he re-enacted his actions on that night, authorities said.

The suspect told police that he struck Chronister on the head with a pistol and then shot him once in the chest and once in the head as he was on the floor.

When Mrs. Blair came out of another room to see what happened, he tied her up, struck her with the pistol and stabbed her and her daughter with a six-inch knife he found in the apartment's kitchen, police said they were told.

Detectives said they have planned to search for the pistol and a bag of clothing Sempsrott said he took from the apartment on the night of the slayings.

Police said Sempsrott told them he gathered everything in the apartment he may have touched and buried the items, along with the pistol[,] in snowdrifts along a road in St. Charles County.

Sempsrott told police he cashed an $85 unemployment check made out to Chronister that he found in the apartment.

Detectives said the suspect told them he purchased the pistol on [sic] the parking lot of a fast-food restaurant the day of the slayings. Authorities said they found four rounds of .22 caliber ammunition behind the front seat of a car Sempsrott told them he borrowed that night.

Authorities said Sempsrott told them he bought the pistol to go rabbit hunting.

Detectives said they have interviewed an acquaintance of Sempsrott who told them the suspect visited him in his outstate home on the night of the triple slaying.

The acquaintance told police Sempsrott arrived at his home about 8:30 P.M. and stayed for about three hours. During the visit, Sempsrott pulled a gun believed to be the one used in the slayings and struck his friend on the head, police said.

The acquaintance overpowered Sempsrott, and Sempsrott stayed at his friend's house, leaving on friendly terms, police said they were told.

Sempsrott's acquaintance told detectives he asked Sempsrott why he struck him with the pistol, and the suspect said he did not know.

Sempsrott told police he arrived at Chronister's apartment at 12:20 A.M.

Police said the suspect told them he and Chronister had smoked several marijuana cigarettes and had played cards before the slayings, but there had been no argument and that he did not know why he killed Chronister, Mrs. Blair and Angela.

Police said Sempsrott, who is unemployed and has a wife and daughter, was in frequent contact with Chronister. According to phone bills, the two men called each other several times each day, with Chronister averaging two or three calls to Sempsrott each day, authorities said.[3]

I later learned that this chilling newspaper account did not include even more gruesome details that Dave later shared with me in his letters and that appear in a key appellate court opinion in this case:

Upon hearing the gun shots Mary Ann Blair, who had been in the master bedroom preparing to go to sleep, ran into the kitchen. Defendant calmly told Mary Ann that he had shot Donald and that she and her daughter should be quiet. Defendant then instructed Mary Ann to gag and tie Angela. Ms. Blair returned to the master bedroom and bound her daughter with items of underclothing. Mary Ann was then ordered into the living room where she was similarly tied with underclothing. After both Mary Ann and Angela were securely bound the defendant took a seat on the living room couch. Mary Ann, wearing only a robe and nightgown, lay directly in front of where defendant sat. At some point defendant untied Mary Ann and ordered her to remove her robe. After defendant retied the woman he cut away her nightgown with a pair of scissors. At trial defendant explained he removed Mary Ann's clothing because if she were to loosen her bonds she would be less likely to escape. Mary Ann now lay naked on the living room floor. According to his own testimony, defendant sat on the couch for thirty-five to forty minutes. He then stood up, walked to the kitchen, put on a pair of gloves and picked up a large knife. Defendant walked back into the living room and stabbed Mary Ann thirteen times. During his attack Mary Ann freed her hands and tried to resist. Defendant responded by smashing the butt of the gun's handle to her forehead. When defendant was sure Mary Ann was dead he went into the bedroom where Angela lay asleep on her mother's bed. Defendant lifted the child from the bed and placed her on the floor. He then stabbed Angela in the throat and strangled her until dead.[4]

Before I knew these ghastly details, I knew only that Dave had committed some sort of nasty crime, as had all the members of the prison group with whom I worked. But not until I read the newspaper account and formal appellate court opinion did I know just how horrifying Dave's crime was. I stared at the photograph of Dave that accompanied the newspaper article I read and felt stunned. Absolutely stunned. I thought perhaps Dave had killed someone inadvertently during a robbery, a fairly common occurrence in the litany of horrors committed by penitentiary inmates. But the actual facts of Dave's crimes were beyond the pale, worse than anything I could have imagined. I had a devil of a time absorbing the information that the Dave I had come to know was the perpetrator of these savage murders. Sometimes events in life just don't add up. But this taught me an invaluable lesson, one I carried into my work with the parole board: initial impressions can be very, very misleading.

I needed to know Dave's version. As I reviewed in my mind the letters that Dave and I had exchanged, it became clear to me that for nearly a year both of us had danced around the topic. I wrote to Dave on December 3, 1983, and told him that soon I would like to ask him some questions about the murders. Until then I had simply asked Dave questions about his childhood, family, acquaintances, jobs, and life in prison. Now I felt the need to ask his permission to broach the topic; I was prepared for him to write back and say that he didn't feel comfortable addressing the murders, and I would respect that. All of us have boundaries we don't want others to cross.

Dave's reply was quick and to the point: "You may ask any question you want. Should there be one I don't want to answer, I simply won't. But I don't foresee that occurring." I was impressed with Dave's candor and willingness to move into this painful, uncharted territory. I decided to start out with a broad question about the circumstances surrounding the murders. Dave seemed to take a deep breath and let the gates open. He confirmed a number of details that appeared in the newspaper article and appellate court opinion, which Dave did not know I had read. He also filled in a number of significant gaps about the events surrounding the murders, including his relationship with the victims.

We have finally come to the point in our relationship I've been dreading. No matter how many times I think about that night I never quite accept that the person doing the killing was me. There's no doubt it was me, but it's hell to live with. I've been tripping the past two days on how to describe the murders to you. I really don't think I can. I don't think there is any way I could make you feel and see what I did.

I guess I need to start with the purchase of the gun. I bought a .22 pistol from a friend of mine, maybe three or four weeks prior to the murders. I bought it for squirrel hunting. Many times you'll shoot a squirrel and not kill it. I didn't like to see them suffer so I got the .22 to shoot them in the head with. My father-in-law showed me how to club them to death, but that seemed worse than them suffering after being shot. We ate the dead squirrels. They are quite good.

I went squirrel hunting in Troy, Missouri, where my friend John lived. John had a .22 pistol I wanted to trade mine for. I wanted his because it looked better, shot better, had a holster, and held nine shots. It was just a better gun.

On the night of the murders I went to John's house to try to trade my .22 for his and some cash to boot. After I left there I was headed home but got the idea to go to Don's instead. I knew he would be home because Mary was at work.

Don was my best friend. We had worked together on two different jobs. I really got into drugs more after meeting Don. We did a lot of partying together. We also went camping, hunting, stuff like that. Don was about 24 or 25.

Don had some sort of breakdown after he was married about a year. He was on a speed run and something snapped. He was admitted to a hospital nut ward for a while. He lost his memory for a short period too.

Mary was Don's girlfriend after his divorce from his first wife. Mary had a daughter, Angie. I did not know Mary well at all. She seemed like a nice person from the few times I was around her. Angie was a normal 4 year old girl. Don would babysit at times and I would drop in occasionally. We would play games with Angie until we were worn out.

Angie was just a child. I could never purposely hurt a child, and find Angie's death so hard to cope with, even after 7 years.

I want you to have some idea as to my state of mind that night. Before arriving at Don's I had taken 8 to 10 dime bags of PCP, I don't know how many mini whites, did one hit of acid, drank a few beers, and smoked many joints. I started about 1:00 or 2:00 P.M. at a friend's house in St. Charles. It was around 11:30 P.M. or a quarter to midnight when I got to Don's apartment. It had to be around that time because Mary got off work at 12, and she got home soon after I got there. I wasn't paying much attention to the time, I guess. If I had realized it was close to midnight I would have probably never gone to Don's, knowing Mary would be home. Not that she would say anything or get mad, but because it would have been bad manners.

Don and I were playing cards when Mary got home, or we were getting ready to at least. Angie was still up so Mary went to put her to bed.

Don and I did some more PCP while Mary was in the other room with Angie. We then got back to our card game. Mary didn't want to play and sat on the couch reading. Angie got out of bed and came into the living room to tell Mary something, and they both went to the bedroom.

Don asked me if I wanted something to drink and went to the kitchen. I walked behind him and I pulled the pistol out and struck him on the head. I have no idea why. None.

Don turned around and I stepped back and shot him twice. Mary came running in to see what the noise was. She asked what had happened and I told her I just killed Don. She asked why and I told her I didn't know.

The baby was crying and I remember telling Mary to put her to bed. Angie had come in to find Mary. Mary took Angie back to the bedroom and then returned to the living room where I was. I made her strip and I tied her hands and feet. I then began to stab her. I don't remember how many times—10 or 12 maybe. It was sickening. She died.

I then went and cut Angie's throat, and that was even worse.

When I was doing all that it seemed as if someone else was doing it and making me watch. I was powerless to stop it from happening. I would not ever want to experience that again. I sometimes think of what I would do if I was forced into a kill-or-be-killed situation here in prison. I have never really settled that question in my mind. Probably won't know unless it happens.

Well anyway, I left Don's and went home. I went directly to the bathroom and took a bath and tried to wash the blood out of my clothes. I then went to bed and passed out. My wife Cindy woke me up 2 or 3 hours later to take her to work. My daughter Michelle was out of school for some reason and I was to babysit. After dropping Cindy off at work I went to a friend's house, put Michelle in her care, and passed out again. I woke up around 10:30 or 11:00 A.M. and took Michelle home to fix her something to eat. When the noon news came on they had the news of Don's, Mary's, and Angie's deaths.

It didn't register at that moment that I was responsible for the murders. In fact, it was not until 2 or 3 days later after being questioned by police that I had any idea that I may have been a murderer. I began to get flashes of what had happened. This grew in time and left no doubt that I had done the killing.

I went to my adoptive parents in Tennessee to think things out. After about a week or so I returned to St. Charles and turned myself in.

||||||||||||||||||||||||||||||||||||||||||||||||||||||||||

Once the horror of the murders settled in, I began to speculate the way any thoughtful person would. It's the way I speculated during parole board hearings when I stared at an inmate who had committed a heinous crime.

Had Dave not been under the influence of a stunning amount of drugs at the time of the murders, the slayings would have been much more puzzling. For several years after moving to Rhode Island, and before my appointment to the parole board, I worked part time in a state hospital forensic unit with men who had been tried for murder and found not guilty because of their severe mental illness. These were men who killed because they hallucinated or were delusional. One man said three eye blinks meant God was issuing a command to kill. Another said that a half-filled water glass was a message from the devil to strangle a neighbor to death. Another patient who was locked in this secure psychiatric facility told me that the sound of a neighbor's typing was clear evidence that she was a communist agent who needed to be eliminated to protect the nation. These are men with forms of psychosis that are not well understood. Labels such as schizophrenia and psychotic paranoia were typically applied to people in the forensic unit. Nearly everyone involved in these cases agreed that these men were not in control of their mental faculties or able to distinguish right from wrong.

Dave's case offered no such clarity, which was often the case with inmates who appeared before the parole board. Granted, by conventional standards Dave was leading a rather marginal, unstable life. He drifted from job to job with hiatuses in between. Dave's marriage was the result of an unplanned pregnancy. By his own admission Dave was beginning to grow more and more dependent on drugs. He was self-medicating, a phenomenon I saw repeatedly in parole board cases. By all accounts Dave's drug binge on the day of the murders caused him to experience psychotic symptoms.[5]

Nonetheless, Dave's case lacked elements I often saw in murder cases. Dave had no history of major mental illness. As the police and prosecutors acknowledged, Dave had no history of violent crimes or behavior. Dave had not been suddenly jilted, fired, or otherwise betrayed, which are often correlates of violent crimes. He had no enemies and sought no revenge. Dave's case was truly an outlier.

Clearly Dave was under the influence of an astonishing volume and variety of drugs. Why? I wondered. What could possibly have led Dave to ingest as much as he did, when he did? How did he explain any of this?

There was no special reason why I took so many drugs that day, no. It was not uncommon for me to do that. It was, though, the first time I had taken so much PCP. That was due to the fact that I had a very small supply of acid. I preferred acid over PCP anytime. I kept taking more and more PCP because I didn't feel like I was getting high. I believe I was so high at that point that I couldn't recognize the fact. When I got to Don's apartment I felt as though I was straight.

I actually remember hitting Don with the pistol and shooting him, and then stabbing Mary and Angie. I remember it all. It took 4 or 5 days for me to accept the fact that I had done all those terrible things that kept running through my mind. The police are not guilty of brainwashing me or anything.

I cannot give you any reason as to why I committed these murders. I do not know and I don't think I ever will. I remember no argument at all; I was not mad at Don. He was my best friend. What can I say?

I do not recall thinking that I had to kill Mary and Angie to get rid of any witnesses. I just did it with no more thought about it than when I shot Don. Sit down and think of something that happened to someone else in your presence. The more you think about it, the clearer the details are. That's the only way I can ever come close to telling you how I felt after the murders happened. There was nothing I could do to stop this terrible bastard from killing Don, Mary, and Angie. It was like a movie almost. I'm out in the audience knowing what's about to happen, but what can you do from the audience? You have to sit and watch along with everyone else.

Yes, I temporarily lost my mind. I have no doubt about that. It does not matter what others think. I know. I know I could never do anything so horrible under normal conditions. It's still hard for me to accept the fact that I did it. But I did, and I will have to live with it.

||||||||||||||||||||||||||||||||||||||||||||||||||||||||||||

In 1982, several months after I began meeting with Dave, *Time* magazine featured a cover story on the dismal status of the U.S. prison system. One week later the magazine published two starkly contrasting letters to the editor in response to this compelling piece about our nation's correctional facilities and their inmates. These snippets have stayed with me, and their pithy sentiments often sneaked into my parole board deliberations:

> To the Editors:
> When considering prisons, it should be kept in mind that every inmate is there by choice. He made the decision to do time the moment he committed the crime.

> To the Editors:
> Our genes and our environment control our destinies. The idea of conscious choice is ridiculous. Yes, prisons should be designed to protect society, but they should not punish the poor slobs who were headed for jail from birth.[6]

The juxtaposition of these two letters is striking, of course. Their authors clearly view the world through radically different perspectives. The first is committed to the view that individuals who violate our criminal laws do so deliberately, willingly, and rationally. In short, criminals know what they are doing and simply take calculated risks to which are attached, at least in principle, well-publicized penalties. From the point of view of the second writer, those convicted of breaking the law are essentially victims of errant genes, trauma, or toxic environmental circumstances that have forced them down life's wayward paths.

I lived this stark contrast during nearly every parole board hearing day. The victims who elected to meet with the parole board usually were traumatized as a result of serious crimes. Some were surviving relatives of murder victims or those killed by drunk drivers. Others were victims of rape, child molestation, armed robbery, brutal home invasions, or domestic violence. Occasionally we saw victims of white-collar crimes, such as people who were defrauded or victims of embezzlement. Nearly always—and quite understandably— victims were unwilling or unable to explain or excuse their perpetrators' misdeeds by exploring the influence of offenders' childhood trauma, psychiatric challenges, congenital illness, financial desperation, or addiction. Victims typically were enraged and eager to convince the parole board that the inmates deserved no mercy. No matter how convinced I was that certain offenders had compelling reasons they had committed their crimes, I didn't dare try to persuade victims to view the offenders with compassion and understanding. That would have been remarkably insensitive. Victims have every reason in the world to feel rage, whatever the determinants of their offenders' crimes.

That said, the contrasting views so clearly articulated in the *Time* magazine letters represent one of the most enduring controversies in recorded history, commonly known as the debate of free will versus determinism.[7] This controversy rattled around my mind during many parole board hearings as I decided how to vote on an inmate's petition for release.

Put simply, on one side are those who argue that all human beings are willful actors who actively shape their own destinies and who independently make rational choices based on personal preferences and wishes. On the other side are those who claim that some human behavior is largely or entirely determined by a series of antecedent events and factors, such that any given so-called choice or behavior is a mere product of these causes, be they psychological, environmental, economic, or physical.

It helps me to know that the free will–determinism debate has ancient philosophical roots, which put my contemporary musings in context when I contemplated my parole board votes. Empedocles and Heraclitus, for example, are early sources of pre-Socratic thought on the meaning of determinism in nature and the idea of natural law. Ideas concerning determinism—especially the influence of divine will—were later given prominence in the fourth century BCE by the Stoics, the Greek school of philosophy founded by Zeno.

The origins of the modern debate about free will and determinism ordinarily are traced to the work of the eighteenth-century French astronomer and mathematician Pierre-Simon Laplace. Laplace's claims about determinism depended heavily upon the scientific theory of particle mechanics. According to his theory, a knowledge of the mechanical state of all particles at a particular time, together with a knowledge of all other forces acting in nature at that instant, makes it possible to discover all future and past states of the world. With this information one could, in principle, discover not only all future and past mechanical states in the world but all others as well, such as the electromagnetic, chemical, and psychological states.[8]

According to determinism, then, problems such as crime, poverty, drug abuse, and mental illness can be traced to historical antecedents that have led inexorably to the person's current difficulties. From this perspective the responsibility for Dave's employment problems, drug abuse, and murders was not his own; rather, it resided in the onset and consequences of previous events in his life. This way of thinking would explain why all offenders, including those who appear before the Rhode Island Parole Board, committed their crimes. It may appear, of course, that Dave and all other offenders I have met exercised rational, independent choices to commit crimes over which they had full control, but according to the hard-core determinists this is only an illusion. Whatever ability offenders have to behave differently is itself the outcome of previous events in their lives. The philosopher John Hospers describes this view well in his essay "What Means This Freedom?"

> The position, then, is this: if we can overcome the effects of early environment, the ability to do so is itself a product of the early environment. We did not give ourselves this ability; and if we lack it we cannot be blamed for not having it. Sometimes, to be sure, moral exhortation brings out an ability that is there but not being used, and in this lies its occasional utility; but very often its use is pointless, because the ability is not there. The only thing that can overcome a desire, as Spinoza said, is a stronger contrary desire; and many times there simply is no wherewithal for producing a stronger contrary desire. Those of us who do have the wherewithal are lucky.[9]

Proponents of the free will school of thought, in contrast, deny that the thoughts, emotions, and behavior of all individuals are at all times a function of previous events over which individuals had little or no control. Adherents to this point of view generally fall short of claiming that no events are determined. Rather, they claim that some events follow from the exercise of free will or choice, that individuals do in fact have the capacity to behave independent of these previous events, although to varying degrees.

I have spent decades working with offenders, and my experience tells me that, without a doubt, how criminal justice professionals, including parole board members, respond to criminals often is a direct function of the professionals' beliefs about the extent to which the offenders sitting before them are (or are not) responsible, in the free will sense of the term, for their misconduct. Police, judges, parole and probation officers, and parole board members often react relatively leniently or punitively, depending on their belief about the offenders' ability to exercise self-control and make free choices at the time they committed their offenses.

That was certainly true for me when I made judgments about an offender's culpability or what lawyers and moral philosophers call mens rea. The concept of mens rea (Latin: guilty mind) emerged in early seventeenth-century England, when judges began to hold that people cannot be found guilty unless there is evidence that they were aware that their conduct was criminal and that they acted knowingly, purposely, and recklessly. At one extreme are offenders with severe psychiatric symptoms who clearly lack mens rea, such as people suffering from schizophrenia who hallucinate and are delusional, people whose behavior is almost entirely or completely determined and far beyond their control. In the 1980s, when I worked in the forensic unit with patients who had committed extraordinarily serious crimes when they heard voices commanding them to kill and rape, I had no difficulty concluding that their heinous behavior was beyond their control.

But at the other extreme are offenders who seem to be cool, calculating, exploitative, and deliberate, embodying the most essential features of free will and mens rea. When I worked at the Missouri State Penitentiary, Warren was one of the inmates in the group with Dave Sempsrott. Warren sent chills up my spine. Like Dave, Warren had been convicted of murder, but the circumstances surrounding Warren's crime were completely different. Warren was not under the influence of powerful drugs. He did not suffer from some sort of psychosis. Rather, Warren was one of the most sociopathic inmates I have ever met. Warren admitted to me that he had worked for an organized crime syndicate based in St. Louis. His principal duties involved intimidating and threatening people who owed the mob money, often because of gambling debt or failure to pay installments on their high-interest loans. Warren seemed like someone pulled directly out of central casting. He was smooth, charismatic, handsome, and engaging. And, it became clear, Warren had no compunction about murdering people who failed to hold up their end of the bargain with his organized crime cronies. Sometimes Warren would leave debtors threatening messages that often included not-so-subtle hints that their loved ones would be seriously harmed if the debtors failed to quickly pay up. Warren had a reputation for breaking bones to ensure that debts were honored. And when all else failed, Warren did not hesitate to pull out a gun and place a bullet between a victim's eyes. Warren was so slick that it took many years before the police and prosecutors could pin any charges on him and make them stick.

One afternoon I visited Warren while he was serving a stint in segregation after he was caught arranging to smuggle drugs into the prison. I stood outside his cell's bars as Warren stretched out on his bunk with his head barely a foot away. We chatted briefly about the circumstances that had led to his segregation. Later in the relatively mundane conversation, I asked Warren whether he had heard the previous day's headline news that an armed robber had shot and killed two clerks who worked at a jewelry store in eastern Missouri. His response startled me: "What's the point of feeling bad? They're dead. They . . . are . . . dead. It's over and done with, and they're no longer around. No point feeling guilty." I did my best to not look stunned. But stunned I was. I had just had an encounter with a man who came as close to exemplifying a free-will offender as any I had ever met. Or at least so it seemed.

But even with inmates like Warren I must admit to some hesitation. An alternative to extreme views of either free will or determinism has become known in philosophical circles as the mixed view, or soft determinism. Those of us who embrace soft determinism tend to feel torn, caught between our intellectual understanding of the factors that lead to criminal conduct (poverty, mental illness, child abuse, domestic violence, substance abuse, racism) and the anger and frustration we feel because we sense that offenders consciously chose to commit their crimes and did not do enough to prevent them.

This view perhaps has the most relevance and currency in the corrections field and for me as a parole board member. This perspective essentially entails three key assumptions. The first is that the thesis of determinism is generally valid and that, accordingly, human and criminal behavior—both voluntary and involuntary—are preceded and caused by preexisting conditions, such that other behaviors are not likely. Dave, for example, murdered three people because of a long and complex series of factors that led him to a terribly dark place.

The second assumption is that genuinely voluntary behavior is nonetheless possible. The third assumption is that, in the absence of coercion, criminal behavior results from the decisions, choices, and preferences of individuals. Warren knew exactly what he was doing when he executed a man who had failed to pay his debt to the mob. No one forced Warren to do the dirty deed. And this is what noteworthy philosophers such as Thomas Hobbes, David Hume, and John Stuart Mill have tried to tell us.

Clearly the degree to which my parole board colleagues and I viewed crime as a product of voluntary, willful choices or as determined, coerced behavior had profound implications for whether we responded to inmates punitively and judgmentally or with a deep, more forgiving appreciation of the toxic circumstances that led to their conduct. Aristotle argued centuries ago that an individual is responsible only for those actions that are voluntary; an action can fail to be voluntary in two principal ways: as the result of compulsion— "I stabbed my wife because of the rage I have felt for years as a result of the horrific physical abuse I suffered as a child"; "My brother pointed a gun at me and told me to start the fire or he'd shoot me"; "My heroin addiction was so out of control that I had to get money as quickly as possible, and that's why I robbed the store"—or ignorance—"I had no idea I could become addicted to gambling"; "I thought she was eighteen years old when we had sex—I had no idea she was fourteen." I am not particularly proud of it, but I admit that some inmates made me angry. Sometimes extremely angry. I had profound compassion for many—particularly those who were clearly mentally ill and who suffered decades of unspeakable trauma at the hands of abusive adults—but some offenders made me livid. Some, like Warren, apparently knew exactly what they were doing when they defrauded an addled elderly relative of her life's savings; hired an arsonist to burn down their place of business to cash in on insurance coverage; stole a psychiatrically impaired neighbor's monthly benefits checks; or stood over a highway bypass with a powerful rifle and shot at unsuspecting motorists just for fun.

In such cases I think it is natural to wish for some sort of retribution. But I know deep down that retribution as a response to serious crime becomes problematic whenever we acknowledge compelling factors in some inmates' lives that caused them to behave as they did and limited their ability to control their behavior and act voluntarily. The eighteenth-century German philosopher Immanuel Kant said it succinctly:

> But what is the mode and measure of punishment which public justice takes as its principle and standard? It is just the principle of equality, by which the pointer of the scale of justice is made to incline no more to the one side than the other. It may be rendered by saying that the undeserved evil which any one commits on another, is to be regarded as perpetrated on himself. . . . This is the right of retaliation (jus talionis); and properly understood, it is the only principle which in regulating a public court, as distinguished from mere private judgment, can definitely assign both the quality and quantity of a just penalty.[10]

So what should I have made of all this in Dave's case and, more broadly, in my efforts to be a truly just and principled parole board member who was obligated to make judgments about offenders' lives? For Dave, who eventually murdered three people, his start in life was difficult: the foster homes, chronic dislocation, child abuse, and absence of stability and consistently nurturing caretakers a child needs to have a decent chance to negotiate life's inevitable challenges, stresses, and strains. But most of us, I suspect, would be willing to concede that despite enduring many unspeakable travails, people like Dave still are responsible for their actions and must not cross the thin but important line into depraved behavior. The trouble is, we disagree wildly about where to draw that line. Even Dave was unsure, as he wrote me in one of his most poignant letters:

> In my own case, I didn't want to kill anyone, didn't intend to, and realized I had done so only after it was done. I guess that's why I hate myself. Because I lost control of myself while on drugs and killed three people. It's simple to say, well, I was on drugs and didn't know what I was doing. But then no one forced the drugs on me. I took them on my own free will. So who's to blame?

The nineteenth-century Russian philosopher and writer Leo Tolstoy may be more erudite in his commentary on this great paradox, but his insight is no more profound than Dave's. For Tolstoy,

> the problem of free will from earliest times has occupied the best intellects of mankind and has from earliest times appeared in all its colossal significance. The problem lies in the fact that if we regard man as a subject for observation from whatever point of view—theological, historical, ethical, or philosophic—we find the universal law of necessity to which he (like everything else that exists) is subject. But looking upon man from within ourselves—man as the object of our own inner consciousness of self—we feel ourselves to be free.[11]

Tolstoy's words often rang in my head when I met with inmates who appeared before the Rhode Island Parole Board, especially those convicted of truly heinous crimes. It was in these cases, especially, that I struggled to understand the nagging and highly consequential tension between good and evil in our world and in the lives of criminals I got to know up close.

2

GOODNESS AND EVIL

In each of us, two natures are at war—the good and the evil.
All our lives the fight goes on between them, and one of them must conquer.
But in our own hands lies the power to choose—what we want most to be
we are.

—ROBERT LOUIS STEVENSON

A T 8:00 A.M. my parole board colleagues and I started our day
in the bowels of what is known in Rhode Island as the Intake
Service Center. The ISC is located on the grounds of a massive state-
operated tract known as the Howard Complex. This campus-like setting includes a large collection of Victorian stone structures, early
twentieth-century colonial-revival brick buildings, and contemporary facilities that serve incarcerated criminals, juvenile offenders,
psychiatric patients, infirm elderly, and people with disabilities.

Often when I drove to the prisons located within the Howard Complex, I thought about how I was part of a long line of people who have
served vulnerable people on these same grounds over hundreds of
years. In Rhode Island and other colonial-era communities, vagrants
and others who did not belong were "warned out" and escorted past
the town line; those who lived in the community faced various forms
of public humiliation or imprisonment, especially if they were considered culprits, impoverished, or diseased. By the mid-nineteenth
century, Rhode Island, like a number of its neighboring states, had
established almshouses for the poor and asylums for people with
mental illness, described by some as social sanitation.

As was common in that era, Rhode Island selected a pastoral site
that, in the horse-and-buggy age, was far—in terms of travel time—

from the urban center in Providence about nine miles to the north. Eighteen frame buildings were constructed in 1870, and that November 118 mental patients were admitted. In 1872 work began on the workhouse and house of correction, the forerunner to the state prisons where I worked.

The Adult Correctional Institute was completed in 1878 as the State Prison and Providence County Jail. The building contained two wings of three-tiered cell blocks flanking an octagonal central administration building. The 250 cells were arranged facing either east or west for unobstructed sunlight and had corridors on two sides so that both sides of each cell were accessible to guards. The prison was opened under the supervision of Warden General Nelson Viall. He had served as commander of a black regiment in the Civil War and personally landscaped the prison grounds.

More than a century later my colleagues and I assembled for the day's hearings at the Intake Service Center, which opened in 1982. I waited for the other board members to arrive in the lobby as I stood directly in front of the prison's reception desk, which was staffed by two correctional officers. I greeted an amiable inmate who was mopping the floor in the lobby area. I recognized him from an earlier parole hearing.

As I waited, I observed a middle-aged woman who was speaking with one of the correctional officers. She held a hanger with clothes she wanted prison personnel to deliver to her son. I overheard her tell the officer that her son was being held without bail on an armed robbery charge and was scheduled to appear in court the following day. The only clothes he had for the court hearing were the shorts and T-shirt he was wearing when he was arrested. The mother said she wanted her son to look good for his court appearance. The woman started crying as she handed the clothes to the officer. The officer reached under his desk and handed her a tissue.

When the entire board had arrived, we passed through a secure metal door that slammed shut behind us, signed the log-in register that an officer in the control booth slipped to us on a clipboard through a narrow opening in the bulletproof glass that separated us, and traded our personal security badges for blue institutional badges that gave us access to the prison's most secure locations. The officer also handed me a panic button that the board could use to summon emergency assistance should an inmate lose control during a hearing or if some other emergency were to arise. We walked through another metal security door before we wended our way through a labyrinth of hallways that led past a series of administrative offices, inmate housing units, and segregation units.

Our escort, a correctional officer, led us up several steps and screamed, "Sixteen!" into an intercom to alert an unseen correctional officer to remotely unlock the door (number 016) that allowed us access to a hallway leading to a high-tech video courtroom.

|||||||||||||||||||||||||||||||||||||||||||||||||||||||||

The Intake Service Center holds offenders from throughout Rhode Island and serves the same functions as most city and county jails. Rhode Island is one of only six states that centralize their jail facilities. This building has the capacity to house 1,118 male inmates who have been charged with crimes and are held before trial. The prison also incarcerates newly sentenced inmates who are awaiting transfer to other state prisons; these new inmates are screened and interviewed before being placed in other high security, maximum security, medium security, and minimum security facilities.

The Intake Service Center also houses inmates who are in protective custody—inmates who have to be segregated from the general population because they have enemies in the state's various prisons or are otherwise vulnerable to serious harassment or threats. Word of an enemy's incarceration can spread instantly; without precautions long-held grudges and vendettas can erupt in a flash. Spontaneous attacks sometimes occur in prison work areas, corridors, dining halls, shower rooms, and recreational yards, often with dreadful consequences.

Seasoned inmates who are concerned about enemies in the prison population know to never let down their guard. I have seen a telltale inmate head gesture thousands of times: alert inmates swivel their heads, constantly scanning their surroundings for any immediate threat.

Other inmates must be segregated because they are cooperating with police or prosecutors and may have testified, or plan to testify, against suspects, accomplices, or other criminal court defendants, some of whom are incarcerated as well. Being known as a snitch in prison can lead to assault or even death.

Occasionally inmates need to be placed in protective custody simply because of their notoriety. Many inmates watch the news; they will know if a new inmate is a well-known youth-group leader convicted of child molestation, a rival gang member charged with the multiple murders of their acquaintances, a former police officer convicted of domestic violence, or a state legislator charged with accepting a bribe. Typically these individuals must be segregated for their own safety.

The Intake Service Center houses a high-tech video courtroom that the parole board uses to conduct hearings with inmates who are incarcerated out of state. Some Rhode Island inmates are transferred to out-of-state prisons because they are considered serious management problems. Many of these inmates have been disciplined repeatedly, usually for violent assaults against correctional officers or other inmates. Some assaults take the form of fistfights and stabbings. Occasionally inmate A murders inmate B. We conducted one video parole hearing for an out-of-state inmate who was in segregation for ninety days because he threw a bag filled with urine and feces at a correctional officer.

A small number of inmates are transferred out of state because they are in the federal Witness Security Program. One parole board calendar included a video hearing for an out-of-state inmate whose location was hidden even from us. Ordinarily we knew ahead of time where an out-of-state inmate was located, including the state and particular prison facility. Before most of these hearings we typically received written summaries of the inmate's disciplinary record, mental health status, and program participation, all listed on the out-of-state prison's letterhead. For this hearing, however, every report we received was deliberately camouflaged. The reports were sent through, and used the letterhead of, a federal office in Washington, DC. The inmate was in the federal Witness Security Program because he had provided extensive information to police investigators and prosecutors about a sex-trafficking ring.

As I read the copious files, I learned that this inmate was now forty-nine years old and had been incarcerated for slightly more than eight years of his twenty-five-year sentence. He had been arrested and charged with helping to organize a thriving sex-trafficking ring on the East Coast. The inmate and his colleagues recruited underage girls by luring them, through websites and social media, with promises of lucrative jobs, love, shelter, and support. The ring targeted girls who were from troubled circumstances, some of whom lived in foster and group homes and were in state custody because they were victims of abuse and neglect.

The documents I reviewed indicated that the inmate had decided to turn on his former cronies and testify against them, mainly to negotiate a shorter prison sentence. As a result of the inmate's subsequent courtroom testimony, the federal government successfully prosecuted three career criminals who had exploited dozens of young girls. The inmate was rewarded with a five-year reduction in the state sentence he had received following his conviction.

In this particular case, in advance of the hearing I had read a chilling collection of police reports, victim statements, and court transcripts. One victim told police that she had been beaten when she did not produce a large enough wad of cash after a slow night. Another victim shared grisly details with the police about how her pimp had branded her arm with a hot iron and tattooed her neck to prove that he owned her. I learned that this sex-trafficking ring had continued for nearly four years before police were able to gather enough evidence to shut it down and arrest multiple perpetrators.

Before the hearing I also read a long and detailed letter that the inmate had written to the parole board begging for his release. In one passage he reflected on his decision to get involved in the sex-trafficking trade:

> As I lay here on my bunk staring through the narrow window in my cell, I can't quite believe I let my life sink so low. When I got caught up in the sex trafficking all I could think about was the easy money and the fast

life. Every day was an adventure, a real rush. I was pretty much my own boss and got whatever I wanted—money, drugs, sex, cars, you name it. I'm embarrassed to say I didn't think for even a moment about all the lives I was ruining, including my own. This is a real wake-up call for me.

I've been getting counseling here, and I'm beginning to realize what led me down this horrible path. I don't want to make excuses, but I'm now understanding for the first time in my life why I've messed things up so badly. You may not know this about me, but my father was in and out of my life while I was growing up. He was very involved in organized crime. I always thought criminal activity was normal. When I was a child I would sometimes eavesdrop and hear my father and his buddies talk about the drug deals, the stolen car rings, the loan-sharking—it just went on and on. For me as a kid, this was real exciting. It wasn't until recently that I began to realize that this is not how most normal people live. I just didn't know any better.

I always had trouble in school. I hated class and had lots of difficulty doing the schoolwork. I dropped out of high school the first chance I got. I was young and stupid, and just figured I would be able to do just fine hustling on the street, just like my dad.

I can't believe I got involved in this racket. I feel very guilty about taking advantage of all those girls. At the time I didn't really care much about them; I just figured I was giving them a way out of their horrible circumstances. Most of them were in bad shape to begin with, living on the street, in foster homes, using drugs, whatever. Somehow I convinced myself I was doing them a favor.

Now I know how twisted my thinking was. I'm sure I made their situations even worse. I know a couple of the girls even tried to commit suicide, things were so bad, and lots of these girls got addicted to drugs. That's on me, and I have to live with that.

When I meet with you next month I hope I can convince you that I've really changed. I know you hear this from inmates all the time. I swear to you it's true in my case.

The inmate's letter seemed quite sincere and insightful. Yet, while sincere remorse and insight are essential, they are not a "get out of jail free" card, particularly given the heinousness of the inmate's crime. There is no guarantee that the inmate's remorse and insight are for real.

||||||||||||||||||||||||||||||||||||||||||||||||||||||||

One of the enduring challenges for me—and, I dare say, any parole board member—was being fair in the face of evil acts. My work in prison led me to think a lot about what evil means and about whether some people are truly evil.

Of course lots of people have long considered these questions. The concept of evil conjures up images of morally reprehensible, pernicious acts.[1] Most major faith traditions assume that evil acts entail some kind of intention and choice (free will). According to Siddhārtha Gautama, the founder of Buddhism, "Killing is evil, lying is evil, slandering is evil, abuse is evil, gossip is evil, envy is evil, hatred is evil, to cling to false doctrine is evil; all these things are evil. And what is the root of evil? Desire is the root of evil, illusion is the root of evil."

In Hinduism the concept of dharma, or righteousness, divides the world into good and evil. The main emphasis in Hinduism is on bad action rather than bad people. The Hindu holy text, the Bhagavad Gita, speaks of the balance of good and evil. When good and evil are out of balance, divine incarnations arrive to help to restore this balance.

Within Islam things that are perceived as evil or bad are either natural events (natural disasters or illnesses) or caused by individuals' choices to disobey Allah's orders. In Christianity evil is any action, thought, or attitude that is contrary to the character or will of God. Satan brings evil and temptation and is known as the deceiver who leads humanity astray. In Judaism evil is not considered part of God's creation but comes into existence through humans' bad actions. Human beings have the ability to choose good over evil actions.

During my career I have met inmates who have committed among the most unspeakable, evil crimes. Lauren Whalen was a twenty-five-year-old mother of a one-year-old boy when she and the father of her child were arrested and charged with sexually abusing their son. I read the graphic police reports before conducting Whalen's parole board hearing at the maximum security women's prison. I could barely breathe. According to the police and prosecutors, Whalen and her boyfriend videotaped themselves engaging in various sexual acts with each other and their infant son and then sold the tapes on the Internet to pornography purveyors. According to one painfully disturbing passage in the police report, Whalen performed oral sex on her son while her boyfriend videotaped the sexual act.

Whalen was charged with first degree sexual molestation and child abuse. She entered a nolo contendere plea (Latin for "I do not wish to contend"), an option for criminal court defendants willing to accept conviction without admitting guilt. The judge sentenced Whalen to twenty years in prison; under Rhode Island law she became eligible for parole after serving one-third of her sentence, which was six and two-thirds years.

I had braced myself for this hearing. Whalen entered the room in her green prison uniform. She was diminutive, wore glasses, and had short-cropped hair. She looked so completely ordinary to me that I had a hard time grasping that Whalen was capable of such a hideous crime. She was not the monster I had imagined, at least by appearance.

Whalen and her attorney took their seats at the head of the table. As is customary, we invited her lawyer to make an opening statement.

Members of the parole board, Lauren Whalen is not here today to defend what she did to her son. She knows there is no excuse. With the benefit of hindsight and several years of mental health counseling, Lauren now understands what led her to commit these depraved acts. She has lost everything. Her parental rights were terminated by the court, her immediate family disowned her, and, of course, she lost her freedom.

We are here today to petition this board to release Lauren so that she can continue healing in a residential program that treats women with major psychiatric and substance abuse problems. We are not asking for leniency; rather, we are asking you to take the time to look beyond the horrible details in this case and to understand Lauren as a person. She is not the monster that appears in the police reports. She is a human being with a tortured past that led to what she fully understands were heinous acts. There's a backstory here, and we think it's relevant to the decision you must make as a board.

Lauren was born in Trenton, New Jersey. When she was two years old, she was placed in foster care after her mother was arrested on prostitution and drug charges. Lauren never knew her father.

Between ages two and fifteen, Lauren lived with five different foster families. When she was thirteen, Lauren moved to Rhode Island to live with a cousin. Unfortunately that didn't work out.

Shortly after her fifteenth birthday, the child welfare department in Rhode Island moved Lauren to a group home for adolescent girls, where she lived until she became an adult at age eighteen. At that point Lauren moved in with her then-boyfriend, whom she met through a mutual friend.

That relationship lasted only six months. It ended when Lauren's boyfriend was arrested for assaulting her. Following that relationship, Lauren became involved with several other men who also sexually abused her.

Members of the board, I share these details with you to help you understand how Lauren's chronic and relentless trauma history contributed to her criminal conduct. In the packet I prepared for the board, you will see copies of three different psychiatric and psychological assessments conducted when Lauren was twelve, fourteen, and eighteen years old. Each of these mental health professionals reached similar conclusions independent of one another: Lauren suffers from severe attachment issues and bipolar disorder. She also tends to self-medicate with drugs to cope with the horror in her life. The reports note that Lauren has never lived with a normal family, has a lifelong history of abuse and trauma, and is so eager to be loved that she tends to become involved with people who pay attention to her but who ultimately exploit her.

And that's what happened in this case. Lauren's codefendant, the father of her child, has a significant criminal record. William has served time for breaking and entering, assault with a deadly weapon, receiving stolen goods, narcotics possession and distribution, and credit card fraud. For him, Lauren was a means to an end; he used her like a puppeteer uses a puppet. The record shows that William introduced Lauren to narcotics and manipulated her, while Lauren was under the influence of drugs, to abuse their son. This was not Lauren's idea, and she is horrified that she reached a point in her life where she engaged in such unconscionable behavior.

As you will hear from Lauren herself, she is filled with guilt and remorse. But for her psychiatric vulnerabilities and trauma history, this crime would not have occurred. Lauren needs help, and lots of it. For her, additional time in prison is not the answer.

The chair of the parole board then invited Whalen to speak. She spoke so softly and meekly that we had to ask her several times to speak up. My hunch is that Whalen was so filled with shame and humiliation that speaking above a whisper seemed nearly impossible. She reiterated much of what her attorney said about her horrific trauma history. Whalen's affect was flat; she seemed shut down. The parole board simply did not have much to work with. In an odd way I felt badly for Whalen, who seemed downright pathetic. I knew she needed lots of help.

On its face Whalen's crime was about as evil as evil gets. There is no denying that a mother who engages in fellatio with her infant son has crossed a moral line that should never be crossed. Yet this stark black-and-white view, while certainly understandable in emotional terms, fails to incorporate the multiple shades of gray that seep into the vast majority of parole board cases. Underneath the raw horror involved in so many inmates' crimes are complex, multilayered nuances that help me understand—although not necessarily forgive—evil acts.

I had to work hard to feel charitable toward Whalen. After she and her attorney left the hearing room, we talked at length about her vulnerabilities. But we focused especially on her horrific sexual abuse of her infant son. In good conscience I could not vote to parole Whalen in light of the depravity of her crime, although I understood—at least I think I understood—how her trauma-filled upbringing had led to her unspeakable crime. My colleagues agreed, and we denied her parole by a unanimous vote.

Factoring in the ways in which so many inmates' dreadful pre-incarceration life circumstances contributed to their crimes was important to me. Attorneys call these mitigating factors. Sometimes

I had difficulty appreciating them, as in the case of Robert Blane. Blane, thirty-six, had been sentenced to twenty-five years for arson. When I first met Blane, he seemed like evil dressed up in a khaki prison uniform; I pictured Blane carefully setting the fire that burned his victims so severely that they could barely function. It was hard for me to listen to one of the victims describe his daily and nightly pain.

At the time of his arrest Blane worked for a man who owned seven rental properties in Providence and Pawtucket, Rhode Island. According to the police report, fire department investigators concluded that arson was the cause of a devastating fire at one of the properties where Blane worked as a maintenance man. The police report stated that fire erupted in the six-unit building around 10:30 A.M. toward the back entrance of the property's basement. The fire quickly spread through the building's stairway; the building was a total loss.

Fire investigators found evidence in the basement of a Molotov cocktail, a common incendiary device used by arsonists. Molotov cocktails are often comprised of a glass container filled with a flammable liquid; a wick extends from the opening. When lighted and thrown against a hard surface, the bottle breaks and sprays the liquid, creating a fireball; fire can spread as fast as one hundred feet per second. In this case investigators found evidence that Blane had taped a packet filled with a hypergolic mixture (one that ignites spontaneously when mixed with another substance) of sugar and potassium chlorate to the outside of a bottle and had added sulfuric acid to the flammable liquid inside the bottle. When the bottle broke, investigators said, the acid reacted with the sugar and chlorate to create a hot flame that ignited the liquid. Two of the building's tenants, a five-year-old child and his father, suffered extensive third-degree burns that required multiple surgeries.

On the day of Blane's hearing we met with the child's father, Alexis Ronaldo. The parole board customarily met crime victims during the morning of the day of the inmate's scheduled parole hearing. Ronaldo limped into the hearing room in the board's administrative offices.

Alexis Ronaldo sat down at the head of our long table and explained that he had difficulty walking because of scar tissue that had formed on his legs as a result of the fire. I noticed that his hands and a portion of his face were also badly scarred. We greeted him and explained that we wanted to hear how the crime had affected his life and whether he opposed or supported Blane's parole.

It's hard to know where to begin. This whole experience has changed my life. Every single day I stare in the mirror and am reminded of the fire. Every day I stare down at my legs and am reminded of the fire. Every day my body aches when I try to do the simplest things. I'm on so many pain medications it's hard for me to keep them straight. Sometimes I wish I had died in the fire.

I used to be a construction worker. I loved my job and was good at it. That's gone too. I'm now on SSI [disability] and can barely make ends meet. I was such a hard worker, and now all I can do is shuffle around our apartment and watch TV. This horror never goes away.

And then there's my son. Do you know what it's like to watch your child suffer? He used to be such a happy kid. Now he is anxious all the time. He has trouble being with other kids. Sometimes other kids make fun of his scars or ask lots of questions. He hates that. He just wants to be normal, but he can't be. Now he spends lots of time in his room by himself playing video games. My wife and I have taken him to a counselor, and that helps a little bit, but he still suffers so much. Sometimes at night he has panic attacks—I think that's what you call them—and he climbs into our bed. A child his age shouldn't be doing that, but we understand.

If it were just me, I could handle this. But seeing my son have to deal with this makes me so angry. I want Robert Blane to serve every day of the twenty-five-year sentence the judge gave him.

Ronaldo wiped tears from his eyes. He then pulled out five photographs he had brought with him. "I want you to see what that man did to me. Take a look at these." The photographs showed him in a hospital bed dressed in a simple green gown. His burn wounds were fully exposed. It was painful to look at the graphic photos. Large sections of the blotched and bloated skin on his face, hands, and legs were various shades of bright pink, intense red, and dark purple. A couple of the photos looked remarkably like pieces of chicken that have been charbroiled and burned to a crisp on an outdoor grill.

At that point during the hearing the chair had to explain to Ronaldo that Blane would not serve the entire twenty-five years, even if we did not grant him early release. Under Rhode Island law most incarcerated inmates are eligible for parole once they have served one-third of their sentence. Even inmates who are not granted parole typically can be released long before the full expiration of their sentence because of "good time" credits. Inmates can have significant portions of their sentence shortened as a result of good behavior and participation in rehabilitation programs. Many victims are understandably shocked to learn that inmates are not going to serve their entire sentence, even if they are not granted parole. Ronaldo's response was typical:

> How is it that Blane gets so much time off of his sentence? That's ridiculous. When I talked to the prosecutor, he never explained this to me. All of this is new to me. I sure wish I had known this when I agreed to support the plea bargain. Blane gave me a life sentence when he set that fire. I want him to serve every day that's coming to him.

At the conclusion of the meeting I told Ronaldo that we never informed an inmate that we had met with a victim or that a victim opposed parole, unless the victim wanted us to share this information. Many victims worry about the possibility of retaliation if the inmates find out that the victims spoke with the parole board and opposed parole; that said, during all my years on the parole board, I never encountered a single instance of such retaliation. It could happen, of course, but the statistical likelihood is low.

I explained to Ronaldo that we would let him decide whether Blane should be told about this meeting. Although many victims prefer to keep this information confidential, quite a few want the inmate to know about their intense opposition to parole. For some victims this is a way to exert some control in a situation where they have had distressingly little control thus far. They want to demonstrate to inmates that they feel empowered and are not intimidated. Some victims deferred to the parole board's judgment about whether to disclose their meeting with the board; others insisted that we share this information with the inmates. Ronaldo was not at all ambivalent about his wishes:

I would like Mr. Blane to know that while he ruined my life, I am not running away. I will be here every time he's up for parole. I want him to know I was here, and I want him to know I will do everything that's humanly possible to keep him in prison.

About an hour after our meeting with Ronaldo, my colleagues and I drove the short distance from our administrative offices to Rhode Island's Medium Security prison. This prison opened in 1992 and can accommodate 1,006 inmates in a half-dozen separate buildings that contain two tiers of cells and common areas. The prison features garment, soap, license plate, upholstery, auto body, and metal fabricating shops.

I walked through the main entrance and waited to be buzzed through the first secure electronic door by the officer in the adjacent control room. From that door I walked into a vestibule that separated me from a fenced-in walkway that leads to the prison proper. The officer in the control booth unlocked a second door electronically, and I walked down an outdoor path toward the lobby of the large prison complex. To my left was a grassy area bordered by a row of shrubs. To my right was a sally port used when inmates are transferred to the Medium Security facility from another prison and when Medium Security inmates return from a court appearance or hospital visit.

At the back end of the prison lobby a prison officer in another control booth took my Department of Corrections badge, traded it for a multicolored prison pass, and then opened yet another sliding metal door. I entered the visiting room, which was filled with rows of bolted tables and chairs. Along one wall are colorful murals painted by inmates and several vending machines. At the front of the room was a small stage on which correctional officers sat to observe inmates and visitors. These officers were trained to monitor inappropriate and unauthorized physical contact and to prevent passage of contraband—especially drugs—from visitors to inmates.

On occasion visitors have conveyed drugs to inmates during a kiss. Before visiting the visitor will put several grams of marijuana, heroin, or other drug into a balloon or condom. She puts the balloon in her mouth and then transfers it to the prisoner's mouth when they kiss. The inmate swallows the balloon and retrieves it from the toilet in his cell after he defecates.

Depending on the hour the visiting room could be filled with a large crowd of inmates and visitors. They inevitably would stare when the parole board walked along the outer edge of the room toward the board's adjacent hearing room.

I never got used to the scene of tiny infants and toddlers visiting their khaki-clothed fathers. It was especially painful to witness their good-byes. On occasion a child too young to understand the reality of the situation would cry and insist that the inmate leave with him. I overheard many inmates tell their young children that their daddy or mommy was "away at school."

IIIIIIIIIIIIIIIIIIIIIIIIIIIIIIIIIIIIIIIIIIIIIIIIIIIIIIIIIII

Robert Blane was the sixth case on that day's calendar. He was represented by an attorney who appeared on behalf of many inmates eligible for parole. I have great respect for this attorney, who always prepared carefully and was a zealous advocate for her clients. Not all attorneys were so thorough, although many were. On occasion I was stunned to find out how little some attorneys seemed to prepare and how much more we parole board members knew about the inmate's circumstances than their lawyer did. Most inmates were well represented; others were not.

As is customary, we began Blane's hearing by inviting his attorney to make an opening statement. She was forthright about Blane's mistakes but did her best to cast him in a positive light, which was difficult given the crimes he had committed.

> Mr. Blane knows he messed up. He does not deny his guilt and he's not here to make excuses for his remarkably poor judgment. However, Robert is here to tell you what he has learned from this nightmarish experience and to help you understand what led him to commit such a serious crime. I will provide a brief overview and then invite you to ask Robert questions. I know you would prefer to hear from him, not me.
>
> Robert was born in Rhode Island. He barely knows his father, who has been in and out of his life. In fact, his father also served time in this very same prison on drug-related charges.
>
> Robert spent a lot of time in foster homes and attended nine different schools by the time he was sixteen. He also spent nine months

at the Rhode Island Training School [a juvenile correctional facility]. He has never had the kind of family support most children take for granted. His childhood history is simply tragic.

What happened here is that when Robert "aged out" of the state child welfare system at age eighteen, he had no place to live, no job, no family, and no high school degree. His whole world consisted of a handful of friends he made in the group home he lived in before turning eighteen. One of his friends had a job working as a maintenance worker at a nearby apartment complex. That's how Robert got the job that led to this mess.

The apartment complex owner, Donald Mason, hired Robert and, according to Robert, started to treat him like a son. Before this Robert never had an adult take care of him. Mr. Mason bought Robert clothes, gave him food, and occasionally took him fishing. When I met with Robert before trial, he told me that at the time he trusted Mr. Mason and would do anything to sustain this relationship. Robert now realizes that Mr. Mason was just grooming him for his own purposes. He abused Robert sexually and, eventually, talked Robert into committing this dreadful crime.

Robert is older now, more mature, and has tremendous insight. Put simply, I see no evidence that releasing Robert on parole would pose a risk to the public. None.

Once Robert's attorney concluded her opening statement, we asked our own questions:

QUESTION: Mr. Blane, we just heard from your attorney. Now we would like to hear from you. What's your version of what happened here?

ANSWER: What my attorney said is true. I know what I did was terrible. I will never deny that. I know I was manipulated by Donald Mason, but I can't blame what happened on him. I should have known better than to get involved with his scheme. I can't believe I was willing to do that. Yes, it's true that he felt like a father to me, and I wanted a real father in my life more than anything; my thinking was completely twisted.

I've learned so much during my time in prison. As you can see from my records, I've completed lots of programs. I've taken the criminal thinking class, substance abuse program, victims impact class, got my GED, and during the past two years I've been in counseling with Jane Tallow, the social worker. I haven't had a serious booking [disciplinary infraction] in nearly four years. I'm a different person now. I really am. I want to prove to you that I have grown up and can become a productive member of society. I hope you will give me that chance.

QUESTION: Where would you live? Where would you work?

ANSWER: As you know, I don't have much family. But about three years ago I found out that I have a half-sister, Maria Borges, I never knew about. Maria read about my case in the *Providence Journal* and figured out that we're siblings. About six months after I got sentenced to prison, Maria wrote me a letter and explained all this to me. She asked me to put her on my visiting list. When we first met, I couldn't believe I actually had a sister—real family. As you can see from my visiting record, Maria visits me a few times a month. She is married now and has two children. We've gotten real close.

QUESTION: Does she know all about your crime? What have you told her?

ANSWER: Maria knows everything. I've been completely straight with her. Plus, she read all the news reports. There's no secrets between us.

Maria wants to help me get a new start in life. She knows better than anyone that I had a rotten deal growing up. She and her husband, Mark, have offered to let me live with them, at least until I can adjust to being out of prison and get a steady job. I've met their kids a bunch of times. They've come to a number of visits here. So, the whole family is on board. I'm very lucky.

My sister's husband, Mark, owns a construction business. He told me I can have a job working there, so I think I'm all set.

QUESTION: Given the amount of time you've spent in prison, what are the challenges you think you will face whenever you're released? What help do you think you might need when you get out of prison, and where might you get it?

ANSWER: I've thought a lot about this. Jane Tallow and I have talked about how hard it's going to be for me and what I need to do to stay out of trouble. I know the worst thing I can do is isolate myself, which was part of the problem when I got into trouble. I need to hang around—I mean spend time with—people who aren't into drugs and stuff. I need to be around positive people who aren't going to drag me down.

QUESTION: Anything else you think you'll need to do to help with the transition?

ANSWER: Not that I can think of.

QUESTION: What I was hoping you would say is that you will need to connect with a mental health counselor so that you have someone to talk to about whatever challenges you face. Do you think that makes sense?

ANSWER: Yes, I do.

QUESTION: Well, I'm a bit concerned that you didn't say anything about that when I asked you what kind of help you think you will need when you get out of prison. Any idea why you didn't mention that?

ANSWER: I'm not really sure.

Toward the end of the hearing I told Blane that earlier we had met with one of his victims, who objected to his release on parole. I then summarized Ronaldo's comments about the effect that the fire had had on his and his son's life, their unrelenting struggles, and their personal agony. I described the nature of Ronaldo's physical and emotional injuries and the photographs that he had shared with us. At that point Blane began to tear up. I handed him some paper towels, and he used one to wipe his eyes.

QUESTION: What is it like for you to hear about the impact of your crime on the Ronaldos?

ANSWER: I feel awful. Just awful. I can't wrap my mind around the fact that I did that to another human being. No one deserves that. I hate myself for what I did. Mr. Ronaldo and his son have every right to hate me and to want me to stay in prison. How can I blame them for that? I hope one day they can forgive me. I don't expect that, but that's what I hope for.

We concluded the hearing with a number of other questions; then Robert Blane and his attorney left the hearing room. We shared our impressions with one another. We acknowledged Blane's impressive progress during his prison stay and his maturation. We agreed that he showed evidence of genuine insight about his crime and its consequences. But we had to balance this positive news with the reality that Blane had served only one-third of his prison sentence. He had been convicted of a heinous crime, and one of his victims, Alexis Ronaldo, strenuously objected to Blane's release. The board voted unanimously to deny Blane's parole. In our minutes (which would be shared with Blane and his attorney) we commended him for his earnest program participation, insight, and disciplinary record. We explained that we were denying parole because of the seriousness of the offense and its effect on the victims. Our only disagreement concerned when to schedule his next parole board hearing. Three of us argued that we should delay his next hearing for two years; one member argued that we should wait three years because of the seriousness of the offense. The majority prevailed.

|||||||||||||||||||||||||||||||||||||||||||||||||||||||||||||

Cases like Lauren Whalen's and Robert Blane's were the most difficult I encountered because I had to consider the impact of their traumatic lives on their criminal conduct. But not all cases were this difficult. Some cases were straightforward; often they involved inmates whose crimes were so unspeakable, so evil, that I could never, ever vote for parole.

The case involving Frank Ballasco was typical. Ballasco, sixty-three, had grown up in Providence. During his teenage years he became enamored of the adults in his neighborhood who were involved in organized crime, specifically La Cosa Nostra.

Ballasco seemed at ease and full of panache in the role of a mobster. He strolled into the parole board hearing room with a nonchalance, hubris, and swagger I rarely saw. His wavy gray hair, facial stubble, wrinkles, and freezing cold stare gave him the look of a seasoned convict, which was what he was.

Many inmates greeted the parole board when they entered the hearing room. Not Ballasco. As a canny career criminal, he had worked hard to cultivate a tough-guy, don't-mess-with-me image, which had served him well during his four separate prison sentences.

I had met Ballasco during several of his previous parole hearings and knew his history well. He had gotten into trouble as a juvenile, mostly for dealing drugs, shoplifting, and gun possession. Between the ages of fifteen and eighteen Ballasco had spent a total of sixteen months in the state's juvenile correctional facility.

When he became an adult, Ballasco joined up with the local organized crime syndicate more formally and plunged himself into a lifetime of criminal activity. His first conviction was for armed robbery. According to the barely legible police report prepared on a manual typewriter, in the early 1970s Ballasco worked for a prominent organized crime figure and was expected to reach out to people who owed the mob money and were late with their payments. One afternoon Ballasco tracked down a local tavern owner who owed a gambling-related debt, walked into the tavern, pulled out a handgun, and demanded payment. When the man refused, Ballasco opened and emptied the cash register near the tavern's front door. "Consider this a down payment," Ballasco said, according to the victim.

Ballasco served eighteen months in prison for that offense. About a year after his release Ballasco was arrested by an undercover detective who had infiltrated a drug-selling ring. Ballasco, still a young man, worked for the ring as a runner, delivering drugs and retrieving payment. He served another two years in prison for that offense. During the next fifteen years or so, Ballasco was in and out of prison for offenses ranging from domestic assault to bribery of a public official to embezzlement. In addition to serving time in Rhode Island's prisons, Ballasco served a total of about three years in federal prisons.

Ballasco's most recent conviction, which had led to his current incarceration, was for bank fraud and murder. Ballasco and one of his associates had falsified mortgage documents, including W-2 forms, to inflate the value of a house that Ballasco had purchased. Soon after, he took out a loan against the inflated value of the house and then defaulted on the mortgage loan. Ballasco murdered his coconspirator when Ballasco learned from his organized-crime connections on the street that his partner was planning to testify against Ballasco in order to gain a shorter sentence from prosecutors.

Here is how the murder unfolded. Under the pretense of friendship, Ballasco invited his coconspirator to attend a New England

Patriots football game. The Patriots' football stadium in Foxboro, Massachusetts, is an easy forty-minute drive from Providence. Ballasco picked up his coconspirator at the man's home and on the way to Foxboro took a detour to a remote state park in northern Rhode Island. Much to the victim's surprise, Ballasco drove into a secluded parking lot, pulled out a handgun, and shot him at point-blank range. Ballasco was convicted following a jury trial and sentenced to life in prison (with the possibility of parole). This was Ballasco's first parole board hearing on the life sentence. Unlike his previous parole board hearings, Ballasco was not represented by a lawyer (either because he could not afford one or he had concluded that hiring one, given his record, would be a waste of money).

QUESTION: Mr. Ballasco, we meet again. You seem to have considerable difficulty staying out of prison. What happened this time?

ANSWER: It's all in the paperwork; you can read it for yourself.

QUESTION: Well, is what's in the police report true? Did you commit the murder?

ANSWER: That's what they say.

QUESTION: My question is whether you admit to the crime or not. Let me ask it again: Did you commit the murder?

ANSWER: I suppose.

QUESTION: What exactly does "I suppose" mean?

ANSWER: It means I don't want to talk about it. It is what it is.

QUESTION: Do you want to be paroled, or would you prefer to serve your life sentence?

ANSWER: Of course I want parole. What do you think?

QUESTION: Please tell us what makes you a good parole risk in this case, especially in light of your significant criminal record.

ANSWER: I'm tired of this life. You'll never see me again.

QUESTION: Mr. Ballasco, I would like to believe you. But I want to show you copies of letters you wrote to the parole board when you were serving other sentences. As you can see here, in both of these letters you told the board how you have learned your lesson, you want to get completely out of the organized crime world, and your criminal career is over. As we all know, things didn't quite work out that way. What makes this time different? Why should we take you at your word now?

ANSWER: I can see I don't have a shot at parole. You guys have already made up your mind.

And with that Ballasco simply stood up and walked out of the hearing room, slamming the metal door behind him. He didn't ask for permission to leave, and he certainly didn't say good-bye. I suppose this was the only way Ballasco knew to convey his disgust and to assert some feeble control in a situation where he knew the outcome.

Although I regret my conclusion, for me Ballasco epitomizes the hardcore criminal who appears to be beyond redemption. He seems evil. A life filled with crime is all he knows. Ballasco has never held a steady job. He has spent most of his life ignoring the rules and doing things his way, regardless of the impact of his conduct on victims. I do not like giving up on human beings, and doing so runs counter to my strong instincts as a social worker. The reality, which took me years to fully acknowledge, is that some inmates' situations feel hopeless to me. It was painful for me to type these words.

And yet, as evil as Ballasco seems, I know that calling him evil is too easy. I have been around long enough to know that people are not born evil. Ballasco's prison file is filled with tales of the trauma and chaos he endured as a child. He did not become a hardened criminal by happenstance or overnight. Ballasco's seemingly evil ways, I told myself, must be the toxic by-products of severe, unspeakable trauma to which he was subjected during his formative years. So once again I found myself staring at multiple shades of moral gray as I tried to sort out whether inmates who have committed the most evil crimes are truly evil people.

||||||||||||||||||||||||||||||||||||||||||||||||||||||

The parole board sees many such cases, where the crimes are so heinous or the inmates' criminal and disciplinary records are so severe that it has no choice but to deny parole. The verdict is all but cast in stone the moment the inmate walks through the hearing room door.

A second pattern of cases is quite different. In these cases inmates have done everything the parole board expects and wants. They have matured during their years in prison, taken earnest advantage of challenging rehabilitation programs, and avoided serious disciplinary problems. Assuming they have decent home and job plans, these inmates often are good candidates for parole.

But between these two extremes is most of the parole board's work, cases with compelling, competing arguments about release. It was not unusual for me to have a tentative opinion in mind—based on my review of the copious records—when the inmate entered the hearing room and then shift my position based on the in-person interview. Sometimes my shift was in the inmate's favor and sometimes not. An inmate who had what appeared to be slim chances of getting my vote for parole would overwhelm me with her insight and sincerity, so much so that I changed my mind. In other cases I found my in-person encounter with the inmate quite discouraging. Based on the inmate's records, I had expected to vote for parole. But during the hearing I found inconsistencies or flat-out contradictions or confabulations in the inmate's version of the crime, evasiveness, or disingenuousness.

By far the hardest cases for me to decide incorporated elements of true evil and goodness, at least as I understand these concepts. And these were the cases in which I drew on my deep-seated belief that many criminals—although not all—have the capacity to alter the course of their lives in fundamental ways. In these cases I wrestled with the facts. I wrestled with my conscience. I wrestled with the potential consequences of whatever I decided.

In my job as a professor I have taught a graduate statistics course for many years. Many students dread the experience, assuming that the course will be filled with arcane mathematical formulas (indeed, there are some) unlikely to be relevant to their professional lives. But I tell them that I choose to teach the course because I think many of the core concepts can sharpen their conceptual skills and significantly enhance the quality of their work. Perhaps my favorite is the distinction between what statisticians call type I and type II errors.[2] Understanding these phenomena shaped my thinking as a parole board member and helped me make the tough decisions.

In research we talk about error, especially when we make predictions. Here's a simple example. Say the local child welfare department receives a report of suspected abuse of a child by his father. A child abuse investigator gathers all relevant information. In the end the investigator must decide whether there is evidence of child abuse and whether the child should be placed in foster care. In effect, she must use her best judgment to forecast the future. If she concludes that the child must be removed from the home and guesses right, she has protected the child. If she concludes that evidence of abuse was insufficient, guesses right, and does not remove the child from the home, she has prevented the trauma commonly associated with placing a child in foster care.

But, as we all know, no one in these circumstances has perfect knowledge or forecasting ability. If the investigator removes the child from his home when there was no actual need to do so, she has traumatized the child and family unnecessarily. That's comparable to what statisticians call a type I error. A type I error occurs when a researcher assumes that compelling evidence exists when in fact it does not.

In contrast a type II error occurs when a researcher concludes that there is insufficient evidence that a phenomenon exists when in fact it does. In the child abuse scenario a type II error occurs if the social worker concludes that the child has not been abused and is not at risk when the opposite is true. That's every child welfare worker's nightmare: failing to remove an at-risk child, because of imperfect knowledge or an error in judgment, and that child shortly thereafter is seriously abused or killed.

Parole board members face the same challenge. They make judgments about whether an inmate is or is not ready to be released from prison. They base their decisions on the best available information, including reams of information in prison files and in-person interviews with victims and inmates. They do the best they can, knowing that their judgment is fallible. If I vote to release an inmate and the inmate does not reoffend, I guessed right, so to speak. The same is true if I decide to continue the incarceration of an inmate who would have committed a serious crime had he been released (although that is impossible to prove).

What kept me up some nights is the risk of type I and especially type II errors. If I voted against parole of an inmate who would have done well in the community, I committed a type I error. I feel badly about that. But what I worried about more was the risk of a type II error: voting to release an inmate who commits a serious crime while on parole. And that happened.

Perhaps *error* is not the best term here; I do not consider it a true error, in the strictest sense of the term, when I used my best judgment and knew that I had considered every available piece of information. It may be more accurate to say that what happened after the inmate's release was not what I had hoped, and I regret that deeply. But I know in my heart that I did the best I could, and the hard reality is that some inmates I voted to release on parole committed new crimes or will do so. I cannot accept the argument that, if that is the case, we should never parole anyone. Keeping inmates in prison longer than they need to be comes with its own set of risks and actually diminishes public protection by increasing the likelihood of future harm. More about that later. Suffice it to say that I never wanted to be wrong when I rendered my vote, and I did my best to avoid type I and type II errors.

So what made Robert Blane's case—the quintessential example of a hard case—and others like it so difficult? In many ways Blane's case exemplifies the tension between free will and determinism. Like so many prison inmates, Blane had a stunningly inauspicious start in life. He was born into a chaotic life. His parents had a tenuous, conflict-filled relationship. Blane's father had himself grown up in an abusive household. His dad spent time in a juvenile correctional facility and was in and out of adult prison because of his chronic struggle with heroin addiction. Blane's mother was sexually abused as a child and, in her teenage years, abused alcohol and cocaine to cope with the trauma. She was also diagnosed with bipolar disorder; the combination—known as a co-occurring disorder that involves both serious mental illness and substance abuse—interfered with her ability to parent Blane. It is no wonder that Blane was badly scathed by his childhood experiences.

I do my best to avoid thinking like a fatalist, but the data are compelling and indisputable: an infant born into circumstances comparable to Blane's is more likely to struggle than a child born into more auspicious circumstances. Research evidence suggests that being the victim of maltreatment during childhood nearly doubles the likelihood that an individual will commit crimes as an adult. In case after case inmates present compelling childhood histories of developmental challenges, school difficulties or failure, interpersonal conflict, hard-to-manage behaviors, physical abuse, neglect, substance abuse challenges, mental health issues, and encounters with the police. The trajectory is not inevitable, but it's far too common.

No one should be surprised that the Robert Blanes of the world get into trouble. In his case Blane sought whatever succor he could find; sadly, the man who took him in was himself a miscreant.

And while the toxic tangle of life circumstances surrounding Blane does not excuse his heinous acts, they certainly helped me understand them. Confronted with Blane's earnest and sincere efforts to address the demons in his life, as evidenced by his stalwart efforts to participate in challenging prison-based rehabilitation programs, his maturation, and the impressive insight that he articulated to the parole board, I felt caught between his crimes and the potential of his rehabilitation.

The Lady Justice statue, sometimes known as Scales of Justice or Blind Justice, is one of the best-known statues in the world, and I often reflected on its image during parole board proceedings. The ancient Greek statue represents Themis, the Titan goddess of justice and law. Well known for her clear-sightedness, she typically (she has been depicted by many sculptors) holds a sword in one hand and scales in the other. The scales represent the impartiality with which justice is served, at least in principle, and the sword signifies the power held by those making the decision. During the sixteenth century, artists started representing Themis with a blindfold to show that justice is not subject to influence.

I don't know that true impartiality is possible, but I did my best. I admit that when some inmates—a small percentage, fortunately—behaved toward the parole board in ways that were disrespectful, arrogant, insulting, and provocative, they pushed my buttons. I know that such behavior often reflects an underlying mental illness, anxiety, sense of vulnerability and fear, or defensiveness, but at times it was hard to feel sympathetic. When inmates acted up during a hearing, I tried hard to remain calm and nonreactive. Often I stopped questioning and asked the inmate to reflect on how he was behaving and to think about the impression he was making on the parole board. Some inmates have the capacity to engage in this sort of reflection and are able to regroup, often after apologizing to the board. Other inmates are either unable to put a harness on their misconduct or choose not to. The occasional inmate, like Frank Ballasco, seems determined to be defiant to the bitter end.

Robert Blane was no such inmate. He was humble, respectful, and saturated with what appeared to all of us to be genuine remorse. I wanted to be sympathetic, yet I could not ignore the anguish-filled testimony by his victim and the patent viciousness of Blane's arson. I call this ambidextrous parole board decision-making: on the one hand, on the other hand. In many cases the scales of justice are tipped steeply to one side; in others they are truly balanced. These were the cases in which I agonized.

|||||||||||||||||||||||||||||||||||||||||||||||||||||||||

Prisons occasionally are filled with goodness. Imagine that. The Rhode Island Department of Corrections partners with a remarkable program, National Education for Assistance Dog Services (NEADS), also known as Dogs for Deaf and Disabled Americans. Inmates who apply to participate in the program must meet strict criteria—typically those who have good institutional records and have avoided serious discipline problems—and undergo extensive interviews. Inmates must make a commitment to participate in the program for at least one year. That eliminates inmates who are serving short sentences and those likely to be released soon; also, the program is limited to male inmates.

Each puppy lives with an inmate handler (a backup inmate participates in case the primary handler is unable to complete the program). Puppies spend most of their time with the primary handler, going to prison classes and groups in which the inmate is enrolled (educational classes, treatment programs), recreation areas, and dining halls. Each puppy sleeps in the primary handler's cell.

NEADS trainers make regular visits to each participating prison to conduct classes for the inmates in the program. In class the inmates learn how to teach their puppy tasks and obedience skills. In addition, they learn how to groom and properly care for their puppy, provide basic first aid, and monitor canine health. The NEADS staff trainers assess each puppy to make training recommendations and assign homework to the handler.

Inmates provide the puppies with socialization experiences and skills by bringing the dogs with them whenever possible. Whether the handler is going to a medical appointment, the TV lounge, or the visiting room, the puppy is usually right by the handler's side. On a number of occasions, while waiting for inmates to be summoned for parole board hearings, I stood in the nearby Medium Security visiting room and observed the puppies, inmate handlers, and NEADS trainers as they put the dogs through their paces. It's a remarkable sight that gave me a glimpse of goodness in the midst of what often seems, and is, terribly grim. In one exercise I watched an inmate pretend to be disabled and roll around the visiting room in a wheelchair. The inmate fell out of the wheelchair and called for the dog. Before running over to the inmate, the dog instinctively searched for a fake cordless telephone nearby, picked it up in his mouth, and brought the phone to the handler so he could summon help.

I could not help but smile as I watched the inmate, Isaac Witte, stroke and praise his dog, a yellow Labrador retriever. Nine years earlier Witte had nearly killed another man in a vicious barroom fight. At an earlier parole board hearing Witte had described in painful detail how he had argued with his victim over, he said, "something incredibly stupid."

I had never laid eyes on Mr. Taylor before that night. Both of us were drinking heavily and playing poker. We were both drunk. Taylor made a few comments to my girlfriend that really ticked me off. My girlfriend was standing next to me and Taylor said something about how her sexy looks weren't going to help me out in this poker game. I told him to keep his mouth shut and that was no way to talk to my girlfriend. Well, we got into it. I shoved him, he shoved me, and we were off and running. He grabbed his beer bottle off of the table and smashed it and started to go after me with the bottle's sharp edges. I grabbed a utility knife I had in a leather case on my belt and threatened Taylor right back. I was working a construction job and had gone to the bar right from work; that's why I had the knife on me. Anyway, it turns out I sliced up Taylor pretty bad. I felt sick when I read the police report. At the time I was so drunk I didn't realize how badly I hurt him.

According to the police narrative and hospital emergency department report, Taylor suffered deep lacerations to his face, neck, and torso. He almost bled to death and required emergency surgery to save his life.

On the morning of Witte's hearing we met with Taylor. Scars ran across his face. Plastic surgery had helped only so much. Taylor said:

Thanks for seeing me. Frankly I'm shocked to hear that Witte is up for parole so soon. Nobody explained to me how he gets time off of his sentence for good behavior and participating in programs.

I don't want this guy out. He's dangerous. Look what he did to me. [Taylor pointed to the scars on his face and neck and then pulled up his shirt to show us scars on his chest. He also passed around gruesome photos that hospital staffers took of him just before and after his emergency surgery. The photos of open lacerations saturated with blood were hard to look at.] What kind of monster would do something like this?

So the guy was upset with me. Does that give him the right to slice me up like a watermelon? It makes me sick just to look in the mirror every day. I will live with these scars and memories forever. Let him do his time. I'm doing mine.

As I watched Witte nurture and work with his NEADS puppy in the most loving way imaginable, I had difficulty reconciling this kind and gentle man with the man who had savagely assaulted Taylor with reckless, alcohol-fueled abandon. Here in this moment was, for me, the compelling juxtaposition of goodness and evil. The scene reminded me of my relationship with Dave Sempsrott, the stunningly kind inmate I had met earlier in the Missouri State Penitentiary, some years after he murdered two adults and a child. Occasionally, it seems, goodness can sprout from evil.

In another NEADS puppy program exercise, an inmate in a wheelchair tells the dog that he is cold. The dog searches the room for a folded blanket, grabs it with her mouth, and places it on the inmate's lap.

In another, a dog accompanies the wheelchair-bound inmate into a nearby lavatory. The dog grabs onto a rope that hangs from the lavatory door handle to open the door. The inmate uses the dog's back for leverage to transfer himself to the toilet and then back onto the wheelchair. The dog is even able to use her paws to activate the sink taps and close the lavatory door with her nose.

The NEADS program is one of the only prison activities for which everyone (inmates, correctional officers, prison administrators, and visitors) shares enthusiasm. Achieving this kind of consensus in prison is nearly impossible. With other programs—such as prison ministries, meditation and yoga, creative writing, and theater—it's not unusual to hear some observers snicker about the do-gooders from the community who want to save inmates and about how many inmates sign up just to obtain more good time (days shaved off of their sentences as a result of program participation) or to impress the parole board. In contrast I have never heard a nasty remark about the NEADS program. Everyone seems to win: the inmates, prison staffers, and the people with disabilities who will be assisted by the dogs who graduate. During one parole board hearing, an inmate who was serving a twenty-year sentence for manslaughter talked about his involvement in NEADS.

This program has been a lifesaver for me. Frankly I think it's done more for me than I've done for my dog, Charlie. Before I came to prison I was living a completely reckless life. I was drinking and drugging; I didn't care about anything but getting high and having a good time. I thought that's what life is all about. I didn't know any better. I know that sounds like an excuse, but it's true. I never really knew my father, and my mother was a drug addict. I dropped out of school in the ninth grade and she never tried to stop me. Imagine that! She was too caught up in her own problems to care about me.

On the night I killed Dan Blair, I was spiraling out of control. I've never had a steady job. I needed money for cocaine and I decided to rob Dan. He was also a drug dealer, and about two months earlier he had ripped me off big time. I figured this was payback time. I was high when I went to Dan's apartment. I never intended to kill him. I had the gun mostly for protection and to scare him. I didn't think Dan would fight me. The gun went off accidentally. I was able to plea-bargain this down to a manslaughter conviction.

Anyway, even during the first few years of my bid [prison sentence] I didn't much care. I figured I would just do my time. As you can see from my prison record, for several years I got in lots of trouble. I was getting booked [disciplined] for all kinds of crap—excuse me, I mean stuff. I got thrown into seg for fighting, mouthing off at COs [correctional officers], hoarding my medication, and refusing to stand for count. I just plain old didn't care.

But then my mom wrote me a long letter that started out with her telling me that she was just diagnosed with lung cancer. She told me about her treatment and how she doesn't know how much longer she'll live. I couldn't believe it. And then she wrote that the one thing she prays for is that before she dies she'll get to spend time with me out of prison and see me cleaning up my life.

That's what did it, for real. That was my wake-up call. And you can see from my record that I've cleaned up my act big time. I haven't had a booking in six years, I've received lots of certificates for programs, and I got my GED. A lot of the COs tell me they can't believe how I've turned things around.

You probably know how hard it is to get selected to be a dog handler in the NEADS program. I didn't think they'd take me, but they did. And I've proved to everyone that I can be responsible. I love this program. I've had three different dogs, and one of the worst things is saying good-bye to them when they graduate. But I've learned so much about myself from this program. The truth is, before being in NEADS, I never really cared about anyone but me. Charlie and my other dogs, they've taught me what it means to really care about someone else. I'm not lying when I say I'd sacrifice my life for these dogs—that's how much they mean to me.

I'm not sure I've ever really loved someone else before this program, except my mom. This program has helped me learn how to care and nurture, and it's also taught me how to be a responsible human being. I know I have to be careful and available all the time; if I mess up, I can mess up the dog and the disabled person the dog is supposed to help down the line. Do you know how amazing it is for me to understand this for the first time in my life? Do you understand?

IIIIIIIIIIIIIIIIIIIIIIIIIIIIIIIIIIIIIIIIIIIIIIIIIIIIIIIIIIIIII

After watching the NEADS dogs and inmates for about ten minutes, my colleagues and I walked through the inmate-filled waiting room that leads to the parole board hearing room. The waiting inmates stared at us as we walked by. They knew that their fate was in our hands.

As I've mentioned, some inmates were represented by private attorneys, although most were not, either because they could not afford one or they preferred to handle the hearing on their own. A few were represented at parole board hearings by public defenders. Over the years I was extraordinarily impressed with the quality of the legal representation these underpaid, overworked attorneys provided to indigent defendants and inmates. They typically had enormous caseloads and precious few resources to conduct the kinds of investigations that would help them make the best case for their clients.

Some public defenders I met were fresh out of law school and viewed this work as a terrific way to gain valuable experience before venturing out on their own. Others—quite a few, in fact—were career public defenders. Most were idealists, in the best sense of the term, and were deeply committed to providing the best legal advocacy possible to society's most vulnerable criminal court defendants. All their clients were poor—which was what entitled them to free legal counsel—and a significant number struggled with mental illness, addictions, or both.

In Rhode Island the public defender's office employs seven full-time social workers to assess clients' needs and collaborate with attorneys who try to convince judges that many clients need mental health and addictions treatment, not prison. In effect, the public defender's office functions as a law firm that includes a visible, active social service unit.

During parole board hearings I sometimes asked an inmate whether he or she had retained an attorney during the criminal court proceedings. A common answer was, "No, I couldn't afford a lawyer, so I had a public defender." The implication was that public defenders are not lawyers, which I found upsetting, given how impressive, dedicated, and skilled public defenders tended to be. I always felt obliged to explain this to inmates. The vast majority of public defenders I have met chose a relatively low-paying career to defend people whom most others revile. Despite the impressive legal acumen and skill that qualify public defenders to pursue much more lucrative positions, they typically have a strong sense of mission and altruism. They are among my unsung heroes.

||||||||||||||||||||||||||||||||||||||||||||||||||||||||||

My efforts to respond to criminals who commit heinous acts forced me to struggle with life's most difficult questions about the nature of evil and goodness. All of us, I suspect, have encountered both. Outside my prison work, my encounters with evil have been once removed. The all-too-steady diet of news headlines about mass executions, sex slavery, beheadings, and torture provides ample evidence of evil. Yet I am heartened by an equally steady diet of news about phenomenally caring, altruistic people who go out of their way, usually without fanfare, to be kind to others. Our world is filled with both—those whose conduct should be erased from the planet and those who exemplify the Yiddish term *mensch*, a true human being. In between, of course, are the rest of us, whose lives are filled with a complicated mix of virtue and vice.

Some years ago I came across a book, *Lest Innocent Blood Be Shed,* that taught me that in the depths of life's worst cruelties one can find veins of goodness. The book's author, a moral philosopher and Wesleyan University professor named Philip Hallie, writes about how his preoccupation with the horrors of the Holocaust inadvertently led him to the discovery of remarkable goodness, in the form of a group of non-Jewish villagers in Le Chambon-sur-Lignon in southern France, a story he stumbled upon during his research on the evils of the Holocaust. The villagers, a group of true altruists, risked their lives to save and protect Jews fleeing Nazi Germany and the Vichy government in France. Hallie writes about how he had spent his academic career studying the nature of evil and in its midst felt compelled to explore the nature of goodness, the kind of goodness he found among the French villagers:

> I knew that always a certain region of my mind contained an aware-
> ness of men and women in bloody white coats breaking and rebreak-
> ing the bones of six- or seven- or eight-year-old Jewish children in or-
> der, the Nazis said, to study the processes of natural healing in young
> bodies. All of this I knew. But why not know joy? Why not leave root
> room for comfort? Why add myself to the millions of victims? Why
> must life be for me that vision of those children lying there with their
> children's eyes looking up at the adults who were breaking a leg for
> the second time, a rib cage for the third time? Something had hap-
> pened, had happened for years in that mountain village. Why should
> I be afraid of it?[3]

Hallie went on to reflect on the complexity of goodness and evil and the tension between them. In *Lest Innocent Blood Be Shed*, Hallie writes about how some of the noblest, most ethical people imaginable—deeply religious residents of Le Chambon—chose to lie to and deceive Nazi sympathizers in Vichy France in order to protect vulnerable Jews. Hallie explores the nature of moral compromise and asserts that neither goodness nor evil always exists in pure form, something I learned repeatedly while working in prisons with inmates who had committed horrific crimes.

> It is plain that the story of the struggle of Le Chambon is of no special
> political or military interest. But it is of ethical interest. The word *eth-*
> *ics* can be traced to the Greek word for character, an individual person's
> way of feeling, thinking, and acting. Ethics is concerned with praising
> some sorts of character and blaming other sorts. In that region of eth-
> ics concerned with matters of life and death (as against, for example,
> sexual or professional conduct), a person who destroys life is blamed
> for doing this unless that destruction can be excused or justified in
> some way; and in life-and-death ethics a person who avoids or prevents
> the destruction of human life is praised for doing this unless his deed
> can be shown to be destructive of human life. In life-and-death ethics
> the person we blame is often called "evil," and the person we praise is

often called "good," although we may use such milder terms of praise and blame as "bad" and "decent."[4]

I read *Lest Innocent Blood Be Shed* while I was working at the Missouri State Penitentiary with Dave Sempsrott. I thought a lot about that book as I tried to sort out how I felt about Dave, his kindness, and his depraved acts. As I paged through Hallie's narrative, I found myself ruminating about the complex juxtaposition of goodness and evil I had encountered among penitentiary inmates and staffers. Sometime later I wrote Hallie a letter and shared my insights with him. I told him how my wife and I had recently visited the German concentration camp Dachau. Hallie wrote back, letting me know how moved he was by my efforts to draw on his book as I struggled with prison-based morality:

> My wife and I visited Dachau, too. My trips to Dachau during the past few years are especially complex as I do research on a German major Schmelling, who tried to do some good. Trying to praise a German soldier under Hitler brings you hard up against the killing camps like Dachau. "A good man in such a regime?" I keep asking myself. I am writing about a good man involved in as evil a cause as man has ever concocted.

When I first read Hallie's words, I could not help but reflect on my own career-long immersion in evil. At the time my relationship with Dave Sempsrott and other inmates in the Missouri State Penitentiary provided the starkest examples. My work forced me to climb inside sordid details linked with murder, rape, armed robbery, molestation, domestic violence, arson, and other crimes. I have reviewed thousands of police reports, court transcripts, letters from victims, and psychiatric assessments that drip with anguish. As part of my parole board duties I met with thousands of distraught victims and heard their plaintive voices. And, like Hallie, I managed to find remarkable goodness embedded in seas of evil and on both sides of the fence: offenders and victims.

I will never forget the case of the inmate Jorge Pires, who was convicted of assaulting Tony Cuozzo. Cuozzo grew up in a mostly middle-class community in northern Rhode Island. He was an average student who did not get into any significant trouble in high school. Immediately after he graduated, he began working in his uncle's thriving pest control business. Cuozzo took courses at the local community college; he hoped to earn a degree in business administration. He was an enthusiastic New England Patriots and Boston Bruins fan and enjoyed going to a local sports bar to watch games and drink. By his own admission Cuozzo started to use cocaine recreationally. Over time he became more and more immersed in the drug culture, unbeknown to his family.

One evening soon after sunset, Cuozzo drove to Central Falls, Rhode Island, to purchase cocaine. He met with a known drug dealer, Jorge Pires, from whom he had bought cocaine on other occasions. According to the police report, Pires and Cuozzo got into a heated argument about money Cuozzo owed Pires from an earlier drug deal. The argument escalated and Pires grabbed a coarse, heavy cinderblock that was near his feet and slammed it into Cuozzo's head multiple times. Pires fled the scene. A neighborhood resident who was walking his dog nearby heard Cuozzo's cries for help and called 911.

The police and a rescue squad responded within minutes and found Cuozzo in a semiconscious state, bleeding from his head and mouth, and only minimally responsive. Cuozzo was transported to a hospital trauma unit in Providence, about a twenty-minute drive from Central Falls, and rushed into surgery. Surgeons inserted a device in Cuozzo's skull to monitor pressure in the brain cavity. They surgically removed and drained the bleeding in his skull. Surgeons had to repair bleeding vessels and tissue. They also had to repair Cuozzo's skull fracture and remove a portion of damaged brain tissue to make room for the living brain tissue. They did their best to maintain blood flow and oxygen to the brain and minimize swelling and pressure.

After Pires fled the scene of the assault, he drove to his sister's house, about thirty minutes away, and pretended that nothing had happened. He took a shower and fell asleep while his sister watched the late-night local news broadcast, which reported on the crime and identified Pires as the suspect. Pires's sister shouted about the news report and woke him up. He turned himself in to police, ultimately pleaded guilty, and was sentenced to twelve years in prison. He was eligible for parole after serving four years.

The morning of Pires's hearing, Cuozzo's father, Daniel, arranged to meet with us on his son's behalf. Daniel Cuozzo walked calmly into the conference room. I gazed at his face for hints of what we were about to hear. Most victims are intensely angry, and that's what I expected here. To my surprise Cuozzo was not angry. In a slow, measured cadence he thanked us for the opportunity to meet with him. His affect was relatively flat. He acknowledged that his son had waded into drug use and had ventured into Central Falls in search of cocaine. I then heard words I never expected to hear from the father of a son who was now permanently brain damaged as a result of a vicious, evil crime:

My son was, and is, a good person. It's true he was where he shouldn't have been, doing what he shouldn't have been doing. Like too many young people, Tony thought he was invulnerable and could handle casual drug use. Little did he know how quickly he would become addicted to cocaine. He worked hard in his uncle's business and he played hard. Sadly, until the crime, my wife and I knew nothing about Tony's drug use. We're not naive; we know many young people use drugs. But we had no clue that Tony was into this scene so deep. Anyway, that's beside the point.

Tony will never be the same. He lives every day suffering from severe headaches and chronic confusion. He has difficulty processing information and often struggles to form words. Tony's personality is nothing like it was. He used to be good natured and outgoing. Now Tony is a mere shadow of his former self. Most days he sits in a chair and stares. Occasionally he watches television, although I doubt he understands much. He's no longer the Tony we knew. We've lost our Tony.

You probably expect me to tell you how I want Jorge Pires to serve every single day of his sentence. I'm not going to do that. My wife and I have prayed on this. We're Christians. We believe in redemption. We want to forgive Mr. Pires. When we sat in the courtroom during Mr. Pires's sentencing, we learned about his troubled life. He was raised—and I use that term loosely—by the state because both of his parents were in and out of jail. We heard Pires's lawyer tell the judge about how Pires sold drugs to survive. Don't get me wrong: we don't like what he did to our son, but we do forgive him. This whole case is just one tragedy piled on top of another. Here's the bottom line: If this board thinks Pires has turned his life around, if you really think he's been rehabilitated, we have no objection to paroling him.

My colleagues and I were stunned. During all the years I met with crime victims, I had never encountered one who was so generous of spirit. In that moment I stared at goodness, a form of which I am not sure I could achieve were I in Daniel Cuozzo's shoes.

I have also been privileged to witness what certainly appeared to be remarkable goodness manifested by inmates who had caused unspeakable harm. The general public tends to imagine that prison inmates are evil; even a cursory review of their litany of crimes can lead to that understandable conclusion. Yet buried in that deep and wide morass of horror are occasional pearls. I have seen a few—not enough, of course, but some. Ronald Stone was one of them.

Stone was sentenced to seven years for overseeing an active heroin distribution operation. When I first met him, he was twenty-seven years old. The parole board denied Stone's first petition for release; we commended him for his prison conduct but wanted him to complete an intensive drug treatment program. Stone admitted that he had gotten involved in the drug trade after becoming addicted to cocaine. We agreed to see Stone again nine months after his first hearing. Shortly before his second parole hearing, he completed the six-month prison-based drug program. That he had learned a great deal was evident during the hearing:

QUESTION: Can you tell us what you learned in the program? What did you get out of it?

ANSWER: I learned a great deal about the nature of addiction and my personal triggers. I suppose you hear this all the time, but I learned that for so long I was in deep denial about the severity of my drug use. I never saw myself as an addict. Now I do. I can say those words and mean them. That's going to help me in my recovery.

QUESTION: What did you learn in the program that will help you avoid relapsing?

ANSWER: Put simply, it's people, places, and things. When I get out, I can't hang around the people I was with when I was using and dealing. If I do, it's probably just a matter of minutes or hours before I'm back in the game. Plus, I've gotta stay away from the neighborhood where I was buying and selling drugs. I can't be a moth drawn to that flame; if I go there, I'm dead, or back here in prison. And then there's the drugs. If I'm around cocaine, there's a big chance I'll relapse. It doesn't take a rocket scientist to know that. I'm smart enough to know that being anywhere in the vicinity of cocaine is, for me, a possible death sentence.

In many respects Stone's case was almost cookie cutter. I was in hearings with thousands and thousands of inmates who, like Stone, dabbled in cocaine or heroin and, despite their best intentions, became addicted. But during Stone's second parole hearing and following his release from prison, I learned about his special goodness. In his prison file was a letter from a senior correctional administrator:

Dear Parole Board:

I am not accustomed to writing letters to the parole board on inmates' behalf. In this case I am making an exception. Inmate Stone has been incarcerated in my facility for a little over two years. About a year ago, one of my assistants told me something remarkable about Stone, something we rarely get to see in prison. I learned that Stone, who spent almost two years in college, started a tutoring program here for inmates who are illiterate. Some of his students have learning disabilities, and some are immigrants who don't understand English very well. What's remarkable about Stone is that he has done this entirely on his own. He never asked for publicity, he never asked any staff for commendation letters to be sent to the parole board, he never asked to get credit for his efforts that could be counted as good time to reduce his sentence.

About a month ago, after I learned about Stone's work, I called him to my office. I asked him about his work and how much time he's been spending doing this. I learned that Stone spends two to three hours nearly every evening working with inmates. I've never seen anything quite like this.

I read the administrator's letter before Stone's second parole hearing and used it to frame a handful of questions:

QUESTION: Were you aware that we received a letter from Mr. Spence about your tutoring program?

ANSWER: No, I had no idea he was sending that. What did it say?

QUESTION: He's really impressed with you. He had no idea you were doing this work until one of his assistants brought it to his attention. I'm impressed too. Tell us what led you to start the program?

ANSWER: It's not really that complicated. During my stay here I've had lots of time to think. I know I messed up bad, and I've hurt a lot of people. I sold drugs to people whose addiction continued or got worse because of me. I now realize that many of the addicts who bought drugs from me got the money to pay me by breaking into people's houses, stealing cars, robbing store clerks, and taking women's pocketbooks. I feel awful about the impact of my crimes.

I have to make amends. I have to do what's right. I was always a pretty good student, so I figured one way I could make amends is to help inmates who can't read. I've been around here long enough to understand that lots of these guys commit crimes because they're poor and need money. Many of them were lousy students, have disabilities, or never learned English. For many, selling drugs and stealing is plain old survival. All of us are hurting lots of people. I just want to do what I can to help these inmates develop a skill that might help them get a job; that might keep them from committing crimes.

Even in prisons one can find people who do what's right.

||||||||||||||||||||||||||||||||||||||||||||||||||||||||||||

During the course of my career working in prisons, I came to believe that between goodness and evil are layers and layers of complexity. Human beings I have come to know, both in and out of prison, rarely are unadulterated good or evil.

My ever-evolving sense of the mix of goodness and evil derives from my understanding of why people commit crimes. There's no simple explanation. I liken the word *crime* to the word *cancer*. Often I hear someone comment that so-and-so has cancer. The word itself tells me nothing about the type of cancer (lung, bone, prostate, esophageal, bladder, skin, testicular, brain, colon, eye, liver, ovarian, or breast), its etiology, treatment options, or prognoses. The word is meaningful only when it's joined with hundreds of others that spell out the important details.

So, too, with the word *crime*. By itself it is relatively meaningless. To be useful the word requires finely textured context: the type of crime (murder, rape, armed robbery, embezzlement, stolen motor vehicle, drug possession and distribution, child molestation, breaking and entering, fraud, domestic violence, gun possession, vehicular homicide, elder abuse, sex trafficking, arson, kidnapping, identity theft), its etiology, rehabilitation options, and the likelihood of recidivism. Understanding crime—and grasping the mix of goodness and evil embedded in crimes—is no less complicated than understanding cancer. We are dealing with complex multivariate equations.

And yet there are patterns—patterns that helped me understand the vagaries of human nature and human beings who commit awful crimes. When I reflect on the tens of thousands of inmates I have encountered, I see reasonably clear patterns.[5] Among the most prominent and relatively easy to detect are offenders who struggle with serious addictions. My strong sense is that most people do not fully grasp the profound link between addictions and crime. Huge numbers of inmates are serving time for crimes related to addiction to alcohol, drugs, and gambling. Extensive research indicates that most inmates are in prison for some addiction- or substance abuse–related reason. Many inmates committed crimes while under the influence of alcohol or drugs. Narcotics, alcohol, and other substances can lead otherwise nonviolent people to commit remarkably violent acts and may exacerbate the tendencies of people who are prone to violence. Many murders, aggravated assaults, armed robberies, domestic assaults, and rapes are committed by people whose judgment is stunningly impaired by substances. Often underlying these inmates' addictions are mental health challenges, undiagnosed or untreated, that the inmate is self-medicating with these substances.

- Hector Aparicio was a heroin addict. He had been incarcerated twice for drug manufacturing and selling. After his last prison sentence, Aparicio was on probation and was enrolled in an outpatient drug treatment program. He worked sporadically for a landscaping company.

  About five months after his latest release from prison, Aparicio relapsed on heroin. This occurred soon after Aparicio learned that his twenty-two-year-old daughter had committed suicide. Aparicio was soon fired from his job because of his erratic attendance and performance. One evening Aparicio walked into a local convenience store, held a gun to the head of the cashier, and demanded money from the cash drawer. The store's manager heard the cashier scream, ran to the front of the store, confronted Aparicio, and tried to wrestle the gun away from him. The gun went off and killed the store manager.

- Lydia Bamberger was addicted to cocaine. She left a friend's party under the influence and began driving home down a four-lane highway. She lost control of her car, crossed the median, and broadsided an oncoming car driven by a young mother who had her infant twins in the backseat. One of the twins was killed instantly; the other twin suffered life-threatening injuries, and the mother lingered in the hospital in a persistent vegetative state.

- Charlene Lau was a hospital nurse who took a leave of absence after a freak accident at home in which she severely injured her back. Lau's doctor prescribed Vicodin, a powerful pain medication derived from opium. Over time Lau became addicted to the Vicodin and began snorting it.

  Lau returned to work and got a new job at a nursing home. To feed her addiction, she began stealing a liquid opioid, Oxyfast, prescribed for three elderly residents who were suffering from severe end-stage cancer-related pain. In an effort to conceal her theft, Lau replaced the residents' pain medication with water and food coloring to match the medication's original color.

It was hard for me to not feel anger toward these inmates when I met them at parole board hearings. Their acts were evil, if we accept the standard definitions of immoral and malevolent conduct. Hector Aparicio terrorized convenience store employees who were simply trying to earn a day's pay. Lydia Bamberger killed one infant and seriously injured another and their mother. Charlene Lau took pain medication from elderly nursing home residents. Yet when I faced these inmates, I tried hard to distinguish between such depraved conduct and the person. Is it possible in some instances to conclude that the inmate's conduct was evil but the inmate is not? I think so.

Addiction, for example, is now widely viewed as an illness and a disease. During the eighteenth and nineteenth centuries, addiction was viewed as a sin, a form of evil conduct. It was not unusual then for people who were considered drunks to be placed in stocks, beaten, whipped, jailed, fined, and otherwise ridiculed. The Ale Houses Act of 1551 made drunkenness a civil offense in England. Repeat offenders were paraded through town wearing a "drunkard's cloak," a barrel with an opening cut in the top for the person's head to pass through. Two smaller holes were cut in the sides for the arms.

Not until the late nineteenth century did significant numbers of physicians begin to view addiction as a disease. Since then we have seen impressive, unprecedented consensus among professionals that addiction occurs when dopamine interacts with the neurotransmitter glutamate to take over the brain's system of reward-related learning. Repeated exposure to an addictive substance or behavior causes nerve cells in the nucleus accumbens and the prefrontal cortex (the area of the brain involved in planning and executing tasks) to communicate in a way that leads people to seek addictive substances.[6] For many, although not all, the needle has moved from the free will side of the dial to the determinism side.

People differ in the degree to which they like or dislike a particular addictive substance or activity, most likely because of differences in physiology and genetics. Some people may enjoy a substance or activity so much that it becomes extremely tempting and difficult to resist; others do not experience this difficulty because they do not experience a similar level of enjoyment. Many of the inmates I have met seem to have remarkably low thresholds of tolerance for addictive substances and activities; with only minimal stimulation they head toward addiction.

If we accept that neurobiology largely determines individuals' addictive tendencies, it makes no more sense to consider addicts evil than it does to consider evil those people with autism, epilepsy, muscular dystrophy, and Parkinson's disease. Yet despite our increasingly sophisticated understanding of the neurobiological determinants of addiction, many of us—me included—sometimes have to fight the instinct to conflate the evil consequences of addiction and the addicted individual.

The same is true of inmates with debilitating mental illness. I do not have in mind the many inmates who are feeling somewhat depressed as a result of their incarceration. Rather, I am thinking about the 15 to 20 percent of prison inmates in nearly every state's prisons who are suffering from serious, disabling mental illness, especially schizophrenia, bipolar disorder, clinical depression, and anxiety disorders.[7] Many of these inmates experience hallucinations and delusions, especially if they are not taking antipsychotic medication. Every prison official in the nation knows that seriously mentally ill inmates are both numerous and challenging.

In a perfect world many inmates with major mental illness would be treated in a psychiatric hospital instead of being incarcerated. Granted, some offenders are so dangerous that they need to be institutionalized, either in prison or a highly secure psychiatric facility. But many inmates I have met got into trouble because of their difficulty managing their mental illness. They stopped taking their psychiatric medication, for example, or they had difficulty accessing psychiatric and other mental health services. I have lost count of the number of inmates with schizophrenia who were actively delusional (experiencing distorted thinking with significant cognitive impairment) or hallucinating (for example, hearing voices that issue commands to commit a crime) when they assaulted someone.

For many, incarceration can intensify and worsen their symptoms if they are not able to get skilled help while in prison. To make matters worse, some inmates with major mental illness get into trouble while in prison—especially by getting into fights with other inmates or failing to cooperate with correctional officers—and get placed in segregation for disciplinary reasons. Placing an inmate with major mental illness in segregation can exacerbate symptoms greatly.

- Don Swaggerty was diagnosed with schizophrenia when he was seventeen. As a young adult, Swaggerty was admitted to a psychiatric hospital on a number of occasions and was able to manage in the community reasonably well when he took his prescribed neuroleptic medication.

  Over time Swaggerty became sexually involved with three young boys in the community. Swaggerty lured them to an abandoned warehouse close to his home and sexually abused them. During a three-month period, two of the boys disappeared and were reported missing. Swaggerty eventually became a suspect, and for several weeks undercover police followed him closely. The dismembered bodies of the two missing boys were found in plastic garbage bags hidden in the basement of the abandoned warehouse.

- Joy Motton began to manifest psychotic symptoms when she was twelve. She lived with her parents until she was twenty, when she became pregnant by a man she met at a local bar. Motton received services from a community mental health center, lived in a supervised apartment, received home-based services to help her care for her newborn son, and was reasonably stable on neuroleptic medication. She was in a stormy relationship with her baby's father.

  During a routine visit at Motton's apartment, a visiting pediatric nurse noticed bruises on the baby's torso; the baby displayed various distress symptoms, suggesting that he may have been physically abused. Evidence presented at trial showed that Motton, who seemed quite confused when she was arrested, had beaten her child.

- Milt Drabowsky was a well-known surgeon. Unbeknown to his wife, Drabowsky was having an affair with a colleague. At one point Drabowsky's mistress threatened to tell his wife about the affair unless he left the marriage.

  During this time Drabowsky was also being treated by a psychiatrist for bipolar disorder. For several days during a one-week period Drabowsky was feeling profoundly depressed and contemplated suicide. He failed to show up for office appointments and stopped spending time with his wife and mistress.

  One afternoon Drabowsky wrote out a suicide note, drove over to his mistress's home, shot her in the head, and tried to commit suicide by poisoning himself with carbon monoxide. Drabowsky did not die and was later convicted of murder.

- Moe Cuellar was a nurse who provided services to patients with HIV/ AIDS. For years he coped with symptoms of bipolar disorder that were usually managed well with psychotropic medication, although recently Cuellar's mood swings had worsened.

  Early one evening Cuellar was driving home from work and stopped at a service station. Another customer had parked his car at an odd angle and in such a way that Cuellar was not able to pull his car next to the gas pump. Cuellar lost his temper and began berating the customer. The customer responded in kind, and the two threatened to harm each other. Cuellar retreated to his car where he kept a handgun in a concealed compartment in the trunk. He grabbed the gun and threatened his adversary, who dared Cuellar to shoot him. Cuellar pulled the trigger and killed the other customer.

  Evidence presented at trial showed that for more than two months Cuellar had not been taking the psychotropic medication prescribed for his bipolar disorder.

- Judy Brandt, thirty-one, struggled with cognitive issues and was diagnosed with intellectual disability (formerly called mental retardation). Brandt lived in a group home for women with similar challenges.

  One evening Brandt got into an intense argument with another group home resident when they disagreed about which television station to watch in the facility's living room. Brandt started screaming at the other resident, who responded by pushing Brandt to the floor. Brandt stood up, ran to the kitchen, grabbed shears that were on a counter for trimming the property's bushes, and stabbed the other resident in the chest. Brandt was charged with assault with a deadly weapon.

When I met inmates whose offenses appeared to be rooted in their addictions or mental illness, or both, it was not hard for me to imagine how their challenges contributed to their crimes. They seemed less evil. Often my questions during parole board hearings addressed these links and the steps the inmate had taken, and could take, to address these debilitating issues (such as addictions counseling and mental health treatment).

But in many other cases inmates' conduct seemed to reflect stunningly poor judgment, without the overlay of addictions or mental illness. My instincts about whether inmates committed crimes because of factors over which they had little or no control, as opposed to committing crimes because of deliberate choices, certainly influenced my thinking about whether they warranted parole. Some inmates need to be held accountable because of their greed, vindictiveness, and other self-serving motives.

Some inmates' offenses arise out of what I call crimes of pure frolic; they did not hurt others as a direct result of psychiatric illness or runaway addiction. Often these crimes have disastrous consequences. Yet most of these inmates do not strike me as evil in the narrow sense of the term. What they did was stupid, unthinking, impulsive, and insensitive but not the product of evil per se. In so many of these cases, what began as misguided tomfoolery escalated into vicious misconduct when the culprits indulged in various forms of reckless abandon, frequently fueled by alcohol and drugs that inhibited their impulse control and impaired their judgment. I often viewed these offenders as callous and careless, but for me these cases do not rise to the level of evil intent.

- Carl Hoffberger and Chip Landau met as juveniles when both were residents of a state-sponsored group home. Both young men had lived in a series of foster homes and group residences after their respective parents' rights were terminated because of neglect and abuse. The two shared an apartment.

  Hoffberger and Landau often sat in the apartment drinking alcohol and smoking marijuana. Early one morning—about 2:00 A.M.—the two were quite inebriated. Hoffberger told Lau he was hungry, and the two men went to a twenty-four-hour convenience store for food. They walked around the store and gathered bread, deli meats, soda, and cookies. At the cash register the drunken Hoffberger took a handgun out of his jacket pocket and playfully told the clerk that it might be a good idea for her to let the pair have the food for free.

The clerk panicked and started screaming. Hoffberger told her to calm down, but that didn't work. The clerk ran out of the store and was about to call 911 on her cell phone. Hoffberger was afraid the police would arrive and find out that he was on probation; he shot the clerk in the back. The victim died.

- Tim Phoebus and Sam Ponson worked together in the shipping department of a large retailer. After work they occasionally visited strip clubs or bars. On weekends the pair occasionally went to a nearby shooting range and, in season, went deer hunting.

  One evening, after visiting several bars, Phoebus and Ponson, both quite drunk, grabbed their rifles and drove to a highway overpass. They concocted a contest to see how many cars they could hit with bullets as they passed beneath the overpass.

  One of Phoebus's shots struck a driver in the shoulder. The driver lost control of her car, veered off of the highway, struck a pole, and died.

Yet another type of criminal who commits offenses that border on pure evil but do not quite rise to that level is the miscreant who commits crimes driven by desperation. These are offenders who conclude that they must commit a crime to work their way out of hopeless circumstances. Typically these offenders reach a point where they feel they have run out of options and must commit a crime to resolve their seemingly untenable predicament. Some crimes of desperation are committed in the context of acute crises. For example, a heroin addict in deep withdrawal may hold up a convenience store to get quick cash and then run to a nearby drug dealer to purchase a quick fix; he panics when a customer confronts him, and he shoots the customer impulsively in response to the threat.

In contrast other crimes of desperation may stem from chronic, cumulative pressure. A man who is informed by an organized crime figure that he must pay off his large loan "in the very, very near future" if he wants to protect his children from serious harm may spend weeks arranging to commit arson-for-profit or embezzle money from his employer to raise the cash the debtor needs so badly.

Many crimes of desperation have a financial stimulus. These offenses are committed in an effort to fix a money-related problem, for example, to obtain cash to pay the living expenses for one's family or to pay off a large gambling debt.

- Gary Orsino had borrowed $19,000 from a local loan shark with organized crime connections. Orsino had a bad credit history, a gambling problem, and was not able to borrow money from conventional banking sources. He felt in desperate need of the money to pay off his mounting debts.

  The loan shark contacted Orsino almost daily, pressuring him to repay the loan and the rapidly escalating interest. Orsino believed he had run out of options and impulsively decided to rob a bank. He put on a ski mask and borrowed a handgun from a friend. Orsino, who had never committed a serious crime, walked into the bank, ordered customers to lie down, handed a teller a note ordering her to hand over money with "no dye pack," and threatened the teller with a handgun. One customer, an off-duty police officer, sneaked up behind Orsino and tried to wrest the gun from him. Orsino shot the officer in the head, killing her instantly.

- Jake Adair invested heavily in the real estate market. Within ten years he had purchased a number of multifamily dwellings in low-income neighborhoods. He also owned two small businesses, an automobile repair shop and a pizza restaurant.

  The local economy weakened badly, and Adair had trouble meeting his various mortgage and rental payments. Sales at Adair's retail businesses dropped dramatically, and he had a hard time finding tenants for several rental units. Adair received a demand notice from his mortgage holder, who threatened to foreclose on his rental properties.

  In desperation Adair contacted a childhood friend who had links to organized crime. Adair arranged to have his pizza restaurant destroyed by arson so that he could collect the insurance coverage. Unbeknown to the arsonist, the pizza restaurant was attached to an apartment with a common wall. On the day of the fire the apartment's tenant was home, recovering from recent heart surgery. The fire destroyed both the restaurant and the apartment, killing the tenant.

- Rob Grimsley was a hearing officer in the state's workers' compensation court. He had been doing this work for nearly twenty-three years. Over time Grimsley's personal lifestyle had become more lavish and extravagant. He and his wife joined an exclusive country club and purchased a pricey beachfront vacation home. They also traveled extensively. Grimsley did not disclose to his wife that they were experiencing serious cash-flow problems.

  Grimsley was approached by a local attorney who frequently represented clients with cases before the workers' compensation court. The attorney and Grimsley knew each other from the country club and occasionally played golf together and socialized. During one lunchtime get-together, the attorney, who was aware of Grimsley's financial challenges, slipped him a sealed envelope containing $5,000 in cash. The attorney, who was under investigation himself for illegal activity, was cooperating with state police investigators when he attempted to bribe Grimsley in relation to a client whose case was about to be heard in Grimsley's court. Grimsley accepted the envelope.

Other crimes of desperation committed by inmates I encountered had little or nothing to do with money and much more to do with interpersonal conflict, for example, vicious assaults that arose out of a desperate attempt to resolve an overwhelming family dispute. The offenders' intense fear may be rooted in anxiety about legal repercussions and risks, the potential loss of a marriage or intimate relationship, or loss of a job. Glaring evil intent may be absent.

- Michael Machado was a city council member generally regarded as a rising star. Like his mother, Machado was elected to the council at a young age. He quickly rose through the ranks and seemed destined to assume a leadership position on the council.

  One evening, after a lengthy city council meeting, Machado stopped at a nearby restaurant, had several drinks, and began driving home. His blood alcohol level was 0.23, nearly three times the legal limit. Machado drove through a red light and slammed into a pedestrian, causing fatal injuries. Machado was so afraid of the public humiliation and legal consequences that he did not stop to help the victim or notify the police. The following morning Machado was arrested for causing a death while under the influence and leaving the scene of an accident.

- Jalen Oates was hitchhiking home one afternoon after finishing his classes at the local community college. A classmate recognized Oates and offered him a ride.

  After chatting some during their ride together, the driver drove to a secluded section of town and made sexual advances toward Oates. Oates reacted angrily and began fighting off the driver's advances. During the scuffle Oates strangled the driver to death.

Intense surges of rage precipitate many crimes, some of which involve, as prosecutors might say, evil malice aforethought. Passionate conflict, fueled by anger and hostility, can erupt in vicious forms, leading to serious injury or death. A significant percentage of rage-induced crimes occur between family members and acquaintances, such as coworkers and neighbors. Federal statistics show that nearly 60 percent of nonfatal violent crimes, many of which include an element of rage, are committed by people who know each other (that is, they are not strangers). Approximately three-fourths of homicides are committed by people known to the victim.

- Edwina Morrall, eighteen, lived with her grandmother. Morrall never knew her father, and her mother was in a drug treatment program.

  Morrall's grandmother was concerned about Morrall's relationship with a thirty-one-year-old married man. She lectured Morrall incessantly about how risky it was for her to be involved with this man. The pair often argued and threatened each other. Morrall later admitted that she sometimes fantasized about her grandmother's death.

  One afternoon Morrall got into a vicious shouting match with her grandmother after she ordered Morrall's boyfriend to leave the home. During the argument Morrall impulsively grabbed an iron frying pan and slammed it against her grandmother's head. The grandmother fell to the floor, started convulsing, lost consciousness, and later died. Morrall panicked, called the police, and reported that a Hispanic man had broken into the home and attacked her grandmother. Morrall later confessed.

- James Orr had been married to his wife for almost seven years. Her sixteen-year-old son from her first marriage lived with the couple; he had dropped out of high school and had developed a substance abuse problem. Orr's stepson worked only sporadically and did not pay for rent or food.

  Orr and his stepson always had difficulty getting along. According to Orr, his stepson always resented his mother's decision to divorce his father and remarry. Orr and his stepson argued constantly; their disagreements often erupted into shouting matches.

  One evening Orr threatened to throw his stepson out of the house when Orr accused him of stealing money from his wallet. The two exchanged punches. During the fight Orr lost control, pinned his stepson, and banged his head against the floor repeatedly, causing severe brain damage.

Some crimes of rage involve people who have no family connection at all. Often these are friends, acquaintances, or neighbors, as opposed to complete strangers.

- Tim Matte was evicted from his single-room-occupancy hotel room. The property owner grew tired of Matte's alcohol abuse and chronically late rent payments. Matte was a Vietnam War veteran who lived on disability income.

  Matte's landlord told him that he would have to leave the property by the end of the week. The two argued; Matte flew into a rage and beat her with his fists. The woman suffered several broken ribs, a broken jaw, fractured skull, and lacerations.
- Dale Shinnick was thirty-one and lived with his parents. He had dropped out of high school, struggled with a learning disability, and had difficulty maintaining steady employment.

  For several days Shinnick and his parents were involved in a feud with a neighbor. Originally Shinnick's parents accused the neighbor of building without permission a new driveway that extended into property they owned. Since then the neighbors had argued repeatedly.

One weekend afternoon Shinnick and the neighbor were outside and began arguing about how best to control a large pool of standing water that extended across the shared property line. Shinnick accused the neighbor of failing to properly grade his property when the controversial driveway was built, and the neighbor accused Shinnick's family of being too noisy. The argument escalated; Shinnick went into his family's garage, retrieved a loaded hunting rifle, and shot and killed the neighbor.

We have become all too familiar with violent crimes committed in workplaces by disgruntled employees and customers. According to federal statistics, in recent years more than a half-million nonfatal violent crimes—rape, robbery, or assault—have been perpetrated annually against people aged sixteen or older while they were at work or on duty. In recent years about five hundred workplace homicides have occurred annually. While some of these crimes are carefully planned acts of vengeance, others are spontaneous acts of rage triggered by adverse employment decisions or infuriating customer service.

- Rob Boyd operated a printing press at a large commercial printer. Boyd made no secret of being gay.

   Two of Boyd's coworkers were homophobic and frequently made snide remarks about gay people within Boyd's earshot. Occasionally these two coworkers would taunt Boyd about his sexual orientation.

   Over time Boyd became more and more frustrated with the harassment, although he never shared his frustration and anger with anyone at work. One afternoon, when the coworkers' harassment was unusually intense, Boyd lost control, grabbed a large metal stake that was lying near the printing press, and stabbed one of the coworkers in his abdomen and thigh. The second coworker fled.

- Jared Unitas bought a new recreational vehicle from a local dealer. After driving his new vehicle for two weeks, Unitas noticed that the transmission was not working properly. Unitas took the vehicle back to the dealer, whose service department attempted to fix the problem. Several days later Unitas returned to the dealer, complaining that the problem had not been fixed. Once again the service department attempted to fix the problem, but Unitas complained soon thereafter that the problem persisted and was worsening.

Unitas made an appointment with the dealer's general manager and insisted on receiving a new recreational vehicle. The general manager explained that he could not replace the vehicle and attempted to convince Unitas that the service department would continue working on the vehicle until it was properly repaired. Unitas became enraged and stormed out of the general manager's office, retrieved a handgun from his car, returned to the general manager's office, and shot the man to death.

Although most crimes of rage involve family members, acquaintances, and coworkers, some involve complete strangers whose paths happen to cross. These unfortunate encounters—many of which do not entail evil acts planned in advance—usually occur in public settings, such as parking lots, highways, restaurants, stores, and sports venues.

• Lonnie Moore pulled onto the highway and headed home after visiting his mother, who had just moved into a nursing home. About five minutes after he entered the highway, a car with a teenage driver and three teenage passengers began to tailgate Moore's vehicle. Moore motioned for the driver to pass. The car with the teenagers pulled alongside Moore's car, and two of the passengers leaned out the windows, made obscene gestures toward Moore, and began screaming at him. Moore blew his horn and returned the obscene gesture. For several minutes the two cars jockeyed for position on the highway.

Eventually Moore slowed down as he neared his exit. The driver of the other car followed Moore off the exit ramp and gently rear-ended his car at the end of the ramp. Moore jumped out of his car and began screaming at the driver and passengers. When the teenagers got out of their car and began to approach Moore, Moore opened his car trunk, retrieved a powerful compound bow he used for hunting, and shot one of the teenagers, killing him instantly.

- Johnnie Lyles was shopping at a large discount department store on a crowded Saturday afternoon. Only two checkout lines were open, and customers were growing increasingly impatient.

  A customer in front of Lyles began yelling at the checkout clerk to hurry up. The checkout clerk admonished the rude customer for her behavior and told her that she was working as quickly as possible; the two continued to exchange heated words. A store security guard walked over and began to escort the customer from the store. The customer resisted, and Lyles stepped in to try to help the security guard. During the brief fracas the unruly customer and Lyles began to scuffle; Lyles grabbed a metal baseball bat from a nearby display and began swinging furiously at the other customer. The bat struck the customer in the head, fracturing her skull and eye socket and causing permanent nerve and brain damage.

- Lew Michaels was an inmate serving a twelve-year sentence for armed robbery. He was placed in the prison's segregation unit for thirty days following a fight with another inmate in the prison's dining room.

  During his stay in segregation Michaels argued with a correctional officer who refused Michaels's numerous requests to shower. Michaels cursed at the officer and threatened to kill him. The argument escalated, and the officer used his portable departmental radio to call for backup; about two minutes later several other officers arrived at Michaels's cell. They opened the cell door in order to restrain Michaels.

  The officers did not know that Michaels had concealed a small razor blade in his hand that he had loosened from a disposable razor; as one of the officers approached him, Michaels slashed the officer's face, just below his eye.

Some inmates I encountered seemed evil in the truest sense of the term. These were offenders who planned in advance to harm others and seemed well aware of their intentions and the likely abhorrent consequences. Exploring these criminals' motives during parole board hearings led me to conversations quite different from those I had with inmates whose crimes seemed to be the by-product of addiction, mental illness, frolic, or spontaneous rage.

Some of the most disturbing evil crimes take the form of carefully calculated revenge and retribution. These offenders act out of sustained anger and a fierce determination to pay someone back for some alleged misdeed. They spend time thinking through how to harm their victims—physically, emotionally, or financially. These crimes are not the product of psychiatric compulsion or driven by addiction; rather, they are the result of manipulative deliberation and plotting.

- Tom Crowley lived with a woman for three years. The couple had an on-again, off-again relationship, although recently they had talked seriously about getting married.

  One afternoon Crowley overheard his partner talking with a friend on the telephone. The partner did not realize that Crowley was in the apartment at the time. She told the friend that she had been having an affair with a former boyfriend and just found out she was pregnant with her lover's child.

  Crowley was furious. He felt angry and betrayed but decided not to confront his partner. Instead, he took time to plot his revenge. One Saturday evening around sunset, Crowley told his partner that he had a special surprise for her. Crowley drove her to a nearby seaside town and told her that he wanted to give her something special to honor their relationship. They walked toward the water's edge and a ledge that overlooked the ocean. Crowley suddenly pushed his partner off the ledge. She and her unborn baby died when she landed on rocks hundreds of feet below.

- Bonnie Grich was employed by a heating and air-conditioning company for sixteen years. Growing up, Grich was the best friend of the daughter of the business's owner. The owner hired Grich as a bookkeeper shortly after she graduated from the local community college.

  Grich had a falling out with the owner's daughter, who accused Grich of flirting with her husband. Soon thereafter Grich sensed that the owner was much more critical of her work and was less flexible with her work schedule. Grich became quite miserable at work and resented the way she was being treated. She began embezzling money from the company's accounts. Grich obtained the funds by creating fraudulent invoices, writing checks to bogus companies, and cashing the checks herself. The fraud lasted about eighteen months. By the time she was caught, Grich had stolen nearly $176,000.

- Terrance Frohwirth, twenty, was a member of a well-known urban gang. The gang was involved with dealing drugs, stealing cars, robbing downtown pedestrians, and shoplifting.

  One of the gang's newest members was arrested by the police in connection with an armed robbery. While being interrogated by the police, the new gang member confessed to several armed robberies and automobile thefts and supplied detectives with the names of his accomplices, other gang members. As a result Frohwirth and three of his fellow gang members were arrested.

  All the defendants were released on bail pending trial. Frohwirth figured out that the new gang member had betrayed him and was furious. One night Frohwirth intercepted the new gang member as he was walking into his mother's home, forced him into Frohwirth's car, drove to a nearby public park, shoved the young man out of the car, and then shot and killed him.

Other inmates commit crimes that are the result of out-and-out greed, exploitation, and opportunism. I have no doubt that some commit crimes with explicit intent, often motivated by a self-centered wish to inflict pain on others. These are criminals who have set their sights on something they want—valuable property, money, sex—and they are determined to get it, no matter the cost to victims. Often these offenders have little ability to empathize with their victims. I must admit that I had difficulty empathizing with these inmates.

Some criminals' evil conduct is in the form of financial exploitation.

- Milton Bowen was fired from his job as the night-shift manager at a large furniture warehouse. According to his supervisor, Bowen had missed work too many times. Bowen deeply resented being fired. He was especially angry that his loss of income limited his ability to buy nice clothes, eat in upscale restaurants, and attend professional sporting events.

Bowen was determined to sustain his lifestyle. He plotted with his brother-in-law to set up a bogus jewelry store. Bowen and his accomplice rented commercial space in a strip mall and arranged for several unsuspecting jewelry salespeople to bring their lines to the storefront to discuss a wholesale purchase. Bowen and his brother-in-law robbed two salespeople at gunpoint and stole all their samples, the total value of which was $279,000.

- Will Bunker dropped out of school at sixteen. He spent most of his time hanging out in the streets with friends. On occasion Bunker worked odd jobs for extra cash. Most of his income came from selling cocaine in the neighborhood. Bunker had been arrested several times for possessing drugs, assaults, and shoplifting.

  Shortly after his eighteenth birthday, one of Bunker's friends told him he knew of a way to earn a lot of money quickly. The friend explained that he knew of a local restaurant owner whose daughter had once dated Bunker's friend; the restaurateur routinely visited a nearby outdoor bank deposit box around 11:00 P.M. to deposit the day's revenue. One night Bunker and his friend lurked in nearby bushes, waiting for the restaurant owner to drive up to the outdoor depository. When the man got out of his car, Bunker and his friend ran up to him, pointed their handguns at him, and shouted for the man to drop his money-filled bank bag. The man resisted, and Bunker shot him in the chest. The man writhed in pain while Bunker and his friend ran off with the money bag. About a half hour later the restaurateur died.

Among the inmates I have met, those involved with organized crime have been among the most callous, cruel offenders imaginable. And I am not thinking of only the stereotypical Italian and Sicilian mafioso types. On the parole board I encountered newer forms of organized crime sponsored by other ethnic groups, motorcycle gangs, and so on.

- For several years Landon Mora was groomed by a local organized crime group to take over its lucrative drug- and sex-trafficking business. At a relatively young age Mora was released from prison and went on to supervise a large-scale and highly profitable cocaine and heroin operation. He and his buddies obtained the drugs from several Mexican connections who smuggled the drugs into the United States. More recently Mora had become involved in sex trafficking of minors.

Mora was arrested during a sting operation conducted by state and federal authorities who were investigating sex trafficking. The investigators responded to ads that Mora had posted on a website known for linking men with minors. Mora began to suspect that police knew about his operation and confronted a man who, Mora believed, had leaked information to the police in order to get criminal charges in his own case reduced. Mora arranged to meet the man in a local park, ostensibly to discuss a new sex-trafficking venture. When the man arrived, Mora shot and killed him.

• Frank Rayford rode with a well-known motorcycle gang. The gang was heavily involved in the drug trade and carefully protected its turf when other motorcycle gangs encroached on the territory. One night Rayford and several of his biker friends were at a bar when members of a rival gang arrived. Tension between the two groups had been simmering for months because of their dispute about which group owned and should control a nearby neighborhood known for a lot of illegal drug activity.

Rayford got into an argument with a member of the rival biker group. In a matter of seconds the two started fighting. The bar manager kicked them out of the bar, and the two adversaries continued to go after each other. Rayford reached into his jacket, pulled out a handgun, fired several shots, and killed the other biker. Another bar patron happened to be walking into the bar at that very moment and was struck in the head by a stray bullet and killed.

• Angela Estrada dated and eventually married Carl Schilling, who was heavily involved in a large burglary and robbery ring that operated in several New England states. Estrada did not have a significant criminal record, but over time she became more and more involved in the ring's activities. On several occasions she coordinated smartphone communications (voice and text) among ringleaders and, using her knowledge from her work in a real estate firm, supplied them with information about potential victims (addresses, location of valuables, and so on).

At Schilling's request Estrada agreed to drive a car that a group of accomplices used in their robbery of the house of a wealthy man with whom Estrada once worked. The robbers abandoned the scheme in midheist when they heard police sirens in the distance (the police were alerted by a silent alarm that the robbers had inadvertently activated). Estrada realized that a landscaper who was on the property had recognized her face and the car; she drove her car right into the employee, who was standing adjacent to the driveway. The man survived the crash but ended up in a persistent vegetative state.

Other inmates exploit their victims sexually. Some sex offenders have diagnosable psychiatric disorders that explain their crimes—paraphilias such as exhibitionism, voyeurism, and pedophilia—but others simply take advantage of victims, knowing full well that their actions are exploitative, manipulative, and opportunistic.

- Bobby Surhoff married for the first time when he was thirty-six. He worked at a car dealership and married a woman he met at work. At the time Surhoff's wife had a fourteen-year-old daughter from an earlier marriage.

  About a year after their marriage, Surhoff and his wife began having difficulty getting along. Both struggled with alcohol abuse and argued frequently. One night Surhoff's wife left their apartment to stay with her mother after an argument. Surhoff walked into his stepdaughter's room as she was getting ready for bed to tell her what had happened. He sat next to her on her bed and told her that he really needed to talk. After several minutes Surhoff began stroking her hair and back and began fondling her. His stepdaughter resisted, but Surhoff told her how close he felt to her, how much he trusted her, and that he would not hurt her. Surhoff told her that it was important for her to learn "what it's like to be a woman" with someone she could trust. Surhoff had her perform oral sex and had intercourse with her. Their sexual contact continued for almost four months, until Surhoff's wife moved out of the apartment with her daughter.
- Stan Phoebus was a college junior and lived in a fraternity house. One Saturday evening the fraternity sponsored a party with a sorority.

Phoebus spent the evening talking with a sorority member. Both drank several beers and shots of tequila. Phoebus slipped Rohypnol—also known as a date-rape drug—into one of her drinks.

At about 1:30 A.M. Phoebus and the young woman listened to music and she began to feel woozy. Shortly thereafter Phoebus had intercourse with her without her consent. The young woman later reported the assault to police, and Phoebus was arrested and charged with rape.

Sorting out evil and goodness among inmates, and the complicated mix of the two, was my biggest challenge as a parole board member. I believe that most people are good in most important respects and that relatively few among us are truly evil. I realize that my decades-long encounters with criminals and truly terrible crime sagas may lead me to exaggerate the prevalence of evil in the world. I try my best to keep my perception of malevolence in check. Sometimes it is hard.

While I was on the parole board, my instinct was to look for the goodness among inmates, those kernels of grace and empathy that lie within many—perhaps even most—offenders I met. I am not naive. I know that some offenders are cruel and some are evil. But most do not seem to be inherently cruel or evil, and most know they have behaved badly and hurt people. Most offenders want to change. They really do.

3

ON BEING A VICTIM

Justice . . . is a kind of compact not to harm or be harmed.
–EPICURUS

J UST BEFORE victims met with the parole board on hearing day, they met with the board's victim advocate. This trained professional explained the parole board's procedures, offered support, recommended supportive services (such as counseling and crisis intervention), and, when victims requested, accompanied them to their meeting with the parole board.

On one particularly memorable morning, I sat at the board's conference table, glanced at the door, and saw a middle-aged woman guide into the room a young man, her son, who was in a wheelchair. Dan sat expressionless and drooled some, his head flopping from side to side. His mom, Ellen, stopped frequently to wipe the drool from his chin. Behind Ellen stood Dan's father, older brother, two aunts, and a representative from the local chapter of MADD— Mothers Against Drunk Driving.

We welcomed the group and told them how much we value the participation of victims and how they are a critically important part of the board's decision-making process. Then we invited them to share whatever they wished about the crime and its impact on them.

Ellen placed a framed photo of Dan on the hearing room table. In the photo he was a beaming sixteen-year-old. He was holding his driver's license, which he had just earned. Dan's life was filled with joy, laughter, and the future's promise. Dan's mother continued:

All of that is gone now. Mr. Marchetti stole away the life we used to have, and he did it in an instant. He needs to pay for his bad decisions.

I have been dreading this day for months. I can't believe that Marchetti is already up for parole consideration. It's only been a little more than eight years. Dan is now twenty-four. Please look at his photo and look at him now. Dan is a mere shell of the person he used to be. Everyone who knows Dan will tell you the same thing: He was pure joy. Dan was every parent's dream. From the day he was born, Dan was kind, goofy, smart, and very, very caring. People loved to be around him. He was the love of our lives. He still is, of course, but in a much different way.

Let me tell you what daily life is like now. Dan needs care twenty-four hours a day. He suffered terrible brain damage as a result of the accident. Dan doesn't understand conversation and cannot communicate. We have to turn him in his bed so he doesn't get bed sores. We have to change Dan's diapers, feed him, dress him, and lift him into his wheelchair. As you can see, he can't even swallow his own saliva. At times Dan groans and groans. We have no idea what he's groaning about; all we can do is try to comfort him.

Compare that to the Dan who used to romp around the house, play soccer, act in school plays, mow the lawn, shovel the snow, and make us laugh. Dan's name is the same, but that's all that's the same. Our lives changed forever when Marchetti chose to drink and drive. According to the police report, he was driving at least seventy-five miles an hour in a thirty-five-mile-an-hour zone. As you know from the police reports, Dan and two friends were walking on the sidewalk—heading to the nearby soccer field—when Marchetti's car jumped the curb and plowed into them.

In some ways it seems like the accident just happened. We were quite surprised when we got the letter in the mail notifying us of this hearing. Yet it also seems like the accident happened a thousand years ago. Before the accident our days sped by. For the last eight years our days have been a steady, slow drip centered on Dan's care. We love Dan and will do everything we can for him. But his father and I are getting older and it's getting harder and harder. We worry about what will happen when we're gone or too disabled to care for him.

I'm not a mean person. I try to do the right things in life and be kind to others. But I can't be kind to Marchetti. He's ruined our lives. Most important, he's ruined Dan's life.

As she spoke, Ellen reached for the tissue box on the hearing room table. She wiped so many tears that we had to give her a fresh one. My eyes welled up too.

When she finished, Dan's older brother, Marcus, spoke. He held Dan's hand as he told us about how much he admired him.

I'm the older brother, but growing up I often felt like Dan was the more mature brother. When I was upset, I often talked to Dan and asked him for advice. When I couldn't figure out math homework, I went to Dan for help. When I wasn't sure which outfit to wear, I asked Dan for his opinion. Dan was my go-to guy. We weren't just brothers; we were best friends.

That's gone now. I've lost my best friend and in so many ways I've lost my brother.

I want you to see this card Dan made for me when I graduated from high school. He was so happy for me. His note is full of love and admiration. Now I'm pretty sure Dan doesn't even know who I am. Please don't release Marchetti. He has no right to go on living a regular life. Look what he's done to us.

The parole board chair offered Dan's aunts the opportunity to speak. We learned that they had flown in from out of state to attend the hearing. They declined the chance to speak, saying that they had accompanied the family to provide support. The meeting ended with testimony from the MADD representative. She spoke in a personal way about MADD's mission and her own intimate connection.

I lost a child to a drunk driver. My twenty-one-year-old daughter was driving home from college for spring break when a drunk driver—a

man who had been arrested five times for driving under the influence and who was driving on a suspended license—ran a red light and
slammed into my daughter's car.

I have been involved with MADD ever since. As an organization we
do our best to strengthen drunk driving laws and support victims' families. Last year more than 10,000 people in the U.S. were killed by drunk
drivers and almost three hundred thousand were injured. Every day, on
average, more than twenty-five people die as a result of drunk driving
crashes—nearly one an hour.

This madness must stop. What happened to Dan and his family has
happened to hundreds of thousands of others. Mr. Marchetti must be
held accountable.

The meeting concluded and the group escorted Dan out of the
room in his wheelchair. I entered a summary of my impressions in
Marchetti's computer file so I could refer to them during our meeting
with him later in the day. My colleagues and I commiserated momen-
tarily, acknowledging the horror of this case, as we prepared for the
next set of victims.

I had read the file in advance, so I knew this would be a difficult
conversation. The victim, Laurie Hinton, now twenty-two years old,
was accompanied by her mother, Yolanda Hinton. According to the
police reports, Laurie Hinton had been sexually molested by her
mother's boyfriend, Terrence Boyd, between the ages of twelve and
fourteen. Yolanda Hinton had divorced Laurie's father and moved in
with Boyd about a year later.

As Laurie Hinton and her mother sat down, I thought of the courage it takes for a young woman to tell this agonizing story to a group
of strangers while sitting next to her mother. And then I tried to imagine what this experience was like for her mother, who was about to
hear her daughter describe the way she was molested by the man
Yolanda had brought into their home:

> One afternoon, just before the Fourth of July that year, my mom was
> working and Terrence and I were home alone. Right around dinner-
> time, Terrence asked me if I wanted to watch TV with him. We'd done
> that many times.

I sat on the couch and we were watching *Wheel of Fortune*. I remember that because Terrence and I argued in a friendly way about who was smarter. I noticed that Terrence was sitting closer to me than usual. I didn't think too much of it at the time, but I did notice.

I had just gotten out of the shower. Terrence said something about my wet hair and began to play with it. Before I knew it, Terrence was telling me how pretty I am and stroking my face. I felt really weird, but I liked Terrence and didn't want to be mean. I just sat there, not knowing what to do.

After a couple of minutes Terrence started to touch my boob. Inside I was freaking out. I kind of froze. He told me how special I am and that we could have a special relationship, just between the two of us. We heard a car pull into the driveway, so Terrence stopped. It turned out someone was just turning their car around.

The next day I was in the kitchen making some dinner. Again my mom was working. Terrence walked up behind me and put his arms around my waist. Just like the day before, I froze. Before I knew it, Terrence had lifted my shirt and started undoing my bra. He asked me whether I had ever seen a man's penis. I didn't say anything. He unbuckled his pants and pulled out his penis and asked me to suck on it. I was so afraid, I did what he asked.

Terrence really messed with my head. He knew that I wasn't getting along real good with my mom. I think he took advantage of that. In a way I wanted to hurt my mom, so I kind of went along with Terrence.

Anyway, this sort of thing happened lots of times. Before I knew it, Terrence and I were having sex in his and my mom's room. We had intercourse lots of times. At the time I kind of liked the fact that I was so special to Terrence, and I loved all the presents he bought me.

Terrence always told me how our special relationship had to be our secret. He told me how upset my mom would be if she knew we were getting together. But right after I turned fourteen I began to realize how wrong this was. I was starting to get interested in boys, and I just knew that what I was doing with Terrence was bad. I told him I wanted to stop, but Terrence told me that if I did, bad things would happen. He started to be mean to me and threatened to tell my mom some of my secrets. Terrence also told me that Mom would never believe me if I told her about Terrence, since I had lied to her so many times before. That's when Terrence started to force me to have sex. It was really awful.

One day at school I was real upset. I knew what I was doing was wrong but didn't know how to get out of the mess. That afternoon I went to the school bathroom and started crying. I didn't want to go back to my Spanish class. About an hour later my teacher, Ms. Ewbank, came looking for me and saw how upset I was. She asked me what was wrong. I couldn't tell her. Ms. Ewbank asked me if I would talk to the school social worker. I said yes and Ms. Ewbank took me to her office.

I decided to tell the social worker everything. She talked to me for a long time and explained that she had to call DCYF [Department of Children, Youth, and Families]. And that's how everything blew up.

During Laurie Hinton's graphic description, I marveled at her composure. She seemed so calm and collected. I could not help but wonder what was churning inside her. I asked about her plans. She said she was a college sophomore and wanted eventually to become a mental health counselor for abused children. How poignant.

The file included a detailed letter from Laurie Hinton's therapist, who described the clinical consequences of Terrence's sexual abuse. The therapist described Laurie Hinton's painful trauma and complex clinical treatment. I learned that shortly after she disclosed the molestation, she started to cut her arms and developed a serious eating disorder. Laurie Hinton was hospitalized in a psychiatric facility for about two weeks when she developed suicidal thoughts. The therapist reported that she became estranged from her mother and was placed in a group home that serves struggling teens. On many days Laurie Hinton refused to go to school; as a result she did not receive her high school diploma, although she eventually earned her GED. In short, Laurie Hinton faced a lifetime of psychological challenges as a result of Terrence's abuse.

The parole board concluded its meeting with Laurie Hinton and her mother—with whom Laurie had reconciled with the help of her therapist—at 9:40 A.M. We had three additional sets of victims with whom we were scheduled to meet that morning. I was already emotionally spent but had to find the wherewithal to focus on the sentiments shared by our next guests.

||||||||||||||||||||||||||||||||||||||||||||||||||||||||

The parole board hears from many, although certainly not all, crime victims.[1] Some victims are too traumatized by the experience to set foot on the prison campus that houses the state's inmates. Even many years later many victims comment on the anxiety they feel when they think about the crime and the prospect of being near the offender; I don't blame them. Other victims do not meet with the board because staffers cannot locate them.

I always felt honored to be able to meet in person with crime victims. These encounters put a human face on the dramatic details that I would have known only through my review of pages and pages of police reports, prison records, court transcripts, and written correspondence. One advantage of being a parole board member in a relatively small state is that geographic distance rarely is a barrier. In many larger states parole board members never meet with victims; it is not possible logistically, although victims may meet or speak with parole board staffers and hearing officers.

Many victims who do meet with the parole board are angry. Very angry. They have been assaulted, raped, molested, robbed, and exploited. Some are the relatives of murder victims or people who were killed by a driver under the influence of alcohol or drugs. The majority of victims want the board to deny the inmate's parole. Some victims, like the Newsome family, feel punitive.

Five members of the Newsome family—two parents and three children—walked into the hearing room. Twenty-two years earlier Barry Newsome had been murdered during a late-night fight in Newport, Rhode Island. At the time Barry, thirty-one, was in an on-again, off-again relationship with his girlfriend, Simone. Based on all the reports, Simone started to date another man but did not tell Barry. He learned about Simone's new relationship from a close friend.

Barry did not handle the news well. He confronted Simone, who then told her new boyfriend, Ron Perkins, that Barry had threatened to harm her if she ended her relationship with him. Perkins drove over to Barry's apartment and started yelling at him to stay away from Simone. The two traded punches. During the fight Perkins ran into the kitchen, grabbed a steak knife, and stabbed Barry, who died at the scene. Perkins fled from the apartment and drove to a friend's house in New Hampshire. The stabbing death made headlines; Perkins quickly became a suspect. Three days later he turned himself in.

Perkins was charged with first-degree murder. The prosecutor argued that Perkins went to Barry's apartment intending to kill him. Perkins, through his defense attorney, argued that he stabbed Barry in self-defense. One day before the scheduled trial Perkins agreed to plead guilty to second-degree murder. As Perkins told the parole board at his first hearing, "I didn't intend to kill him. I only pled guilty after my lawyer told me that, if I went to trial, I ran the risk of a first-degree murder conviction and a much longer sentence. I didn't want to roll the dice."

At our meeting with the victims Gloria Newsome, Barry's mother, began speaking on behalf of the family:

> Thank you for seeing us. This is the third time we've come in for these parole hearings. We'll be here for every single one.
>
> I think you know how we feel. Mr. Perkins took my precious son— and their precious brother—away from us. Barry didn't go looking for trouble. He worked hard and he loved Simone and their son, our grandchild, Stephan. Yes, Barry and Simone had their issues, but Barry told me they were working on them and that things would be fine. The next thing we knew, Barry was dead.
>
> Not only have we lost Barry, we've also lost our grandson. We loved that child from the day he was born. But after Barry died, Simone took Stephan out of our lives too. We have no rights. Twenty-two years ago Ron Perkins made his bed. Please make him lie in it until the last day of his sentence.

Other victims were more fearful than punitive. Shelly Ressler came to her meeting with the parole board accompanied by her six-year-old daughter, Nicole. Ressler was brutally abused by her former husband and Nicole's father, Darryl Gaubatz. According to the police reports, nearly five years earlier Gaubatz had walked into the apartment he shared with Ressler and Nicole at about midnight. Gaubatz, who had a history of heroin and cocaine abuse, was under the influence. Ressler confronted Gaubatz about his chronic substance abuse and threatened to leave him, taking Nicole with her. The police report stated that "Ressler was bleeding from her mouth and forehead. She stated that Gaubatz grabbed her by the throat, threw her to the floor, punched her with his fists, and slammed her head into the floor."

Ressler began the meeting by describing in detail what had happened. Her testimony, five years later, was consistent with the details in the police report. Ressler's graphic description was painful to hear; Gaubatz's abuse of her was horrific. But I could not help but think to myself, "Why are you saying all of this in front of your six-year-old child?" Nicole was old enough to grasp some of the details about the way her father had brutally abused her mother. I certainly understand that at some point in their lives children have a right to know, and may even need to know, the painful truth about such traumatic events. But as a parent of two daughters, I was deeply concerned about the impact that this recitation might have on Nicole.

I had a bad feeling in the pit of my stomach. I glanced at Nicole a number of times as Ressler spoke. I had difficulty reading the stone-faced expression on the child's face. Most victims who bring children with them to their parole board meetings decide to leave them in an adjacent room, out of earshot, with a relative or acquaintance.

Ressler talked about the physical and emotional pain she had felt since the assault. I expected Ressler to share her anger, as many domestic assault victims do, but that did not happen. Instead Ressler focused on her relentless fear and anxiety.

> I know Darryl is the prisoner, but every day I feel like one too. I used to be a happy-go-lucky person. I had a good job at Stop & Shop and used to love to go dancing. I used to take Nicole to the park down the street. We loved to feed the ducks at Roger Williams Park.
>
> Now I hate to leave my apartment. I have panic attacks and live in fear. I don't want to let Nicole out of my sight. She used to play with friends at their homes but not anymore. I'm just so afraid that when Darryl gets out he's going to come after me.

I asked Ressler whether she had seen a mental health counselor to help her cope with her anxiety. "I saw somebody for a while, but I stopped going," Ressler said. "It helped me some, but I couldn't really afford the copay, and finding someone to be with Nicole was a problem." Then I asked Ressler whether she would like to talk to the parole board's victim advocate to get the names of counselors who do not require a copay (for example, agency-based service providers who have funding from government or nonprofit agencies to assist crime victims). Ressler declined the offer. "I don't like to leave my home," she said. She talked about how difficult it was for her to come to the parole board meeting. I encouraged her to keep the offer in mind and reassured her that the board's victim advocate would always be willing to assist her.

I felt quite sad about the difficulty Ressler was having in coping with the debilitating aftermath of her abuse and the difficulty she was having reaching out for help. She seemed to be suffering from her own form of incarceration. And I felt terribly glum when I thought about the impact all this was likely to have on Nicole. Over the years Nicole was at risk of developing her own symptoms, behavioral issues, and mental health challenges. As in so many parole board cases, there are many ripples in the pond, and these ripples tend to be turbulent.

Occasionally I was thoroughly surprised by victims' sentiments. Such was the case with Roseanne Burkett. Burkett, too, was a domestic violence survivor. Her former live-in partner, Lon Lyles, was serving a ten-year sentence. Lyles had struggled for years with bipolar disorder and alcoholism. According to the police report, on the night of the assault Lyles and Burkett were arguing about whether she should abort an unplanned pregnancy. Burkett wanted to have the baby, but Lyles was adamant that the couple could not afford to raise a child. Burkett told the board that Lyles "lost it" and started pounding her belly. She tried to fight him off, but Lyles continued the assault. Lyles eventually stormed out of the apartment, and Burkett called 911. She suffered serious internal injuries and miscarried as a result of the abuse.

To my great surprise Burkett told the parole board how much she loved Lyles and would like him released from prison.

I know what he did was wrong. He knows it too. Lon is a good man, he really is. I know he loves me. What happened that night wouldn't have happened if Lon had been taking his medication. He had been taking those bipolar pills, but about a month before all this happened he stopped taking them. Lon told me he was feeling much better and he didn't want to take those pills anymore. He complained that the pills made him drowsy and gain weight. Soon after that I noticed his mood swings had started again. I was afraid something like this would happen.

I want Lon home again. I need him. I'm having trouble paying the bills. I'm afraid I'll get evicted if I don't get some help soon.

I asked Burkett whether Lyles had ever abused her before the assault that led to his conviction and prison sentence. "Yes," she said, "but only a few times." I asked her to say more about these other occasions—when they occurred, the type of abuse involved.

I guess it's happened about four or five other times. I think it's because of his mental problems. Lyle told me his father was the same way.

I know he loves me and doesn't mean to hurt me. We usually have problems when we've both been drinking.

When I visited Lyle last week we had a real good talk. He promised me it won't happen again. He told me he'll be good and get help.

I knew Burkett meant well and loved Lyles deep down. It was certainly possible that Lyles would get the help he needed and would never again abuse Burkett. But my professional experience and well-known crime statistics told me the odds were not in her favor. I worked with inmates time and again who solemnly swore that they would never abuse their partner again. In the moment they seemed to be sincere. However, recidivism is all too common. Most of the reputable studies I have reviewed suggest that, on average, an abused woman will leave her abuser six or seven times before she finally leaves for good.

I asked Burkett whether Lyles had asked her to meet with us in order to ask the board to release him. She hesitated for a moment, perhaps wondering whether her answer would work against Lyles. "Yes," she said in a quiet voice. "Yes."

||||||||||||||||||||||||||||||||||||||||||||||||||||||||

When I first started working in the corrections field in the 1970s, there was little focus on victims. Oh, how that has changed. In the United States the modern crime victims' rights movement began in the 1960s, in part as a result of the civil rights and women's movements. These early efforts led to the inauguration of rape crisis centers and domestic violence shelters, along with coalitions of national organizations.[2]

Another key impetus was the 1973 U.S. Supreme Court decision in *Linda R.S. v. Richard D.* In this landmark decision the court acknowledged the then-prevailing view that a crime victim cannot compel a criminal prosecution because "a private citizen lacks a judicially cognizable interest in the prosecution or non-prosecution of another." But the court then suggested a remedy by stating that Congress could enact laws that would provide victims with legal standing.[3] Since the court handed down its opinion in *Linda R. S.*, most states have amended their constitutions to include crime-victim rights provisions and have enacted crime-victim rights statutes.

About a decade later, in 1982, President Ronald Reagan's Task Force on the Victims of Crime issued the most forceful statement on the subject in U.S. history. The report's introduction included a clarion call:

> Before you, the reader, can appreciate the necessity of changing the way victims are treated, you must confront the essential reality that almost all Americans, at some time in their lives, will be touched by crime. Among the most difficult obstacles are the myths that if people are wise, virtuous, and cautious, they will escape, and that those who are victimized are somehow responsible for their fate. These are pernicious falsehoods. First, for every person mugged on a dark street at 3 A.M., many more are terrorized in their homes, schools, offices, or on main thoroughfares in the light of day. Second, to adopt the attitude of victim culpability is to accept that citizens have lost the right to walk

their streets safely regardless of the hour or locale; it is to abandon these times and places to be claimed as the hunting preserves of the lawless.

Violent crime honors no sanctuary. It strikes when least expected, often when the victim is doing the most commonplace things.[4]

The victims' rights movement was up and running.

In the federal system Congress passed the Victim and Witness Protection Act in 1982 and subsequently passed a series of laws that gave successively greater legislative recognition to the rights of crime victims. The Victims of Crime Act, passed in 1984, continues to fund victim services through fines and fees levied against federal criminal offenders. In 2004 President George W. Bush signed the Crime Victims' Rights Act, which established the rights of crime victims in federal criminal proceedings and provided mechanisms for victims to enforce those rights.

In addition to these legislative efforts, various courts have also recognized the importance of crime victims' participation in criminal court proceedings. For instance, in *Payne v. Tennessee*, the U.S. Supreme Court explicitly recognized that crime victims are not nameless or faceless nonplayers in the criminal justice system.[5] As a result of these statutes and court rulings, victims' rights now include the right to information; be present at criminal justice proceedings; due process (the right to notice of, and opportunity to be heard at, important criminal justice proceedings); financial compensation for losses suffered as a result of a crime, such as restitution and/or compensation/reparations; protection; and privacy.

|||||||||||||||||||||||||||||||||||||||||||||||||||||||||||

The crime victims I have met suffer in diverse ways. The physical injuries are obvious. Victims lifted their shirts and rolled up their sleeves to show me and my colleagues stab wounds, bullet holes, and scarred-over lacerations from razor-blade slices. Some removed their hats to show us their caved-in skulls, the result of domestic assaults with baseball bats and other makeshift weapons. Some rolled into our meetings in wheelchairs; others limped in with canes.

But many, perhaps most, victims' injuries are invisible. Many victims report debilitating anxiety and clinical depression. Some report developing alcohol or drug problems as a result of their efforts to numb their chronic emotional pain. Some show no outward sign of their internal torment and anguish.

Andrea Unseld walked confidently into the board's hearing room. This was the first time I had seen a victim accompanied by a dog. Within minutes I learned that the canine was her psychiatric service dog, Coby. Coby accompanied Unseld 24/7, virtually without exception, and enabled her to cope with her intense and chronic anxiety and posttraumatic stress. Ironically Coby was trained in a prison program.

Eight years before our meeting Unseld's husband, Will Bellamy, had raped and beaten her. They had married soon after Unseld learned that she was pregnant. Their newborn was clearly mixed race; Unseld and Bellamy are both Caucasian. When Bellamy realized he was not the biological father of the infant, he flew into a rage. He tied Unseld to a chair and beat her relentlessly. Eventually he left their apartment. A neighbor who had a key to the apartment heard Unseld's groans and let herself in. She freed Unseld and called 911. Unseld was rushed to the hospital and underwent emergency surgery to address several serious fractures, internal bleeding, and organ damage. Unseld began her comments to the parole board haltingly:

> I'm sorry if I seem a little nervous. I flew in last night from North Carolina, where I now live. I have family in Raleigh, and after this happened I decided to move near them. It's just too hard for me to live around here—too many memories, too many triggers.
>
> It's hard for me to talk about what's happened. I get upset just thinking about it. I hope you don't mind, but I've put my thoughts on paper. It'll be easier for me to read you my letter. Is that okay?

Most victims do not prepare written statements, but some do. We reassured Unseld that it would be fine for her to read her letter.

> Dear Parole Board:
> It's hard to know where to begin. When I met Will about nine years ago I thought he was my knight in shining armor. We met at a friend's

backyard party in Georgia, where Will was stationed in the Army. Will seemed to have it all, and he swept me off of my feet. He was kind, considerate, and gentle. My family loved him.

Will and I dated for almost a year before we decided to get engaged. Shortly after we were married Will was deployed, so that was tough. But we got through that. We were able to talk a lot and I was thrilled when he got home and we could start our life together.

Things were good for about another year and a half. That's when they started to go downhill. Will started to spend more and more time with his Army buddies. He was drinking a lot more and we began to argue a lot. I didn't like his drinking and I thought some of his friends were a bad influence. When Will came home drunk he would yell at me. Sometimes Will would hit me. One time he grabbed my cell phone and started searching my messages. He accused me of having an affair. When I denied it, he threw my phone across the room so hard that it broke into pieces. I would say that was the beginning of the end. I felt really sad and lonely.

The truth is that at the time I wasn't having an affair, but soon I couldn't take it anymore and started a relationship with a man who had been flirting with me at my job. I knew it was wrong, but at the time I was so miserable. This relationship with Damon was the only good thing in my life.

One thing led to another and I found out that I was pregnant. I wasn't sure whether the child was Will's or Damon's. I was pretty sure it was Will's, so I decided to just wait it out. I was terrified, because I knew that if the child was Damon's, Will would know instantly, since Damon is a dark-skinned Cape Verdean man.

When the baby was born, Will just went after me soon after I came home from the hospital. You probably know that he raped me, tied me up, and beat me. I know I made a mistake, but I didn't deserve to be treated like this.

Ever since, my life has been a nightmare. I can't sleep, I don't want to leave the house, and I'm afraid all the time. My body hurts every day. I've had two surgeries to repair my shoulder, which Will dislocated when he beat me. The doctor told me I probably need one or two more operations.

I worry that Will will come after me when he gets out of prison. I brought a copy of a letter Will wrote from prison last year to one of his cousins, Randy. Randy and I still talk and are friends, and he knows what Will did to me. Randy said he thought I should see the letter. You can see what Will says about me and how much he hates me. [Unseld handed the letter to the parole board. It was filled with comments about how Bellamy hoped his former wife "rots in hell" and how "she better watch her back."] That's why I'm afraid. I'm scared he'll find me and beat me again. That's why I moved to North Carolina.

Please don't let him out. Please.

Some victims dwelled on the financial injuries they incurred. Victims of home invasions talked about stolen articles—especially laptop computers, electronic tablets, high-end cameras, flat screen televisions, and jewelry—and what insurance policies did not cover. Victims whose cars were stolen talked about the increase in their insurance premiums and the deductibles they had to pay. Embezzlement victims talked about the amount of money they had lost; in one case an embezzlement victim talked about the long-term family business that went under because of dire cash-flow problems. Ex-spouses of inmates talked about how their bank accounts were drained to pay off mounting gambling debts.

In one memorable case a married couple, Dora and Mitch Loughery, met with the board. Without her husband's knowledge, Dora had written checks totaling $12,350 to a tarot card reader. Dora Loughery began by telling the board that she was deeply ashamed, humiliated, and embarrassed to be meeting with us. Mitch Loughery held his wife's hand as she did her best to contain her sobs. At the time she had been feeling depressed following her mother's death, so she sought out the tarot card reader on the advice of a friend. She and her mother had been extremely close. There was more to the story.

> At the same time my home health-care business was in bad shape. My business provided services to people who were very sick and disabled. Most of our patients were low income, so we depended very heavily on state Medicaid payments. Well, that rate hadn't been increased in a long time, and I just couldn't pay the bills. I kept this secret from my husband, who had been telling me for years that we couldn't afford to keep the business. I couldn't bear to lose the business and my mother at the same time. I didn't know what to do.

Stupidly I decided to follow my friend's advice and see the tarot card reader, Earline Monroe. And that's how it all started. Now I know how gullible I was. Earline was so nice and sincere. Right from the start she had amazing insights about my challenges. I was hooked, almost like it was an addiction.

Well, after about six readings, Earline told me that I was under the spell of a curse. She explained that the Seven of Swords tarot card was sending me a message about deception and cunning in my life. Earline assured me she could get rid of this dreadful hex. She told me that it would take time, and lots of effort, but it was definitely possible.

Earline told me that she would need $500 to start the process, and that it probably wouldn't cost much more than that. She explained that she would go through a special ceremony to place the hex in a capsule, which she would bury. Well, every time I met with Earline she had a new update about challenges she encountered getting rid of the hex. And each of these times she needed more money to be sure that she could get rid of the hex permanently.

I can't believe I fell for this. But at the time I was desperate, and before long I was in over my head. Before I knew it I had given Earline thousands of dollars. I trusted her, but I knew my husband would think this was crazy, so I kept it secret. When I finally realized I had been scammed, I decided to tell my husband. I wouldn't have blamed him if he had left me. But here he is. He's such a saint. I'm not sure I deserve him.

Some of the most touching victim testimony I heard came from people who talked about their spiritual injury. They may not have used this language, but I think what these victims had in common was their deep and painful sense of moral injury and betrayal. Typically these victims talked about their loss of trust in other people and their heartfelt dismay about some human beings' capacity to hurt others. Many of these victims spoke in spiritual terms about their profound sense of loss, that they felt robbed of their previous belief in others' goodness.

Most of these victims did not indict all of humanity; instead they tended to focus on the intense disappointment and emotional hurt they now felt for the first time and as a direct result of their victimization. Most such victims did not use religious terminology or concepts, but their imagery and conceptualization certainly had a keen spiritual quality. Such was the case with seventy-two-year-old Jan Shue—a retired grade-school teacher—whose house was broken into by Earl Manning, who had a long criminal record and was serving a six-year sentence.

> Nothing like this has ever happened to me. I've never been on these prison grounds, even though I live only a twenty-minute drive from here.
>
> I live a very quiet life, especially since my husband, Max, died about nine years ago. Since I retired from teaching, I have volunteered at the hospital and help organize the Green Thumb Garden Club. I spend lots of time with my three grandchildren and do all the normal things— shop, clean, and so on.
>
> I've always liked and trusted people. I've tried to be kind to people, and people have always been kind to me. I know some people are cruel, but until this I've never seen it up close. Earl Manning changed that. Breaking into my house was bad enough. But did he need to hold a knife to my neck? I suppose I'd feel differently if he had just stolen my things and run. But that wasn't enough for him. He scared me so badly that I had heart attack symptoms and had to be hospitalized. I've recovered from that, thank goodness, but there's one thing I haven't gotten back: my belief in people's basic goodness. That's gone.

||||||||||||||||||||||||||||||||||||||||||||||||||||||||||

Most crime victims I have met are irate. Some, remarkably, are not, and some talk earnestly about their willingness to forgive the offender. This never ceases to amaze me, and I marvel at some victims' willingness to forgive and generosity of spirit. My conversations with forgiving victims led me to think hard about the nature and meaning of forgiveness.[6] Today I think forgiveness is a far more complex and nuanced concept than I did years ago.

Thinking broadly, forgiveness is some form of positive response to wrongdoing. According to the ancient Greeks and the Hebrew and Christian Bibles, forgiveness is a personal response to having been injured or wronged; it is a condition one seeks or hopes is bestowed upon one for having wronged someone else or one's self. The *Oxford*

English Dictionary defines *forgivable* as that which "may be forgiven, pardonable, excusable."

My commonsense understanding of the word *forgiveness* entails an effort to repair a ruptured relationship. A parent may choose to forgive a child who has misbehaved, and a wife may forgive a husband who has strayed, in order to recalibrate their relationship. But in the context of my work in prisons, most victims had no wish to resume or sustain a relationship with the offender who caused them harm. In most instances the victim and offender had no previous relationship. The exceptions, of course, were cases of crimes among family members, friends, or coworkers. In these instances there was the possibility, if not the probability, that victims would wrestle with issues of forgiveness.

Victims' diverse understandings of forgiveness may be a function of their previous relationship with the offender, if any; their religious and spiritual beliefs about the importance of forgiveness; and, to paint with a broad brush, their personality. For some victims, having a deep personal connection and previous relationship with the inmate makes forgiveness possible. For some the passage of time applies some salve to the wound and allows victims' hearts to open to the possibility of forgiveness. Some victims are never able to forgive the offender.

Sometimes victims are willing to forgive because the offender has apologized or the victim knows about the offender's personal struggles that contributed to the crime. Such was the case with Maryann West, who was assaulted by her longtime boyfriend, Stu McKenzie.

There's no excuse for what Stu did to me. He stole my jewelry and cash. He sold the jewelry real fast at the Eastside Pawn Shop. That broke my heart. I lost the necklace my mother gave me when I turned eighteen. He also stole and sold my wedding ring from my first marriage. My former husband died, so that ring meant a lot to me.

I'm not happy that Stu stole money from me, but at least that can be replaced. That jewelry can't, and that hurts.

Stu really is a good person. But when those drugs get hold of his life, he turns into a demon. When he's clean and sober, and realizes what he's done, he always apologizes. I know he feels awful.

Stu needs help, and he knows it. He promised me he's going to re-hab to work on his addiction. This is the first time he has begged me to help him get help. This is new. So please parole him to a treatment program. That's what he needs. I can forgive what he did to me as long as he is serious about getting help.

For other victims, having had a long-standing relationship with the offender made matters worse. In some cases the commission of a serious crime in the context of a close personal relationship is the ultimate betrayal and destroys any forgiving instincts the victim may have otherwise. Sally Doyle's sentiments were prototypical; her teen-age daughter, Diana, was molested by Doyle's boyfriend, Ben Ohl.

This man is a monster. I thought I knew him, but he played me for a fool. I'd been with him for almost nine years. He told me and Diana that he loved us. He told Diana he loved her like a daughter. Well, now we know the truth. Ben's a liar. He's a con artist. I couldn't see it at the time, but now I see how he used me to get to my daughter. He's ruined her life. Diana hates herself, and it's because of him. She used to be a good student; now she won't go to school. She used to smile. Now she thinks about killing herself. I've lost count of the number of times Diana's been in the mental hospital.

I bet when you see Ben he'll convince you that he's worked hard in prison and addressed his issues. Don't believe him. He'll try to fool you just like he fooled me. He's slick. Please don't let him out.

For other victims, not knowing the inmate before the crime seems to free them up to forgive. They have no emotional baggage that gets in the way. Some victims can view the inmate's misconduct in a silo of sorts; the inmate and his conduct stand on their own merits. That's what happened when the parole board met with Rob Ferry, whose car was stolen by Warren Hightower.

I didn't know Hightower from Adam. Until I saw him in court the day he pleaded guilty, I had never laid eyes on him.

When I sat in the courtroom, I heard Hightower's attorney describe his life leading up to the theft. By the end of his lawyer's presentation to the judge, I kind of felt bad for the guy. Yes, I'm upset he stole my car, and that was a real hassle. But part of me understands what got him into that way of life. I mean, Hightower had no chance in life. I heard how he was born with drugs in his system and was abandoned by his mother, who had a terrible heroin problem. I heard how he went from one foster home to another. I heard how he never knew his father. I heard how Hightower was homeless by the time he was eighteen.

Of course he shouldn't have done what he did to me, but this guy was just trying to survive. I sure wish he had gone to some program for help, but now I sort of understand why he stole my car.

I hope this guy's getting help. If you think he is, and he's serious about changing, I forgive him and have no objection to parole. But that's only if you think he's serious about changing.

For others the inmate's stranger status—an odd form of anonymity, despite whatever close contact they had during a brief period of time surrounding the crime—makes it easier for victims to sustain their anger and resentment and oppose the inmate's release on parole. The impersonality makes it that much easier to hate the inmate. This was what happened to Sybil Counts, whose pocketbook was stolen and who was assaulted by Christine Warley.

That bitch is low life. I can't believe she's already up for parole.

Do you know what happened to me? I was coming out of Shaw's market with groceries and, right before I got into my car, Warley comes up behind me fast and grabs my pocketbook, which I had sitting in the shopping cart seat. I tried to pull my bag back and we got into a bad tussle. Before I knew it, Warley pushed me to the ground, kicked me hard, and ran off with my bag. She only got caught because the store's security cameras recorded what happened and the police recognized her.

That woman's got a record like you wouldn't believe. The detective told me Warley was on probation when she assaulted me. Can you believe that?

There's no way in the world this woman should be getting out. She's a menace, a one-woman crime wave. I don't care what kinds of problems she's had. She deserves prison. I want her to serve every day, every minute that's coming to her. If she wants help, let her get it after she finishes her full sentence.

||||||||||||||||||||||||||||||||||||||||||||||||||||||||||||

Some victims draw deeply on their faith traditions when they contemplate forgiving the inmate. Every major religion has its unique take on forgiveness. Buddhists believe that reconciliation, and forgiving others as well as ourselves, is an important step on the path toward a better life and enlightenment. Giving up hatred and forgiving the harm done to us by others allows us to move on and to achieve peace of mind.

In Hinduism, in the *Rig-Veda,* the ancient Indian sacred collection of Vedic Sanskrit hymns, forgiveness of wrongdoers is discussed in verses dedicated to the deity Varuna. Forgiveness is considered one of the six cardinal virtues in Hinduism. For Christians, Colossians, the twelfth book of the New Testament, states, "Bearing with one another and, if one has a complaint against another, forgiving each other; as the Lord has forgiven you, so you also must forgive." For Jews the Torah says that it is acceptable to rebuke someone who has caused injury, but one should not sustain hate: "You shall not hate your brother in your heart. You shall surely rebuke your fellow, but you shall not bear a sin on his account." Confucius said, "He who refuses to forgive breaks the bridge over which he, too, must cross." And in Islam the Qur'an states, "If a person forgives and makes reconciliation, his reward is due from Allah."[7]

My understanding of forgiveness is that its principal outcome is to absolve the offender, at least to some degree, and to allow the parties to move on with their lives. I saw some inmates cry when the parole board informed them that their victim had forgiven them. One case involved Bart Jones, who murdered Jason Dickey during a drug deal that went bad.

The parole board met with Dickey's surviving sister, Lacey Garry, who was now raising Dickey's two children. She spoke at length about how both Jones and her brother were involved in the drug trade. She knew that Jones did not mean to kill her brother, and she hoped he was getting help. She asked the board to tell Jones that, "as a Christian," she forgave him. The board met with Jones about two hours later and told him what Garry had said. Jones broke into tears. As he spoke, Jones had to pause frequently to catch his breath.

I can't believe she said that. [pause] Did she really? [pause] Oh, my god! [long pause] I never, ever expected you to tell me that. I feel so relieved. What I did to her brother was a terrible thing. I regret it every day. [pause] I'm not the person I was twenty years ago when I killed Jason. I will take that to my grave. [pause] No matter what the board decides today, I will be able to sleep better tonight.

I also heard a relatively small but significant number of victims talk about how their decision to forgive the inmate was what they needed to do in order to release the intense anger and angst they had carried with them in the years following the offense. In this respect forgiveness is in the victim's best interest, or at least so it appears; such forgiveness is a therapeutic gesture that for some seems to be an essential element of their efforts to heal from the trauma they have endured and to cope with relentless anxiety, depression, and stress, as in the case of Alice Hawkins.

Alice Hawkins had been robbed early one February morning by Tom Lorick as she was returning to her college dorm after attending a party. As Hawkins described it,

Marla and I were about a block away from the party when we heard footsteps coming up behind us. For a moment I thought it was one of the other students heading back to campus from the party. But before I knew it, I felt someone's hands around my neck. A man—who turned out to be Tom Lorick—yelled at me to stop walking. My bag was slung over my shoulder and across my neck. Lorick yanked the bag. When the strap didn't snap off, he pulled it over my head and shoved me to the ground. I hit my head on the sidewalk and, it turns out, got a severe concussion.

All I remember is that Marla started screaming for help. From what I've been told, the police showed up a few minutes later and called for rescue; it's hard for me to remember exactly what happened. I ended up spending two days in the hospital.

Ever since then I've struggled with anxiety and headaches. I never used to have those problems.

What's really interesting is that after this happened, I decided to take a course on the sociology of crime. I was an art history major, so this was new territory for me. At the same time I decided to see a therapist to help me deal with my anxiety from the assault. Both experiences taught me so much. My therapist helped me work through my fears and taught me ways to cope with and manage anxiety. I'm doing much better now.

The course I took really opened my eyes. I would never excuse what Lorick did to me, but I now have a much better understanding of how these things happen. In court, at Lorick's trial, I learned about his heroin addiction. I heard about how he's been to prison twice before this case. Apparently he was a construction worker for years after graduating from high school. His lawyer said that during one of his jobs Lorick fell off a ladder and shattered his leg. His doctor gave him narcotic pain killers, which eventually led to his first addiction.

My understanding is that Lorick lost his job because of his injury and lost his medical coverage. He couldn't afford to pay for his pain medication. In court he testified that his brother gave him some heroin to help him manage the pain since it's much cheaper on the street than narcotic pills. Lorick testified that he quickly became addicted to heroin, and he ended up robbing me when he was dope sick and needed money fast.

Of course what Lorick did to me was awful. But learning about him and, in my course, about how some criminals aren't really bad people but sometimes end up doing terrible things because of their addiction, I now think much differently about what happened to me than I did when the crime occurred.

In court Lorick actually apologized to me. When he was on the stand, he looked right at me and started to cry. He begged me to understand that he's not the kind of person who wants to hurt others. He wanted me to know that he's sorry for what he did to me and that he wants help.

I talked to my therapist a lot about whether to come here and whether to oppose parole. I've actually gotten to the point where I can handle Lorick's getting parole. A big reason is that this is a way for me to get out from the burden of this case that has gone on for years. I am ready to let go . . . at least I think I am.

But in some cases a victim's forgiveness is the product of manipulation by their offender. Often this occurs in the context of domestic violence cases. Al Haymond was serving a six-year sentence after being convicted of assaulting his live-in girlfriend, Tina Gilburg. The couple had lived together for four years before the assault. Haymond had a long criminal history, including charges of illegal drug possession, drug dealing, receipt of stolen goods, shoplifting, robbery, and domestic violence. As a juvenile he had also served time in the Rhode Island Training School on drug-related and breaking-and-entering charges.

I asked Gilburg how she had met Haymond and whether she was aware of his criminal record when she decided to move in with him.

We met at work. I was a cashier and he was in the shipping department. At first we just hung out in the lunchroom with other people, things like that. Eventually Al asked me to go to a bar with him after work. I kinda liked him right from the start, and he was real nice to my two kids.

I knew about his record. I was a little concerned, but the truth is, most of the men I know have records. I just felt like Al was different, that he was a good man.

Then I asked her about the abuse.

I remember it real well. It was about six months after we moved in together. He came home from hanging out with his buddies, and I could smell the alcohol. That had never happened before. I figured it was no big thing. But then Al started making comments about how messy the apartment was. I told him to shut up and mind his own business. If he didn't like the mess, he could clean it himself. My kids are good, but, yeah, they do make a mess.

Anyway, things got bad during that argument and Al slapped me upside my head. It hurt. I told him he's to never lay his hands on me again. Al didn't like that, and he walked over and yelled "Like this?"

and hit me again. I grabbed my kids and left the apartment. We stayed at my sister's place over on Covington Street.

The next morning Al called me on my cell phone and apologized. He realized he done wrong and he promised it wouldn't happen again.

Things were good for a few months, but then Al got drunk again and started after me. He called me all kinda names. I couldn't take it no more. After Al punched me in the face, I ran from the apartment and called the cops. He got arrested and got ninety days.

At first I didn't let Al live with me when he got out. But probation was requiring him to go to classes so I figured he was getting help. I decided to give him another chance.

Things was good again for about six months. Then this case happened. Al got fired from his job, and we was having money problems. We were behind in the rent. Al got drunk again and it got real bad. I told him he had to get out the apartment but he refused. I threatened to call the cops and Al went berserk. He lunged at me, pushed me against the wall, and threatened to hurt me real bad if I called the cops.

I felt like I couldn't take it no more. I pushed Al away and ran into the hallway and down the stairs. I ran outside, got in my car, and locked the doors. I called 911 and told them what happened. Then I drove to my sister's again. The short of it is that Al got arrested and got this sentence.

Here's the thing. I know you might think I'm crazy, but I want Al out on parole. I think this time is different. Me and the kids have been visiting him. He's promised me—all of us—that he's gonna get help. He knows he got a problem. Here are the letters Al done wrote me from prison.

I still love him.

QUESTION: How many times has Al hit you?
ANSWER: Maybe six or seven.
QUESTION: Do you have a restraining order against Al?
ANSWER: I used to. I don't now.
QUESTION: Have your children witnessed any of the abuse? Have they seen Al hit you?
ANSWER: Yes, a few times.
QUESTION: Does that concern you?
ANSWER: I suppose.

What Gilburg did not know, but my parole board colleagues and I knew, was that during this particular prison sentence Haymond was getting visits from another woman, Tracy Barnowski, with whom Haymond was having an affair around the time of his arrest for assaulting Gilburg. In fact, Haymond had been placed in segregation for having fondled Barnowski during one of their visits. Also, Haymond had written a letter to Barnowski that said in part: "I can't wait to get rid of that bitch. Tina and me is over. It's you and me now, babe. I'm pretty sure I can get her to tell the parole board how much she wants me out. I'll let you know, babe."

For forgiveness to be authentic, it is vital that the offender be sincere. Forgiveness offered by victims in the face of inmates' disingenuousness and manipulation compounds the tragedy.

||||||||||||||||||||||||||||||||||||||||||||||||||||||||||||

Victims were always in the forefront of my mind when I met with inmates. When inmates discussed their crimes during our hearings, I always looked for hints that they had thought about the impact of their offenses. Many inmates empathized with victims and reflected on the harm they had caused. Other inmates were so self-centered that they commented on victims only when prompted by parole board members—not a good sign.

The statistical reality is that only a small percentage of victims choose to meet with the parole board. My conversations with them just hours before I met with their offenders weighed heavily on me and often influenced my vote.

But many crimes have no named victims; there was no one for me and my colleagues to meet. These cases have victims in the general sense, but they are more abstract. You and I—the general public—are the victims. Inmates who embezzled money from a state agency where they once worked victimized *us*. Inmates who vandalized public property victimized *us*. Inmates who accepted bribes while in public office victimized *us*. And the toll is big.

People sometimes refer to so-called victimless crimes. Among the most common involve inmates who are serving time on illegal drug possession and drug distribution charges where no one is identified in police reports as a victim. We should not kid ourselves; we are all victims of such crimes, and I always kept that in mind during hearings. I have read countless police reports that sound like this:

On July 2, XXXX, at approximately 1830 hours, Detectives Smith and Jones were monitoring the area of Robbins Street in an unmarked police vehicle. While on Steele Street, the detectives were stalled in traffic and observed a tall Caucasian male (later identified as Lawrence Curtis, DOB XX-X-XXXX) standing outside of the passenger window of a late-model Honda Accord (registration RI XXX-XXX) which was occupied by a Caucasian male (later identified as Richard Parker, DOB X-XX-XXXX). Both detectives observed Curtis reach into the Honda Accord and remove a large plastic bag of suspected narcotics from a white tube sock and hand the bag to Parker. Detectives continued to monitor the Honda Accord and then observed Parker hand Curtis a large amount of U.S. currency.

Both detectives exited their unmarked police vehicle and approached both subjects. Both detectives were wearing t-shirts with POLICE on the front and back of the shirts. Detective Smith approached Parker on the sidewalk area as he was stuffing the currency in his back right pants pocket. Detective Smith ordered Parker to show his hands. Detective Smith placed Parker in handcuffs.

Detective Smith approached Curtis, who was attempting to conceal the suspected narcotics in a plastic bag that contained laundry. Detective Smith asked Curtis to exit the Honda Accord. Curtis exited the vehicle, and Detective Smith placed him in handcuffs and seized the suspected narcotics.

A call for assistance was aired over channel X for a transport vehicle. Parker was transported to police headquarters by a patrol unit. Curtis was transported to police headquarters by the detectives. The Honda Accord was towed from the scene.

While at police headquarters, Detective Smith conducted a field test on the suspected narcotics (62.7 grams net) with a positive result for heroin. The remaining heroin was sent to the state toxicology lab for further analysis.

Detective Jones seized $2,700 in U.S. currency from Curtis in the cell block area pending a forfeiture hearing. The white tube sock was delivered to the property room. At the time of his arrest Parker was wearing a home confinement bracelet placed on him by Superior Court for an earlier offense. He also has an immigration detainer. Curtis was charged with delivery of heroin (1 ounce to 1 kilo) and held for court. Parker was charged with possession with intent to deliver heroin and possession of heroin (1 ounce to 1 kilo). Parker was held for court.

There is no named victim in this report, no one who is going to ask to meet with the parole board for a victim's hearing. But all of us pay a steep price in such cases. Let's go through the list:

- Police departments devote significant resources to narcotics investigations. Taxpayers foot the bill for officers' and detectives' salaries and benefits, administrative supervision and overhead, clerical staff salaries and benefits, office facilities and maintenance, police cars and maintenance, surveillance equipment, cell block staffers, and so on.
- Suspects who are arrested have a right to a lawyer. Many of the inmates I saw were indigent at the time of their arrest. Often they relied on lawyers who worked for the public defender's office. This office is expensive to run. The budget includes lawyers' salaries and benefits, administrative and clerical staffers' salaries and benefits, office facilities and maintenance, and so on.
- Cases are expensive to prosecute. The budget for the prosecutor's office includes prosecutors' salaries and benefits, administrative and clerical staffers' salaries and benefits, office facilities and maintenance, and so on.
- Criminal courts are expensive to operate. The budget includes judges' salaries and benefits, administrative and clerical staffers' salaries and benefits, office facilities and maintenance, security, and so on.
- Many offenders are placed on probation. Probation office budgets include probation officers' salaries and benefits, administrative and clerical staffers' salaries and benefits, office facilities, transportation costs (probation officers spend many hours visiting probationers at their homes and job sites), and so on.
- Many offenders are incarcerated. Prisons are extraordinarily expensive to operate. Budgets include salaries and benefits for correctional

officers and supervisors, doctors, nurses, counselors, teachers, maintenance staffers, and food service personnel; medication; security equipment; inmate uniforms, shoes, jackets, coats, hats, underwear, and glasses; food; basic toiletries; utilities; cars and trucks; gasoline; office supplies; maintenance equipment and repairs; educational materials; office, dining hall, and visiting room furniture; and so on.

- Most inmates meet with a parole board. Parole board budgets include members' salaries, administrative and clerical staffers' salaries and benefits, office facilities, transportation expenses (mileage reimbursement for travel to and from prisons, housing and food expenses), and so on.
- Many inmates are released on parole. Parole office budgets include parole officers' salaries and benefits, administrative and clerical staffers' salaries and benefits, office facilities, transportation costs (parole officers spend many hours visiting parolees at their homes and job sites), and so on.
- Many offenders are placed in residential and outpatient counseling, addictions, and other programs as a condition of their sentence. Most inmates are low income and do not have personal funds or insurance coverage to pay for these expensive services. Many of these service providers are paid with funds that come from federally and state-funded contracts and grants for mental health and addictions treatment, which means they are funded by taxpayers.
- A significant number of inmates are homeless at the time of their release from prison. When there is no alternative, many offenders are referred to a residential facility or program for people who are homeless. In addition to housing, many of these programs offer social services, such as vocational training, mental health counseling, and addictions counseling. Most of these programs are funded by large federal grants and contracts (for example, from the U.S. Housing and Urban Development, Department of Justice, and the Substance Abuse and Mental Health Services Administration) and state contracts and grants, which means they are funded by taxpayers.

Over the years I have read many scholarly analyses that estimate the costs of crime to society.[8] Not surprisingly estimates vary, but there are some noteworthy patterns. Key among them are that in the

United States the cost of crime is somewhere between 2 and 6 percent of the gross national product (the monetary value of all goods and services produced within a nation's geographic borders over a specified period of time). That is a staggering figure by anyone's measure.

Researchers who study crime and its impact on the broader society typically distinguish between so-called external costs and social costs. External costs are those costs that offenders have imposed on victims (individual victims and the broader society). For example, the external costs of an armed robbery might include the value of the stolen goods, lost productivity and employment for injured victims, medical care to treat the injuries, emotional harms sustained by the victims, and the value of time spent dealing with the consequences of the armed robbery (negotiating with credit card companies about fraudulent charges, canceling credit cards, notifying credit rating companies, obtaining a new driver's license, etc.). Likewise, the external costs of a home invasion might be increased premiums for homeowners' insurance, the time and money required to repair broken doors and windows and replace stolen items, the cost of psychotherapy to deal with the fear and anguish caused by the intruder, and so on. Lawyers sometimes say that compensation for all these external costs is required to "make the individual whole."

In contrast social costs pertain to the impact of crime on the broader society. Social costs are an example of what economists refer to as externalities—a side effect, or consequence of an activity, on third parties. Crime-related social costs include what is required to fund police departments, public defenders' and prosecutors' offices, courts, prisons, probation and parole departments, parole boards, rehabilitation programs, and other supportive services. Some costs, such as stolen property and police officials' salaries, are tangible; others are intangible, such as the emotional harm and stress to victims.

|||||||||||||||||||||||||||||||||||||||||||||||||||||||||||

Month after month, year after year, I listened intently as thousands of victims shared stunningly intimate details about their lives and the impact crime has had on them. It felt like a sacred privilege when victims led me through the door to their suffering, giving me access to the remarkably personal details that we typically share only with our spouses, intimate partners, closest friends, clergy, and psychotherapists. I often wonder what it is like to talk to complete strangers about having been raped, molested, or robbed. I hope I provided victims with a sense of safety, trust, and perhaps insulation. During meetings with victims, I knew, in each and every moment, that I was dealing with the most intense pathos life can produce as we talked about victims' efforts to cope with the worst kinds of personal violations imaginable.

Often when I sat with crime victims, I thought of the words attributed to the sixteenth-century English Protestant clergyman John Bradford: "There, but for the grace of God, go I." I tried to imagine what it would be like to be a crime victim who shares with a panel of strangers what it was like to have been sexually molested, robbed by a man who pointed a gun at my head, or had my home broken into. I deeply admire victims who are able to share their struggles with paralyzing clinical depression, debilitating anxiety, overwhelming fear, and chronic physical pain that crime created. That takes a special kind of courage.

My worst moments, by far, were my meetings with victims who reminded me of the people I love the most, especially my wife and daughters. When I met a middle-aged woman who was thrown to the ground by an armed robber who accosted her in a shopping mall parking lot, I pictured my wife being loaded into the ambulance by emergency medical personnel. When I met young women who had been sexually assaulted or victims of horrific domestic violence, I pictured my daughters trying to cope with the relentless agony that permeates victims' lives. On the one hand, I needed to be careful to avoid letting my imagination bias my decisions about inmates' petitions for parole; the offenders deserved as much objectivity and neutrality as I could muster. However, I also had a duty, I think, to be as empathic with victims as possible, to immerse myself in their pain and anguish as best I could, and then factor that into my parole board votes. It was a delicate balance, to be sure.

My other frequent, nagging thought when I met with victims concerns life's remarkable fragility, unpredictability, and randomness. It is not a good feeling. Like most people, I would prefer that life's

challenges be manageable. I do not like the idea of unanticipated crises and disasters. I feel terribly vulnerable when I hear news about
an airline pilot who flew his passenger-filled plane into the side of
a mountain, a completely innocent bystander who was struck by a
stray bullet fired by one gang member toward another, a recreational
swimmer who was bitten by a shark and lost her arm, and college students who plunged to their deaths while gathered on an apartment
building balcony that collapsed as they celebrated the end of their
semester. Knowing that such tragedies can occur in all our lives—at
any moment—is unsettling, to say the least.

So many crime victims were simply and innocently in the proverbial wrong place at the wrong time. Had there been a ten-minute delay in their timing, had they taken a right-hand turn instead of a left-
hand turn, had they gotten sick that day and stayed out of work, they
would have escaped the horror that crime has visited upon their lives.

Hearing about such random tragedies is agonizing. Some of the
meetings I had with victims were so very painful that I was not certain
I could keep my composure during our time together. For one memorable meeting a large family filed into the hearing room: the parents
of the victim (he did not attend the meeting), assorted cousins and
family friends, and the uniformed police chief who investigated the
case when she was a major in the department. The mother of the victim began:

> As you must know from all of the reports, our son, Victor, has major
> disabilities. When he was molested by Donald Welch, Victor was re-
> ceiving services from the North County Disabilities Center.
>
> When he was four, Victor was diagnosed with pervasive develop-
> mental disorder. He has lots of problems. Victor has difficulty with ver-
> bal and nonverbal communication, social interaction, and adjusting
> to changes in his surroundings. He spends lots of time flapping his
> hands and banging his head. Victor has lots of temper tantrums and
> difficulty sleeping, and he's fearful so much of the time. We love Victor,
> but he's a handful.
>
> The North County program was great—that is until Donald Welch
> did what he did. Every weekday the bus [Welch drove] would pick
> Victor up at our home and take him to North County. His days there

were filled with physical therapy, occupational therapy, speech therapy, and lots of recreational activities. Most of the time, Victor was excited about going to the center. He was eager to see the staff.

For many months after Victor started attending North County we saw major progress. He was having fewer tantrums and was communicating better. We were so relieved that Victor was well cared for, and this also provided us with some respite.

But last March we noticed a big change in Victor. He began smiling less and his tantrums became frequent again. All of a sudden he had trouble sleeping and had frequent nightmares. Victor sometimes refused to eat, which is a problem we hadn't seen before. He started to torture our cat and was masturbating frequently.

We just knew something was wrong, but we didn't know what to do. We told Victor's social worker, Sandra, about our concerns. Sandra was very astute. She interviewed Victor and figured out that Welch had been fondling Victor. We're not sure exactly how long the abuse was going on, but we're pretty certain it went on for at least several months.

It's hard for me to say this: there's also evidence that Welch had Victor perform oral sex on him.

Victor's mother sobbed as she shared these odious details. Her husband held her hand, and her sister stroked her back to comfort her. Listening to these dreadful facts was excruciating for me. Child sexual abuse is always horrible, but there was something especially loathsome about the way Welch abused Victor.

I did not know how to climb into the pain that Victor's family and acquaintances shared, one after another. It was one of the worst mornings of my professional life. But I knew I had to make the climb.

There, but for the grace of God, go I.

4

PUNISHMENT, RETRIBUTION, AND SHAME

It is said that no one truly knows a nation until one has been inside its jails. A nation should not be judged by how it treats its highest citizens, but its lowest ones.

—NELSON MANDELA

MOST INMATES I met had committed serious crimes. They had hurt people badly and violated the public's trust and sense of safety. Intellectually I know that many criminals commit crimes because of their severe trauma history, mental illness, and out-of-control addiction. Often I had compassion for their dreadful, often lifelong, challenges and did what I could to help them get the treatment they desperately needed. But, I admit, in some cases my intellect took me only so far. My heart aches badly for so many of the victims I met—and many I never met but read about in police reports, correspondence, and court documents—that I had a deep-seated wish to punish the offenders who sat across from me at the hearing room table.

One particular parole board hearing day started like most others, or so I thought. As usual my colleagues and I met with victims who chose to meet with us. The second victims' meeting of the morning was unlike any I had encountered. Most victims with whom we met suffer as a result of a violent crime. This case was a bit different.

The owner of a local cemetery, Bob Pellington, met with us to share his distress about the crime that Donna Shula had committed along with her boyfriend. I had read the police report and knew this was an unusual case. Pellington began:

I've owned Longview Cemetery for thirty-four years. I've never seen anything like this. Imagine what it's like to get a call in the middle of the night from the police informing me that they received a report of serious vandalism. I dressed quickly and headed over to the cemetery. I learned that someone—at the time I didn't know who—walked onto the grounds in the vicinity of 2:30 A.M. and stole ninety-one brass flower vases that were attached to gravesites. Good heavens, who would do a thing like that?

Each vase costs about $325, so we're talking about a total of around $30,000. And that doesn't begin to count the heartache this caused for all of the relatives of the deceased. Imagine what it's like to find out that the vase you ordered for a loved one, many of which had personally engraved messages, was stolen. My staff and I had to track down all of these people and break the bad news. Some of them started to cry, they felt so violated. For many families, placing flowers in these vases is a deeply emotional way to connect with their loved ones. So we've had to deal with the emotional anguish as well as the financial issues.

I had heard about these sorts of thefts at cemeteries around the country. Our professional association has sent out alerts. Thieves gather up large numbers of these vases and take them to scrap metal dealers. I've heard that each one is worth just a few bucks when they're melted down.

About two hours later, after we had completed our meetings with victims, my colleagues and I drove over to the women's prison that housed Donna Shula. When I got out of my car, I noticed six female inmates in dark green prison uniforms tending a large garden adjacent to the parking lot. The garden would have been the pride of any homeowner. These inmates, who are generally considered low risk, had to earn the privilege of this coveted outdoor assignment based on their institutional conduct and criminal record. The inmate gardeners I have spoken to relish the opportunity to have time outside the institution's harsh confines, get their hands dirty, and nurture vegetables and flowers. For many inmates this is horticulture therapy. They dread stormy weather during gardening season, because it means they are stuck inside and subjected to the usual prison constraints. However, because of her prison disciplinary record, Donna Shula was not allowed to participate in the program.

After I admired the inmates' garden for a brief moment, I headed up the concrete stairs to the prison's main entrance. From a small lobby adjacent to the control center, I could see into the spacious visiting room. It held a collection of toys that inmates' young children play with during visits. Just beyond the visiting room's large windows are large swaths of fencing and razor wire. It's quite a contrast.

I walked down the hallway, past a door with a formal, engraved sign that announces Urine Room. This is not the women's lavatory. Rather, it is the room where inmates who are being tested for illicit drugs fill their personalized cup.

Illegal drugs in prison are a huge challenge, and they often create a problem for inmates who appear before the parole board. When I reviewed inmates' files in advance of their parole hearings, it was not unusual to read a disciplinary report stating that the inmate had been placed in segregation after a urine sample tested positive for opioids or some other contraband substance. The parole board's long-standing policy is to consider parole release only for inmates who have not been disciplined within the preceding six months. Inmates who test positive for use of an unauthorized substance automatically forfeited the possibility of parole release.

People who aren't familiar with prison culture are often surprised to hear that illegal and unauthorized drugs find their way into institutions. Given how secure prisons are, how is it possible to smuggle drugs in? In fact, the myriad ways that drugs find their way into prisons are a testament to the ingenuity of inmates (and some unscrupulous staffers). Some drug-trafficking schemes that have been reported nationwide are rather simplistic; others are downright brilliant.

- A civilian accomplice tosses a tennis ball or dead bird embedded with drugs over the security fence into the minimum security prison's recreation yard. Inmates who are in on the plan may stage a fight to distract correctional officers while another inmate retrieves the missile after it lands.
- Visitors stash drugs in a balloon or condom, hold them in their mouths, and pass them to an inmate during a kiss. The inmate

swallows the object and retrieves the defecated contents for personal use, sale, or both.

- Family members may send inmates books with drugs inserted in the lining of covers.
- Drugs may be hidden under postage stamps on envelopes that friends and relatives mail to inmates.
- Crooked staffers—particularly those who have security clearances and thus bypass scrutiny—bring drugs in their duffel bags, satchels, coolers, lunchboxes, toolboxes, pocketbooks, and compartments sewn into their clothing or belts.
- Visitors purchase packaged food or drinks from visiting room vending machines and place drugs in the items before handing them to inmates.
- In a more sophisticated variation, seasoned visitors buy items from a grocery store identical to items in the vending machines, place drugs in the packages, then smuggle the food into the institution. The visitor buys an identical item from the vending machine, covertly switches the items, and gives the inmate the smuggled package with the drugs inside.
- Visitors who bring infants to visit inmates hide drugs in the baby's diaper, which they retrieve during a diaper changing.
- Some drugs in pill form can be dissolved into a paste and painted into a children's coloring book, which an inmate's child then brings to a visit.

Donna Shula was one of the many inmates serving time for a crime that arose from drug addiction. Her addiction to cocaine and heroin was so severe that on two occasions she tested positive for opioids while incarcerated. Each time Shula was placed in the prison's segregation unit for thirty days. On both occasions Shula received contraband drugs from visitors (once from her sister and once from a friend, both of whom struggle with addiction).

The correctional officer ushered Donna Shula into the hearing room. She sat down and placed her tattoo-covered arms on the table. Shula glanced around the room and fidgeted, looking anxious. She then described the circumstances that had brought her to prison. Key features of Shula's journey are sadly common, especially concerning the ways in which her heartbreaking, chronic trauma paved the way for her prolonged substance abuse and periodic crime sprees.

QUESTION: Tell us, please, what brought you to prison. How did you get involved in this theft of cemetery vases?

ANSWER: To tell you the truth, this never would have happened if I didn't have a drug problem. I was hanging with a bad crowd. All of us are addicts. My boyfriend has done time in prison and I followed his lead. I'm really ashamed of myself.

QUESTION: What are your drugs of choice when you're on the street?

ANSWER: Mostly crack and heroin. Before that it was mostly Vicodin and oxycodone. By the time I was arrested I was in real bad shape. The only reason we went into the cemetery and stole that stuff is that we were dope sick. We needed money bad and we knew this was an easy way to get it.

QUESTION: When did your drug abuse start? How did that happen?

ANSWER: It was right after my sixteenth birthday. Being at home was a nightmare. My mom's boyfriend had been sexually abusing me for a couple of years, but I was afraid to tell anyone. I started skipping school, staying out at night, running away—I was a mess. One night I met a guy who turned me on to Vicodin. Before long I was hooked. For a couple of years I relied on friends to give me drugs or traded sex for drugs. It was terrible, but I didn't know what else to do. Then I met Jon, the guy who got me involved in this case. I can't believe I let things get this bad.

QUESTION: What have you learned as a result of this experience?

ANSWER: I never want to go back to that way of life. Never. I've got a real good counselor here. I sort of knew before this that being sexually abused for so long has a lot to do with my drug use. I know I was using drugs to deal with the pain. But my therapy here is real good. It's helping me understand myself and my triggers better and come up with ways to stay clean when I get out.

QUESTION: That's great, but I see in your disciplinary record that you've tested positive twice in here for drugs and got sent to segregation. What's that all about?

ANSWER: It's true, but that was pretty early in my sentence, when I was still thinking like an addict. You'll see that things have been better for the past year or so.

Understandably Shula's crime makes people—lots of people—angry. She entered a cemetery and stole dozens of brass flower vases from gravesites. The judge sent her to prison because this was not her first offense. Shula had previous convictions for shoplifting, drug possession, and drug dealing. She was placed on probation for those cases with mandatory drug counseling. However, she relapsed and returned to drug use. When Shula was arrested yet again—in this case for theft—the judge decided that she needed to serve time in prison, especially given the financial cost and deep emotional hurt caused by her crime.

I struggled with such cases. On its face Shula's crime is terrible. It pains me to think of the distress she caused many families. At the same time Shula did not commit a violent crime; she never stabbed or shot anyone or broke into someone's home. Shula deserved punishment, to be sure; she also needed help to cope with her serious drug addiction. The enduring questions for me in such cases are, What is the role of punishment? How much punishment is warranted?

||||||||||||||||||||||||||||||||||||||||||||||||||||||||||||

I certainly understand that many criminals need to be punished. Punishment may not always deter future crime—more about that later—but it may be necessary in order to satisfy the compelling need of victims and the broader society for some sort of retribution in response to heinous acts.

My work in prisons led me to think hard about the complicated concepts of punishment and retribution. And clearly my views and my parole board votes were directly connected.

Historically, moral and political philosophers have embraced one of several perspectives on the issue. Some argue that punishment is justifiable when its aim is to produce a specific desirable consequence, such as rehabilitating an offender or deterring the offender from committing crimes in the future (known as specific deterrence). Even the most ardent supporters of punishment recognize that it may be a last resort, given its destructive qualities. The eighteenth-century philosopher Jeremy Bentham put it succinctly in his 1789 classic, *An Introduction to the Principles of Morals and Legislation*: "But all punishment is mischief: all punishment in itself is evil. Upon the principle of utility, if it ought at all to be admitted, it ought only to be admitted in as far as it promises to exclude some greater evil." Thus from this point of view Donna Shula's significant punishment was necessary to deter her from crime in the future and to announce to the broader community that those who commit such crimes will face similar consequences. Using an offender's punishment to discourage others from committing crimes is called general deterrence.[1]

Years ago I read the dialogue between Socrates and Polus in Plato's *Gorgias*. This is perhaps the earliest argument that punishment is morally justifiable as an effort to cure the offender:

> **SOCRATES:** Of two who suffer evil either in body or in soul, which is the more wretched, the man who submits to treatment and gets rid of the evil, or he who is not treated but still retains it?
>
> **POLUS:** Evidently the man who is not treated.
>
> **SOCRATES:** And was not punishment admitted to be a release from the greatest of evils, namely wickedness?
>
> **POLUS:** It was.
>
> **SOCRATES:** Yes, because a just penalty disciplines us and makes us more just and cures of us evil.

Another perspective on punishment focuses on the value of retribution for its own sake, that is, punishment is necessary to convey the community's anger, indignation, and resentment toward the offender.[2] Evidence that the punishment cures or deters the offender or deters others is not necessary; what matters is that members of the broader society have an opportunity to condemn the offender for the misconduct and restore the moral balance. Thus Donna Shula needed to get the strong and certain message that the community condemned her conduct, and punishment was the vehicle required to communicate this message. This popular sentiment has its roots in the philosopher Immanuel Kant's nineteenth-century musings in his *Philosophy of Law*:

> Juridical punishment can never be administered merely as a means for promoting another good, either with regard to the criminal himself or to civil society, but must in all cases be imposed only because the individual on whom it is inflicted has committed a crime. For one ought never to be dealt with merely as a means subservient to the purpose of another, nor be mixed up with the subjects of real right. . . . The penal law is a categorical imperative; and woe to him who creeps through the serpent-windings of utilitarianism to discover some advantage that may discharge him from the justice of punishment, or even from the due measure of it.

A third perspective—one that I embrace—blends these two views and acknowledges the legitimate right of the community to express its indignation and resentment toward those offenders who have the ability to exercise some measure of control over their behavior (this would not include, for example, offenders whose serious psychiatric illness prevents them from appreciating the difference between right and wrong). However, reasonable constraints must temper these understandable instincts; any punishment imposed on an offender must serve a constructive purpose with respect to some beneficial and realistic consequence, such as public safety, deterrence, and rehabilitation. In other words, principled—not draconian—punishment serves multiple aims, which may vary from circumstance to circumstance and case to case.[3]

Moral indignation may be particularly important in some circumstances—for example, when a prominent politician accepts a bribe meant to influence her handling of proposed legislation, or when a man makes a deliberate decision to sexually exploit his stepdaughter. In other cases deterrence and rehabilitation are compelling considerations—for example, when a loving, caring mother who is earnestly trying to conquer her drug addiction shoplifts in order to feed her hungry children or when a homeless man suffering from untreated schizophrenia is arrested after he starts a fire for warmth and accidentally burns down the warehouse where he sought shelter during a blizzard.

In my parole board deliberations I aimed for what is best described as just deserts. Here, too, I think it is helpful to reflect on early understandings of this complicated concept that, at least in principle, underpins the administration of justice and the concept of punishment.

The principle of just deserts has ancient origins, dating at least as far as the Torah, the Qur'an, and the Code of Hammurabi. These classic views, based on remarkably different faith and ideological traditions, share a common conceptual thread. Perhaps the best-known characterization is *lex talionis*, or the law of talion (commonly known as the principle of "an eye for an eye"), a precept of ancient Hebrew scripture.[4] Prominent—albeit chauvinistic—references in the Torah include:

When men strive together, and hurt a woman with child, so that there is a miscarriage, and yet no harm follows, the one who hurt her shall be fined, according as the woman's husband shall lay upon him; and he shall pay as the judges determine. If any harm follows, then you shall give life for life, eye for eye, tooth for tooth, hand for hand, foot for foot, burn for burn, wound for wound, stripe for stripe.

If a malicious witness rises against any man to accuse him of wrongdoing, then both parties to the dispute shall appear before the Lord, before the priests and the judges who are in office in those days; the judges shall inquire diligently, and if the witness is a false witness and has accused his brother falsely, then you shall do to him as he had meant to do to his brother; so you shall purge the evil from the midst of you. And the rest shall hear, and fear, and shall never commit any such evil among you. Your eye shall not pity; it shall be life for life, eye for eye, tooth for tooth, hand for hand, foot for foot.

He who kills a man shall be put to death. He who kills a beast shall make it good, life for life. When a man causes a disfigurement in his neighbor, as he has done it shall be done to him, fracture for fracture, eye for eye, tooth for tooth; as he has disfigured a man, he shall be disfigured. He who kills a beast shall make it good; and he who kills a man shall be put to death.[5]

Similarly the Qur'an makes explicit references to principles of *lex talionis* in its formulation of Islamic law. Islamic law provides for exact retaliation (*qisas*) and payment of blood money (*diyah*) in response to wrongdoing: "And We prescribed to them in it that life is for life, and eye for eye, and nose for nose, and ear for ear, and tooth for tooth, and for wounds retaliation. But who so forgoes it, it shall be an expiation for him. And whosoever judges not by what Allah has revealed, those are the wrongdoers."[6]

Such sentiments also appear in Aeschylus's *Agamemnon* (458 BCE). Clytemnestra's husband, Agamemnon, is fated to die for slaying their eldest daughter, Iphigenia:

> The spoiler is robbed; he killed, he has paid.
> The truth stands ever beside God's throne
> Eternal: he who has wrought shall pay; that is law.

The Code of Hammurabi (ca. 1728–1686 BCE) also contains similar prescriptions. The code includes the first written evidence for penalizing offenses with an exact talion: For personal injury the code prescribes taking an eye for an eye (no. 196), breaking a bone for a bone (no. 197), and extracting a tooth for a tooth (no. 199). Other sanctions are less exact and identical, for example, cutting out the tongue of an adoptive son who has denied his adoptive parents' status (no. 192), cutting off the breasts of a wet nurse who, without informing the parents, contracts for another child to replace a child who has died (no. 194), and cutting off the hand of a son who strikes his father (no. 195).

As the following two cases illustrate, the Code of Hammurabi was uniquely elitist in that it legislated different consequences and penalties depending on the involvement of different classes—nobles, commoners, and slaves.

> 209: If a man strike a free-born woman so that she lose her unborn child, he shall pay ten shekels for her loss.
> 210: If the woman die, his daughter shall be put to death.

211: If a woman of the free class lose her child by a blow, he shall pay five shekels in money.

212: If this woman die, he shall pay half a mina.

213: If he strike the maid-servant of a man, and she lose her child, he shall pay two shekels in money.

214: If this maid-servant die, he shall pay one-third of a mina.

229: If a builder build a house for someone, and does not construct it properly, and the house which he built fall in and kill its owner, then that builder shall be put to death.

230: If it kill the son of the owner, the son of that builder shall be put to death.

231: If it kill a slave of the owner, then he shall pay slave for slave to the owner of the house.

Clearly as a society we have moved far from the strict law of talion (the principle that punishment should be equivalent or identical to the offense committed), and thank goodness for that. Today's criminal court judges typically follow sentencing guidelines that prohibit penalties approximating an eye for an eye, a tooth for a tooth, and so on, although some might argue that in states authorizing the death penalty in murder cases, the law of talion still reigns.

Perhaps the closest we get today to the principles of talion are restitution orders that judges sometimes impose on offenders who have caused a victim some kind of financial harm. In these cases judges may consider the costs associated with stolen property, property damage, insurance deductibles, embezzlement, crime-related medical and psychotherapy costs, lost wages, and crime-scene cleanup and require offenders to comply with payment plans. Of course many offenders are poor, which limits their ability to make full restitution payments. And incarcerated offenders may not be able to make payments while they are in prison, beyond minimal amounts deducted from their prison-job wages. These cases may call for community service (for example, participating in community cleanups, volunteering at a shelter), another form of restitution.

- Rhonda Grimsley was arrested by police and charged with embezzlement. She pleaded guilty to embezzling $61,542 from her former employer, a prominent family-owned waste-management company. The company had contracts with a large number of retail businesses to haul their waste. Grimsley, who was the company accountant for nearly twelve years, admitted in court that she had created a scheme to divert payments made by the company's clients for her personal use. She created bogus invoices in an effort to camouflage her scheme.

Grimsley presented to the judge a formal report prepared by a psychiatrist that documented her spending addiction and bipolar disorder. Grimsley's attorney was able to negotiate a plea deal that included two years in prison and two years of home confinement, along with a restitution order.

Once she was released from prison and placed in the home confinement program of the Department of Corrections, Grimsley started a new job helping to manage a cousin's popular restaurant. Grimsley began making monthly restitution payments in order to retire her debt to her former employer.

Grimsley will need many years to satisfy the restitution order—not exactly an eye for eye but as close as we are likely to get.

IIIIIIIIIIIIIIIIIIIIIIIIIIIIIIIIIIIIIIIIIIIIIIIIIIIIIIIIIII

One of the nagging challenges in criminal justice—especially with respect to imposing sanctions and punishment—concerns socioeconomic and racial disparities. For a variety of complex reasons, inmates are disproportionately poor and people of color.[7] When I walked through the congested corridors of my state's prisons, I could not help but notice this stark reality—a pattern one sees in nearly every prison in the United States. Inmate file after inmate file is filled with tales of poverty. Relatively speaking, few affluent people are in prison, especially state prisons. And there is no denying that throughout this nation's history, the criminal justice system has discriminated against people of color. National surveys conducted by the U.S. Department of Justice report that while African Americans and whites may be subject to traffic stops by police at similar rates, African Americans are three times as likely to be searched after being stopped. Studies also suggest that law enforcement emphasis on drug-related policing in communities of color has resulted in African Americans' being prosecuted for drug offenses far out of proportion to the degree that they use or sell drugs. And it is well known that African Americans—especially young men—are incarcerated at extraordinarily high rates and that these rates of imprisonment are not the result of their higher rate of involvement in crime. As Michelle Alexander, a civil rights litigator and legal scholar, notes in her powerful book *The New Jim Crow: Mass Incarceration in the Age of Colorblindness*, "African Americans are not significantly more likely to use or sell prohibited drugs than whites, but they are made criminals at drastically higher rates for precisely the same conduct."[8]

While greater involvement in some crimes accounts for higher rates of incarceration for African Americans, thoughtful and credible scholars and criminal justice professionals recognize that a significant proportion of the disparity is not entirely a function of disproportionate criminal behavior. And this is on the minds of some inmates.

Franklin Rayford appeared before the parole board for the first time after serving twenty months of his five-year sentence for violating probation on an earlier conviction and for resisting arrest. According to the police report, undercover narcotics officers responded to calls from Rayford's neighbors about what appeared to be illegal drug selling from his nearby apartment. Neighbors reported seeing people going into Rayford's apartment throughout the day and night and leaving shortly after their arrival. One neighbor reported seeing Rayford leave his apartment on a number of occasions, hand bags of suspected drugs to car drivers and passengers who drove up to his address, and accept handfuls of cash. Undercover officers in plainclothes and unmarked cars conducted surveillance of Rayford's apartment for two days. Before beginning their surveillance on the second day, officers arranged for what in the trade is known as a controlled buy.

A controlled buy refers to a type of drug investigation in which a police officer is first searched to confirm that the officer is not carrying contraband. The officer is then provided with prerecorded and marked funds to purchase drugs and taken to a prearranged area for the transaction. Police maintain continuous surveillance, and once the transaction is complete, they again search the officer and field-test the drugs obtained from the target of the investigation. Most controlled buys are recorded using small devices that can be hidden on the officer's body, otherwise known as wearing a wire. Some controlled buys are made by confidential informants who are cooperating with the police. Often these confidential informants have criminal records and are facing charges; they may choose to cooperate with the police to negotiate a more favorable deal for themselves.

When the undercover officers confirmed that Rayford had just completed an illegal transaction, they announced that they were police, displayed their badges, and ordered Rayford to the ground. Rayford ran from the officers, one of whom caught up to him about a block away. Rayford fought with the officer and had to be subdued. During the scuffle Rayford punched the officer in the face and twisted his arm. Rayford suffered a head injury and multiple contusions when the officer forced him to the ground. Both Rayford and the officer were taken to a nearby hospital for emergency treatment.

At trial Rayford denied that he was selling drugs. The recording device malfunctioned and did not include any evidence that could be used against Rayford. When the officers arrested Rayford, he did not have drugs on him, only several hundred dollars in cash. The judge ruled that the evidence was insufficient to convict Rayford on the drug-dealing charge but found him guilty of gun possession, resisting arrest, and violating his probation.

At the parole board hearing Rayford was adamant that he had not been selling drugs when he was arrested.

QUESTION: What's your version of what happened in this case?
ANSWER: Look, I know I have a bad record. There's no point denying it. But I didn't sell no drugs this time, and the judge didn't convict me of that. I shouldn't of run, man, I know that. But them cops have it out for me, you know what I'm sayin'? They lookin' for every chance they got to rope me in, you know what I'm sayin'? I'm a black man with a record, and I got set up on this one. That's the truth. I

had the gun for my own protection, that's all. And when they caught me after I ran, they let me have it good. My head still hurts.

In this sort of case I was not in a position to judge the veracity of the inmate's version of the offense and its ugly aftermath. As parole board members often told inmates who challenged details in police reports, we were not in a position to retry their case. Board members do their best to separate fact from fiction, but in the final analysis the board must depend heavily on official descriptions of the events that led to arrest and conviction. I recognize that for some inmates, this seems grossly unfair. This is yet another of the challenges parole boards everywhere face.

In Rayford's case his extensive criminal record worked against him. Even if I had accepted his adamant denial that he was selling drugs when he was arrested—which was difficult for me in light of his many drug-selling convictions—he had been caught with a gun. That was enough for me and my colleagues. Parole denied.

The good news is that significant numbers of principled, conscientious professionals from the ranks of the police, courts, prosecutors, defense attorneys, and corrections staffers have worked diligently toward eliminating discrimination at each stage of the criminal justice process. We are not there yet, of course; too many headlines report unwarranted police shootings, planted evidence, mistreatment of inmates by guards, and other miscarriages of justice that have racial overtones. But during my career I saw real progress, albeit not enough. Growing numbers of police departments and departments of corrections are conducting training in an effort to prevent racial profiling. Judges throughout the United States convene in conferences to discuss sentencing and other racial disparities in the criminal justice system.

Perhaps the greatest advances pertain to court sanctions and punishment. When I began my criminal justice career in the 1970s, discrimination seemed rampant; criminal defendants who were poor people of color often were sanctioned more severely. In the 1970s the concept of sentencing guidelines emerged; the goal was for criminal court judges to impose sentences based on strict criteria, in order to enhance consistency and reduce disparities. The guidelines are not a panacea, but they are a critically important move in the right direction.[9]

That said, we still have much work to do to strip discrimination from the criminal justice system. Long before judges impose sentences on convicted offenders, there are lots of opportunities for discrimination. While most of the many police officers I got to know over the years work hard to be fair when they decide whether to arrest a suspect, there is no denying that police discrimination is a serious problem in many communities. Also, prosecutors exercise a great deal of discretion about which cases to prosecute, so here, too, there is room for modest or unbridled discrimination.

Until some significant reforms in recent years, many courts relied on so-called indeterminate sentencing, in which judges used their discretion about a minimum and maximum sentence and a parole board used its judgment about an appropriate release date. Most thoughtful observers concluded that this approach had led to some wildly disparate sentences in cases that were similar with respect to the nature and severity of the offense, the defendant's criminal history, mitigating circumstances, and so on. The overarching goal of pioneering sentencing reform efforts was to curb discretion within reasonable limits in order to reduce disparities and discrimination and enhance proportionality in sentencing.

The harshest critics accused some judges of engaging in arbitrary and capricious sentencing. As a result of sentencing reform, many states and the federal government adopted structured sentencing policies and guidelines designed to control the discretion of sentencing judges. A number of states adopted determinate sentencing policies that offer judges a limited number of sentencing options and include additional penalties for use of a weapon, a previous criminal record, or infliction of serious injury. Other states and the federal government adopted sentencing guidelines that incorporate crime seriousness and previous criminal record in a sentencing grid that judges use in determining the appropriate sentence. These grids typically include a detailed list of relevant factors and a point system. Other reforms enacted at both the federal and state level include mandatory minimum penalties for certain types of offenses (especially drug and weapons offenses).

Not surprisingly the states have adopted diverse sentencing protocols. There is more uniformity at the federal level. In 1977 Senator Edward M. Kennedy introduced the Criminal Code Reform Act. The purpose of SB 1437 was to establish a federal commission on sentencing, which would be authorized to develop sentencing guidelines for U.S. district judges. Kennedy introduced versions of his sentencing reform bill in the next four congresses, until it was finally enacted as the Sentencing Reform Act of 1984.[10]

The measure created the U.S. Sentencing Commission (USSC), which was authorized to develop and implement presumptive sentencing guidelines designed to eliminate discrimination and enhance truth in sentencing and greater uniformity. The law stated that departures from the guidelines would be permitted with written justification and provided for appellate review of sentences to determine whether the guidelines were correctly applied or whether a departure was reasonable. The federal sentencing guidelines promulgated by the USSC went into effect in 1987.

The federal guidelines are complex. The first guidelines manual consisted of more than three hundred pages of directives; the manual is now nearly six hundred pages long. Judges and other criminal justice officials calculate the sentence using a standardized worksheet that, at least in principle, leads to uniformity. Although the federal sentencing guidelines are fairly rigid, they are not inflexible. The guidelines provide for some discretion by judges between the minimum and the maximum sentence for each combination of offense seriousness and previous record. Also, defendants who plead guilty may qualify for a significant reduction in the guideline range for "acceptance of responsibility." Defendants who provide "substantial assistance"—that is, information that leads to the prosecution and conviction of another offender—can also be sentenced outside the applicable guideline range. This type of departure is especially common in cases involving drug offenses.

||||||||||||||||||||||||||||||||||||||||||||||||||||||||||||

Of all the parole board cases I dealt with, some of the most difficult involved murder. Meeting with surviving family members and acquaintances was among the most painful tasks I faced. Invariably these cases led me to reflect on the essential purposes of punishment and incarceration.

For reasons I will spell out, I do not support the death penalty. However, I will concede that a handful of cases are so heinous that they have made me think twice (and more) about the issue and provide considerable grist for debate. Chief among them is the Boston Marathon bombing that occurred on April 15, 2013, a short drive from my home. The Tsarnaev brothers, Tamerlan and Dzhokhar, killed three and wounded 264 people. Shortly after the bombing the suspects killed an MIT policeman, carjacked an SUV, and exchanged gunfire with police in Watertown, Massachusetts. Tamerlan was shot several times in the exchange, and Dzhokhar ran over him with the stolen SUV during his attempted escape. Tamerlan was pronounced dead at the scene. Dzhokhar was found guilty and sentenced to death.

Recently I read this newspaper account about a deeply disturbing case in Nevada. This is the kind of case that shocks our collective conscience and fuels support for the death penalty. I was relieved that it would not fall under my board's jurisdiction.

A North Las Vegas man abandoned the 17-year-old stepdaughter he impregnated, police said, leaving the teen to give birth alone at home while looking after her 3-year-old sister, who eventually starved to death.

Jondrew Lachaux's arrest report, made public Wednesday, revealed callous acts that police said started as abuse, and eventually killed his own flesh and blood.

The toddler died in early March, North Las Vegas police spokeswoman Chrissie Coon said.

Her body was left untouched about two weeks, police said. The teen and baby, meanwhile, lived in the house as her sister decomposed.[11]

And then there is the case of Dave Sempsrott, my pen pal for thirty years, who shot and killed his best friend, bound and stabbed his friend's girlfriend to death, and then murdered the girlfriend's four-year-old daughter. If ever there was a case for the death penalty, this would be it, I often thought. In 1977, when Dave committed the murders, Missouri was not a death penalty state. Missouri had placed a moratorium on the death penalty in 1968 because of legal challenges and reinstated it in 1977—only five months after Dave committed those murders—when the state legislature passed a new law modeled after death penalty statutes in other states that had been upheld as constitutional by the U.S. Supreme Court. Dave knew that he had barely escaped being eligible for the death penalty and nearly certain execution, as he made clear in one of his letters to me: "I know I'd be on death row if Missouri had the death penalty when I killed Don, Mary, and Angie. Sometimes I wish they could kill me, to get me out of this living hell. I can't really say I don't deserve it."

Did I want to see Dave executed? No, in part because I oppose the death penalty and in part because I knew that Dave was being punished severely by his life sentence, with no parole eligibility, and that he no longer posed a threat to the general public. Do I understand why many people wanted the State of Missouri to execute Dave for his unforgivable and heinous crimes? Yes; these are legitimate sentiments.

The death penalty debate in the United States has raged for decades.[12] My state, Rhode Island, does not have the death penalty as an option. The last person executed in Rhode Island was Johnny Gordon, who was hanged on February 14, 1845. Gordon was executed for the mysterious murder of Amasa Sprague, a prominent mill owner who had used connections in the state senate to have Gordon's pub shut down. Although Gordon's two brothers were also charged with the murder, John was the only one who could not produce a strong enough alibi to avoid conviction. Following the conviction Gordon received the support of the state's labor movement, and petitions were filed with the state government asking for clemency. On appeal the state's general assembly upheld the conviction in a 36–27 vote. Governor James Fenner then reviewed the case but also declined to grant Gordon relief, and the execution was carried out.

Many believe that anti-Irish sentiment contributed to Gordon's conviction. In fact, on June 29, 2011, former governor Lincoln Chafee issued a formal pardon of Gordon, stating that "there is no question he was not given a fair trial. Today we are trying to right that injustice."

Rhode Island abolished the death penalty for all crimes on February 11, 1852, becoming one of the first states to do so. The abolition lasted until 1873, when the general assembly reinstated the death penalty for the crime of murder committed while serving a life sentence. Following the U.S. Supreme Court's 1972 decision in *Furman v. Georgia*, which led to a moratorium on the death penalty throughout the United States, Rhode Island rewrote its death penalty law to include a mandatory death sentence for murder committed while under confinement in a state prison. However, the mandatory death sentence was declared unconstitutional by Rhode Island's Supreme Court in 1979, and on May 9, 1984, the general assembly removed the death penalty from Rhode Island law.

Our nation's history on this issue is complicated. Britain influenced America's use of the death penalty more than any other country did. European settlers brought the practice of capital punishment with them. The first recorded execution in the new colonies was that of Captain George Kendall in the Jamestown colony of Virginia in 1608. Kendall was executed for being a spy for Spain. In 1612 Virginia governor Sir Thomas Dale enacted the Divine, Moral and Martial Laws, which provided the death penalty for even minor offenses such as stealing grapes, killing chickens, and trading with Indians.

Laws regarding the death penalty varied from colony to colony. The Massachusetts Bay Colony held its first execution in 1630. The New York Colony instituted the Duke's Laws of 1665, which made certain offenses punishable by death, such as striking one's mother or father or denying the "true God."

The first attempted reforms of the death penalty in the United States occurred in 1778 when Thomas Jefferson introduced a bill that would have revised Virginia's death penalty laws.

> And whereas the reformation of offenders, tho' an object worthy the attention of the laws, is not effected at all by capital punishments, which exterminate instead of reforming, and should be the last melancholy resource against those whose existence is become inconsistent with the safety of their fellow citizens, which also weaken the state by cutting off so many who, if reformed, might be restored sound mem-

bers to society, who, even under a course of correction, might be rendered useful in various labors for the public, and would be living and long continued spectacles to deter others from committing the like offences.

The bill proposed that capital punishment be used only for the crimes of murder and treason. It was defeated by only one vote.

Dr. Benjamin Rush, a signer of the Declaration of Independence and founder of the Pennsylvania Prison Society, also challenged the belief that the death penalty served as a deterrent. Rush gained the support of Benjamin Franklin and Pennsylvania attorney general William Bradford. Bradford subsequently led Pennsylvania to become the first state to consider degrees of murder based on culpability. In 1794 Pennsylvania repealed the death penalty for all offenses except first-degree murder.

In the early part of the nineteenth century, many states reduced the number of their capital crimes. In 1847 Michigan became the first state to abolish the death penalty for all crimes except treason.

New York built the first electric chair in 1888 and in 1890 executed William Kemmler, who had been convicted of murdering his common-law wife with a hatchet. Nevada introduced the use of cyanide gas in 1924. Gee Jon, a Chinese immigrant convicted of murdering a rival, was the first person executed by lethal gas. The state first tried to pump cyanide gas into Jon's cell while he slept, but this proved impossible because the gas leaked out of the cell. A makeshift gas chamber was then constructed at the prison's butcher shop to complete the execution.

By the 1950s public sentiment in the United States had begun to turn away from capital punishment. Many allied nations either abolished or limited the death penalty, and in the United States the number of executions dropped dramatically. In the late 1960s the Supreme Court began to address issues concerning the way the death penalty was administered. Two 1968 cases were key. The first was *U.S. v. Jackson*, in which the Supreme Court heard arguments regarding a provision of the federal kidnapping statute requiring that the death penalty be imposed only upon recommendation of a jury. The court held that this practice was unconstitutional because it encouraged defendants to waive their right to a jury trial to ensure they would not receive a death sentence.

The second important case in 1968 was *Witherspoon v. Illinois*. The Supreme Court held that a potential juror's mere reservations about the death penalty were insufficient grounds to prevent that person from serving on the jury in a death penalty case. Jurors could be disqualified only if prosecutors could show that the jurors' attitude toward capital punishment would prevent them from making an impartial decision about punishment.[13]

The issue of the arbitrariness of the death penalty was brought before the Supreme Court in 1972 in the landmark case of *Furman v. Georgia*. Furman was burglarizing a private home when a family member found him. He attempted to flee and in doing so tripped and fell. The gun that he was carrying went off and killed a resident of the home. Furman was convicted of murder and sentenced to death.

Furman, bringing an Eighth Amendment challenge, argued that capital cases resulted in arbitrary and capricious sentencing. In a 5–4 vote the court held that Georgia's death penalty statute, which gave the jury complete sentencing discretion without any guidance as to how to exercise that discretion, could result in arbitrary sentencing. The court held that this approach to punishment under the statute was therefore cruel and unusual and violated the Eighth Amendment. Thus, on June 29, 1972, the Supreme Court effectively voided forty death penalty statutes around the nation, thereby commuting the sentences of 629 death row inmates and suspending the death penalty because existing statutes were no longer valid.[14]

With the *Furman* case the Supreme Court made it possible for states to rewrite their death penalty statutes to eliminate the problems cited in this important capital punishment challenge. Advocates of capital punishment began proposing new statutes that they believed would end arbitrariness in capital sentencing. Florida took the lead, rewriting its death penalty statute only five months after *Furman* was decided. Shortly thereafter, thirty-four other states enacted new death penalty statutes.

After a ten-year moratorium on executions because of Supreme Court decisions, the State of Utah revived the practice by killing

Gary Gilmore, who had been convicted of murders in the cities of Orem and Provo, by firing squad on January 19, 1977. In 1994 President Bill Clinton signed the Violent Crime Control and Law Enforcement Act, which expanded the federal death penalty to about sixty crimes, some of which do not involve murder. Currently thirty-one states, the federal government, and the U.S. military have the death penalty.

I am pleased to live and work in a state that does not have a death penalty. I do not consider myself to be soft on crime; my opposition to the death penalty is rooted in other reasons.

Volumes have been written both for and against capital punishment. It is likely that the debate will never be settled. It is best to accept that large numbers of thoughtful, reasonable, and principled people will disagree on the issue (along with many people whose views are not thoughtful, reasonable, or principled).

Clearly human beings have struggled with this issue for a long, long time; my struggle is not particularly unusual. I have tried to read a wide range of classic and contemporary commentaries. The Bible makes a number of well-known references to punishment by death, and many proponents cite these passages to advance their argument in favor of the death penalty. Prominent examples include:

> He that smiteth a man, so that he die, shall be surely put to death. And if a man lie not in wait, but God deliver him into his hand; then I will appoint thee a place whither he shall flee. But if a man come upon his neighbor to slay him with guile; thou shalt take him with guile; thou shalt take him from mine alter, that he may die. And he that smiteth his father, or his mother, shall be surely put to death. And he that stealeth a man, and selleth him, or if he be found in his hand, he shall surely be put to death. And he that curseth his father, or his mother, shall surely be put to death. . . .
>
> And if any mischief follow, then shalt give life for life, foot for foot, burning for burning, wound for wound, stripe for stripe. . . .
>
> If an ox gore a man or woman . . . if the ox were wont to push with his horn in time past, and if it hath been testified to his owner, and he hath not kept him in, but that he hath killed a man or a woman; the ox shall be stoned, and his owner shall be put to death.[15]

Thou shalt not suffer a witch to live. Whosoever lieth with a beast shall surely be put to death. He that sacrificeth unto any god, save unto the Lord only, he shall be utterly destroyed.[16]

And to the children of Israel, you shall say: Any man of the children of Israel or of the strangers who sojourn among Israel, who gives any of his offspring to Molech, shall surely be put to death; the people of the land shall pelt him with stones. . . .

And a man who commits adultery with [another] man's wife, committing adultery with the wife of his fellow the adulterer and the adulteress shall surely be put to death. And a man who lies with his father's wife has uncovered his father's nakedness: both of them shall surely be put to death; their blood is upon themselves. And a man who lies with his daughter in law both of them shall surely be put to death; they have committed a depravity; their blood is upon themselves. And a man who lies with a male as one would with a woman both of them have committed an abomination; they shall surely be put to death; their blood is upon themselves. And a man who takes a woman and her mother it is evil counsel. They shall burn him and them in fire, and there shall be no evil counsel in your midst. And a man who lies with an animal, shall surely be put to death, and you shall kill the animal. And a woman who comes close to any animal so that it will mate with her you shall kill the woman and the animal; they shall surely be put to death; their blood is upon themselves. . . .

A man also or a woman that hath a familiar spirit, or that is a wizard, shall surely be put to death: they shall stone them with stones: their blood shall be upon them.[17]

The Code of Hammurabi also mandates capital punishment for a wide range of offenses, including theft of temple property (no. 6), kidnapping (no. 14), abetting the escape of a slave (no. 15), robbery (no. 22), hiring a substitute for military service (no. 33), adultery (no. 129), harboring outlaws (no. 199), and mother-son incest (no. 157). Islamic law requires stoning to death as a penalty for adultery.

Plato also supported the death penalty in *Laws*: "But suppose the law-giver finds a man who's beyond cure—what legal penalty will he provide for this case? He will recognize that the best thing for all such people is to cease to live—best even for themselves. By passing on they will help others, too: first, they will continue a warning against injustice, and secondly they will leave the state free of scoundrels."

As one would expect, contemporary death penalty proponents typically cite the appropriateness of a retributive response to heinous crime. Offenders who commit these crimes, proponents argue, deserve the ultimate penalty, and the public has a right to impose the ultimate penalty as a reflection of its collective rage and vengeance. But death penalty opponents typically advance several key counterarguments:

- Execution is fundamentally inhumane.
- Capital punishment undermines the sacredness of life. All human life—even that of a person who commits heinous crimes—has intrinsic value; it is immoral to kill another individual under any circumstances.
- Mercy is ethically superior to revenge or vengeance.
- The death penalty does not alleviate the fear of violent crime.
- The death penalty does not protect society more effectively than other alternatives, such as life imprisonment without parole.
- The death penalty does not restore the social order breached by offenders.
- Society's response to a crime should not necessarily be proportionate to the harm caused by the criminal (an eye for an eye, a life for a life).
- The death penalty does not effectively deter serious crime.
- The death penalty is not imposed with fairness and discriminates against the poor and ethnic and racial minorities.
- The death penalty is not imposed in such a way as to prevent the execution of innocent death-row inmates.

Most arguments against the death penalty are philosophical and theological. These are the enduring, gut-wrenching, passionate, and ultimately unresolved debates about the relative morality and immorality of capital punishment. These issues do not lend themselves to any sort of reasonable empirical test.

In contrast we can explore empirically the arguments of critics that focus on the deterrent value of capital punishment, discriminatory application of the death penalty, and the potential execution of innocent people who have been sentenced to death—and the available data are troubling.

Over the years a number of scholars have conducted diverse studies of the deterrence value of capital punishment. Most studies include comparisons of homicide rates in death-penalty and non-death-penalty states that are considered similar with respect to other key attributes, such as geographic region, unemployment rates, per capita income, and ethnic and racial composition.

The famed criminologist Thorsten Sellin conducted the most significant early studies of the deterrent value of the death penalty. In the 1950s Sellin examined homicide rates from groups of matched death-penalty and non-death-penalty states. His results were compelling in that they demonstrated the inconsistent correlation between the death penalty and homicide rates. Ohio, a death-penalty state, had the highest homicide rate; Michigan, a non-death-penalty state, and Indiana, a death-penalty state, had identical homicide rates. Iowa, a death-penalty state, had the lowest homicide rate, but it was nearly the same as the rate for Wisconsin, a non-death-penalty state. In another comparison North Dakota, a non-death-penalty state, had a lower homicide rate than South Dakota and Nebraska, both death-penalty states. Finally, Maine, a non-death-penalty state, had a slightly higher homicide rate than two death-penalty states in New England, New Hampshire and Vermont, but the homicide rate in Rhode Island, a non-death-penalty state, was considerably lower than Connecticut's, which was a death-penalty state.[18]

Since Sellin's groundbreaking study, various other scholars have examined homicide rates in death-penalty and non-death-penalty states, using diverse methodological approaches to control for extraneous differences between these states. Viewed as a group, these studies find that Sellin's original conclusion holds up: capital punishment does not seem to have a general deterrent effect on homicide.[19]

This does not surprise me. During parole board hearings I often asked inmates who had killed their victim some variation of the following questions: At the time you committed the crime that led to this sentence, did it occur to you that you might get caught, arrested, convicted, and sent to prison? Did that lead you to hesitate when you considered committing this crime? Rarely did I hear inmates respond with a clear, unequivocal yes. Nearly always I heard responses that resemble these:

> I was so high at the time I murdered her, I wasn't thinking at all about getting caught. The whole thing happened in a split second.
>
> DARWIN, CONVICTED OF MURDERING THE
> MOTHER OF HIS THREE CHILDREN

> I was having a great time at my cousin's party. I have no idea how much I had to drink that night, but I know it was a lot. I never should have gotten in my car and driven anywhere. I just wasn't thinking clearly.
>
> LANCE, WHOSE BLOOD ALCOHOL CONTENT WAS .17 WHEN HE WAS
> ARRESTED AFTER KILLING THREE PEOPLE IN A CAR CRASH

> My boyfriend and I were so dope sick that night, we would have done anything to get some money—we needed more heroin bad. I feel bad about breaking into Mrs. Thomas's house and shooting her. But I wasn't in my right mind; I barely remember what happened.
>
> BRANDY, CONVICTED OF BREAKING AND ENTERING
> AND ASSAULTING AN ELDERLY WOMAN

> Me and my boys were running wild that night, you know what I'm sayin'? The day before one of the Holland Street Gang guys shot up my brother's place. We just felt like we had to retaliate. We wasn't thinkin' at all about what might happen.
>
> JOSEPH, A GANG MEMBER CONVICTED OF
> MURDERING A RIVAL GANG MEMBER

Yes, there are inmates who knew exactly what they were doing when they decided to commit their crimes. They understood the risks and potential consequences. But in my experience a staggering percentage of inmates commit their crimes on impulse, under the influence of drugs or alcohol, or in a fit of rage or desperation. Most of the offenders I met did not conduct a carefully considered precrime calculus or anything resembling a cost-benefit analysis.

With regard to the death penalty in particular, the added daunt-ing problem is that throughout history it has been applied inconsis-tently, arbitrarily, and discriminatorily—not in every case, of course, but often enough that any staunch proponent of capital punishment should pause and reflect.

One famous study, conducted by William Bowers and Glenn Pierce, assessed the probability of a defendant's receiving a death sentence in Florida, Georgia, Texas, and Ohio. The researchers found that black offenders who murdered white victims in Florida were thirty-seven times more likely to receive a death sentence than blacks who killed other blacks; in Georgia black offenders who murdered white victims were thirty-three times more likely, in Texas eighty-seven times more likely, and in Ohio fifteen times more likely to be sentenced to death than blacks who killed blacks.

In another compelling study, this one by Michael Radelet and colleagues, researchers examined homicide cases in twenty Florida counties and found that killers of whites were significantly more likely to be sentenced to death than were killers of blacks. And in a study of eight states conducted by Samuel Gross and Robert Mauro, researchers found that for all homicides both the race of the victim and the combination of the victim's and offender's race had an ef-fect on the likelihood that a defendant would be sentenced to death. In Georgia killers of whites were nearly ten times more likely to be sentenced to death than were killers of blacks, in Florida they were almost eight times more likely, and in Illinois six times more likely. Black offenders were significantly more likely to be sentenced to death if they killed a white rather than a black victim. And these are the results of a mere cross-section of such studies of the impact of race on death penalty sentences. There are more.[20]

Complicating matters is the mounting and distressing evidence of wrongful convictions that lead to the death penalty, cases in which innocent people have been sentenced to death. Consider the work of the Innocence Project, a national litigation organization founded at the Benjamin N. Cardozo School of Law, Yeshiva University, and dedi-cated to exonerating wrongfully convicted individuals through DNA testing and reforming the criminal justice system. Every year more than three thousand people write to the Innocence Project for the first time asking for help, and at any given time the project's staffers are evaluating six thousand to eight thousand potential cases. The Innocence Project estimates that between 2.3 percent and 5 percent of all prisoners in the United States are innocent, and some have been sentenced to death. Since 1989 more than three hundred people in thirty-seven states have been exonerated through the project's post-conviction DNA testing. More than 70 percent are people of color (African American, Latino, or Asian).

If that's not convincing enough, consider the work of the Center on Wrongful Convictions, part of the Bluhm Legal Clinic at the Northwestern University School of Law. The center receives nearly two hundred inquiries a month seeking staffers' assistance. Along with the University of Michigan Law School, staffers created the National Registry of Exonerations, which provides detailed information about every known exoneration since 1989, now totaling more than sixteen hundred cases. And with special regard to capital punishment, the Death Penalty Information Center reports that since 1973 more than 150 people have been released from death row based on evidence of their innocence.[21]

Those are sobering figures, and they are among the reasons I oppose the death penalty. But capital punishment opponents must still grapple with an overarching moral question. In theory we could establish a criminal justice system that imposes the death penalty consistently and without arbitrariness or any hint of discrimination. In theory we could establish safeguards that prevent the execution of innocent people. Then what? If we subtract from the equation the basis for any and all objections related to unfair, inconsistent, arbitrary, and discriminatory administration of capital punishment, can we still mount reasonable and persuasive objections to the death penalty?

I think so. I can accept that thoughtful people are going to disagree on the issue. Some will favor capital punishment because it offers society the purest, most basic, and unfiltered way to express its understandable rage and honor its legitimate retributive instincts in response to the worst of crimes. We can debate this issue forever without consensus. In fact, I do not believe retribution is inherently immoral; I think society has a legitimate right to express its outrage in response to many crimes and that principled forms of retribution have a place in the criminal justice system. In select parole board cases I was more than willing to convey my heartfelt anger to inmates who committed unconscionable, despicable, and cruel acts that caused incomprehensible harm. But I do not believe that my wish, our wish, for retribution ought to be satisfied by capital punishment.

There is one more key point. Apart from my belief that capital punishment is hard to defend on moral grounds, I have often argued that execution provides some inmates who commit heinous crimes with an easy way out. I have encountered some prisoners who find the prospect of lifelong imprisonment so odious—the daily grind and torment of prison life, ever-present tension and potential for conflict, annoying politics of inmate-prison staff relationships, occasional brutality, monotony, confinement in a tiny cell twenty-three hours a day while in segregation, deprivation of life's common creature comforts—that lethal injection, the electric chair, and the firing squad begin to look like appealing alternatives. For some—not all—people who commit heinous cries, my retributive wish is for them to suffer in prison minute by minute, hour by hour, day by day, night by night, week by week, month by month, year by year, and decade by decade. I want them to get up in the morning dreading what awaits them—the relentless repetition, frustrations, disappointments, the aches and pains of imprisonment. I want them to lie in their narrow, hard bunks at night replaying their bad choices, reflecting on the misery they have inflicted on others, and wrestling with their agony. I want them to endure the slow, slow drip of lifelong imprisonment. That is what I want for people such as Farid Fata.

Farid Fata was a physician and oncologist who was sentenced to prison for violating more than 550 patients' trust and raking in more than $17 million from fraudulent billings. In court Fata admitted to pumping poisonous chemotherapy drugs into patients for years, telling them they had cancer when they didn't. He overtreated terminal cancer patients rather than letting them die peacefully. He also undertreated actual cancer patients in order to profit from their misery.

Fata wept uncontrollably in court as he apologized for his actions, admitted to fraudulently billing Medicare, insurance companies, and hundreds of patients through misdiagnoses, overtreatment, and undertreatment. In some cases Fata gave patients nearly four times the recommended dosage of aggressive cancer drugs; in at least one instance a patient was given toxic chemotherapy for five years when the standard treatment was six months.

Fata lied to patients about their cancer prognoses by claiming they required chemotherapy when they simply needed observation; he convinced others that they needed infusion treatment by telling them that they had to receive "maintenance chemotherapy" to stave off cancers already in remission. Prosecutors called Fata the "most egregious fraudster in the history of this country." Fata was convicted and sentenced to forty-five years in federal prison, where there is no possibility of parole. His release date is October 19, 2052. Fata will be about eighty-eight years old.[22]

Some inmates—a small percentage, in my experience—are so cruel and vicious that life imprisonment without the possibility of parole *is* retributive justice. In some cases execution is the undeserved, easy alternative, the path of least resistance, which should not be an option.

||||||||||||||||||||||||||||||||||||||||||||||||||||||||||

I started the day at Rhode Island's High Security prison, which houses the most dangerous, difficult-to-manage inmates and those who must be in protective custody because of their notoriety or because they have enemies housed in the state's other prisons. As I strolled up the main walkway, I glanced at the narrow windows in the cells that face the parking lot. The windows are 5.5 inches wide. Remarkably in 1986 an inmate serving a twenty-five-year sentence for second-degree murder squeezed through his cell window and escaped. According to prison reports, the five-foot-seven, 120-pound inmate shattered the window in his cell by using a heavy metal bar from the back of a chair. After squeezing through the window—a rather astonishing feat—the inmate climbed over a barbed-wire fence and made his getaway. Local police caught the escapee about two hours later in a neighborhood about one mile from the prison. He was returned to the very same building, although this time to a cell without a view.

After completing the usual security protocol at the control center, the correctional officer released an electronic lock, and I walked into a small vestibule that smelled of fresh paint. The officer then released a second door at the back of the vestibule, and I walked into a corridor adjacent to the prison's visiting area. It looks like a scene from a movie; because this high security prison limits physical contact between inmates and visitors, a row of small booths with telephones and seats is set on each side of security glass.

The officer in the control center released yet another electronic door, and I stood outside the parole board's hearing room. While I waited for another officer to open the room, I noticed an inmate mopping the adjacent hallway floor. I recognized him immediately. About four years earlier I had met this inmate at a professional meeting at a prominent mental health agency. At the time he was a senior administrator responsible for programs for adolescents with major mental illness. The meeting had been called to develop a formal application for federal funds to provide innovative services to this vulnerable population.

When I saw this inmate wearing his blue prison uniform and pushing the mop, I had a flashback to our earlier meeting and the shock I felt when, several months later, I learned that he had been arrested in a cheap motel for cocaine possession and engaging in a sexual relationship with a minor who was in state-sponsored foster care. I remember feeling horrified, especially because this man had been a professional colleague, although we had not worked together.

Seeing him in prison brought it all back; I felt a deep pang in my heart. I learned that he was in protective custody because he testified against a codefendant in his case who orchestrated a number of large narcotics transactions.

We acknowledged each other in the prison's hallway and exchanged cursory pleasantries. I asked him how he was doing, and he muttered, "Okay. I guess." I decided to let it go at that and simply wished him well, knowing that before long he would appear before the parole board for his hearing.

My colleagues and I settled into the hearing room, set up our laptops, reviewed the day's hearing calendar, and waited for our administrative staffer to usher in the first inmate. I will never forget this hearing. Bernard Ayala was serving a twelve-year sentence for conspiracy to distribute narcotics. At the time of his arrest Ayala was a police officer—a cop who was leading a double life. When he was on duty, Ayala was an undercover officer who infiltrated the local drug scene. When he was off duty, Ayala crossed the line and became a dirty cop.

During my career I have been invited many times to train police academy cadets and seasoned members of several police departments. Typically I am asked to lecture about the challenges faced by police officers that, when not handled well, can lead to serious impairment and unethical conduct. I show them video clips of cases from throughout the United States of former police officers who crossed the line, destroyed their careers, and were sent to prison. I tell them that from 1992 to 2008 nearly two thousand New York City Police Department officers were arrested, an average of 119 a year, according to annual reports prepared by the department's Internal Affairs Bureau. Most of those investigations involved drugs, theft, or crimes like fraud, bribery, or sex offenses, committed both on and off the job. I tell them about the former Memphis, Tennessee, police officer who was sentenced to prison after being convicted of stealing cash from drivers he pulled over and searched. I tell them about the former Columbia, Missouri, officer who was convicted of first-degree murder in the death of his gay lover who talked about revealing their relationship to the police chief. I tell them about the former Woodbridge, New Jersey, police officer who was convicted of sexually assaulting a teenage boy during a three-year period. I tell them about the twenty-two-year veteran of the Conroe, Texas, police department who was convicted of bank robbery. I tell them about the former Chickasaw, Alabama, police officer who committed suicide after being convicted of sexually assaulting his ten-year-old stepdaughter.[23] I watch the cadets' and officers' eyes widen and jaws drop as I move through the litany of cases, a mere subsample.

And then I move to a collection of local cases.[24] The room is always very, very quiet.

Bernard Ayala is a case study par excellence. As a former police officer, Ayala could not serve his sentence in the prison's general population; it was simply too risky, given the number of inmates he either arrested or knew from his undercover work on the street. He was housed in the High Security prison for his own protection.

Ayala walked into the hearing room and sat down. He did not smile; he looked tense, uncomfortable, and laser-focused on the proceedings. This was his first parole board hearing.

QUESTION: Obviously yours is a very complicated and unusual case. Please tell us what happened.

ANSWER: It's hard to know where to begin. I'm ashamed to be sitting here. I used to be your professional colleague. Now I'm an inmate. I've ruined my life, and it's my own fault. I was a good cop, but I sure messed things up. You know, when you're in the academy you hear stories about cops who become dirty. Like everyone else, I never thought it could happen to me. But it did.

For the first twelve years or so I did everything by the book. I got great evaluations. I was a team player. I did my job and I did it well. I got promoted. I was proud to be a cop.

Things changed about six years ago. My marriage started to fall apart. My ex-wife and I knew each other in middle school and high school. We were twenty when we got married. We had two kids while we were in our early twenties. We thought we were so grown up. Of course, we weren't and were in over our heads.

At the time I was working two jobs—managing a convenience store and learning the insurance business from my uncle—and we were barely making ends meet. I started taking courses part time at the community college and gradually finished my BA in criminal justice. I applied to the police academy and was accepted, but I sat on the waiting list for nearly six months. Finally they formed a new class and I started.

I loved everything about the academy. It was a dream come true.

About a year after I was on the force, my wife and I started having trouble. We argued a lot, and she hated it when I went out with some of my buddies from the department. I guess you could say we started growing apart.

Well, things really headed downhill when I got involved with a woman and cheated on my wife. We met when I was in uniform and investigated a break-in at her home. We really hit it off, and I made up excuses to have to interview her for more information about the break-in. Before I knew it, we were involved.

I now realize it was about then that I also began to turn into an alcoholic. When things got real bad with my wife, I would go out and drink. I never thought I'd become an alcoholic, but that's what's happened.

Things took an even worse turn about nine months after I started working undercover. One of the challenges of being undercover is not getting sucked into the criminal element. I had to be real friendly with these guys who were dealing drugs, but I couldn't be their friend.

What happened is that I got into real bad financial shape. I had a couple of apartment rental properties that were vacant for a while, and I had serious cash-flow problems. I fell behind on our mortgage payments and thought the bank might foreclose on our house. I kept all this from my wife.

I needed money bad, and I knew I could borrow some from one of the big drug dealers I was hanging with as an undercover. I can't believe I actually did it, but I did. I borrowed $10,000 and then had trouble paying him back. What happened is that we worked out a deal; I never told him I was a cop, but I did tell him I had real good connections with a dirty cop and could help him set up one of his rival drug dealers to get arrested. Long story short, I gave this guy confidential information I had; it worked out good for him and I got out of my debt.

The problem was that he ended up getting arrested, and he gave the detectives information about me in order to save his own neck. Little did he know he was turning in a dirty undercover cop: me. And that's how I got here.

Every single day, every single night, I beat myself up over this. I am disgraced, humiliated, and ashamed. I've lost my marriage and my house, and my kids are suffering big time. I deserve to be in prison. Don't get me wrong—I want parole. But I get why I'm here.

It was painful for me to listen to Ayala's anguished and tortured description of his horrific, self-destructive trajectory. This was a text-book example of how an otherwise accomplished individual's life can spiral out of control. I was staring at a unique kind of tragedy. But, no matter how bad I felt for Ayala, I had to exercise my judgment about whether it was time for him to be released from prison. Did I think he posed an ongoing risk to the general public and was likely to recidivate? No. Did I think Ayala had genuine insight into his crime and the circumstances that led up to it? Yes. And then I asked myself the hardest question: Did I think he had been punished enough and should be granted parole after serving only one-third of his fifteen-year sentence? No. In good conscience I could not vote to parole Ayala. Justice required that he serve more time, especially because of his former status as a police officer who was sworn to uphold the law. My colleagues agreed. We denied parole and scheduled Ayala for another hearing in two years.

With the exception of inmates who are truly psychopathic or sociopathic—those who experience no guilt in conjunction with their crimes and seem unable or unwilling to empathize with their victims—the most common denominator I have noticed among inmates like Ayala is a deep sense of shame. It is as true for the car thief with a ninth-grade education and learning disability as it is for the former lawyer or state legislator who accepted a bribe. In such cases I often reflected on Charles Dickens's words in *Great Expectations*: "Heaven knows we need never be ashamed of our tears, for they are rain upon the blinding dust of earth, overlying our hard hearts. I was better after I had cried, than before—more sorry, more aware of my own ingratitude, more gentle."

||||||||||||||||||||||||||||||||||||||||||||||||||||||||||||

Shame is a complicated concept, mostly commonly understood as a feeling of guilt, regret, or sadness we get when we have done something wrong. Most, but certainly not all, of the many thousands of inmates I have met feel a deep sense of shame. They know they have messed up, and they really do feel some combination of guilt, regret, and sadness. It's truly the rare inmates who are so arrogant, narcissistic, and sociopathic that they do not experience shame.

Over time I have come to think that the shame that most inmates feel can be a constructive force in their lives, if they will let it. For other inmates shame can be so disabling that it is hard for them to move past it and grapple in a positive way with the demons in their lives. I encountered some inmates who were so wrought with shame that they shut down and, to use more formal language, became clinically depressed. That degree of depression can be paralyzing for any human being, inmate or not.

But for many inmates shame is the impetus for genuine personal growth, the catapult that helps them turn their lives around. It doesn't happen often enough, but it does happen, far more than most people know. In fact, I know many offenders who were released from prison and have done well. Many used large portions of their prison time to talk to mental health professionals, participate in rehabilitation groups, and search their souls. Newspapers and Internet newsfeeds rarely report these good stories.

IIIIIIIIIIIIIIIIIIIIIIIIIIIIIIIIIIIIIIIIIIIIIIIIIIIIIIIIIIIIII

I have been particularly struck by the shame experienced by the relatively small number of inmates who once led prominent professional lives. Before his conviction Kevin Singleton was a well-respected priest in a local parish. Over time, however, church officials became concerned about accounting irregularities and rumors about the priest's inappropriate relationship with a male teen. After a thorough investigation and criminal charges, Singleton entered a guilty plea to embezzling more than $120,000 from church coffers. Evidence showed that he used some of the money to travel to tropical resorts with teenage boys. During the parole hearing Singleton cried as he told us about his "descent into an emotional hell." Singleton described his "crisis of faith" and his "moral lapses" that led to his crimes.

Several weeks later the board conducted a hearing for a former high school English teacher who was arrested after rumors circulated that he was producing pornographic films featuring male teens. At the hearing the former teacher shared with the board gory details about how he was sexually abused as an adolescent and had spent a lifetime trying to cope with that trauma.

> I know what I did was wrong, and I'm ashamed of myself. I was in a
> position of trust and a role model for my school's students. I let my

own issues get ahold of me and I lost all perspective. It's almost like I was a passenger on a runaway train that was going so fast I had no idea how to get off. I'm not trying to make an excuse; that's just the way it seemed.

I've been in the sex offender treatment program for almost three years now. You can see from the counselor's report that I've made great progress. For the first time in my life, I've talked about my own victimization. This is the first time I've asked for help, after a lifetime of keeping to myself and leading a secret life. I feel like a burden has been lifted. I know it may sound strange, but I needed to come to prison to tackle these issues.

I encountered comparable candor from a former psychiatric nurse, Ron Dauer, who had been sentenced to thirty years in prison following his conviction on a second-degree murder charge. The shooting occurred in the parking lot of a popular sandwich shop located on a heavily traveled road. Dauer had gone to the shop intending to meet with Lance Harlow, an acquaintance who was employed as a clerk. The two argued about a small debt that Harlow owed Dauer. Harlow pushed Dauer out of the store and told him to "stay away. You're not welcome here."

According to police and court reports, Dauer drove away and met another acquaintance, Larry May. Dauer and May drove back to the shop and confronted Harlow. Dauer grabbed a gun from his car, fired a shot through the store window, and killed Harlow.

At trial Dauer and his attorney argued that he should be found not guilty because of his "diminished capacity" at the time he shot Harlow. Dauer, his attorney, and expert witnesses presented evidence in an attempt to show that for many years Dauer had struggled with bipolar disorder and that at the time of the shooting Dauer was not taking his psychotropic medication and was in the midst of a manic episode. Expert witnesses for the prosecution testified that Dauer was not so impaired at the time of the shooting that he was not in control of his actions. Dauer was found guilty and sentenced.

At the parole board hearing Dauer was remarkably coherent and articulate. He fully admitted that he had stopped engaging in treatment for his bipolar disorder several months before the shooting.

Dauer was properly medicated at the time of the parole board hearing and spoke insightfully about a pattern that I know is all too common among people who suffer from this serious illness: Some people feel so much better following a period of stable treatment and psychotropic medication that they conclude they no longer need the medication. Once they are off the medication, their symptoms tend to reemerge, and too often their behavior spins out of control, often in the extreme. That was what appeared to have happened to Dauer. Properly treated, he understood the toxic pattern and dynamic. But in the throes of unmedicated bipolar disorder, Dauer's judgment was severely impaired, to the point that he shot and killed a man during a dispute. How tragic and ironic that a once-prominent professional, with training in psychiatric disorders, fell victim to his own psychiatric illness and as a result killed a man.

Not all formerly prominent inmates are so insightful and forthcoming. Later that same year the board conducted a hearing for a disbarred lawyer who had been convicted of bank fraud. The records indicated that the lawyer had colluded with a real estate agent and filed a series of bogus documents that inflated the assessed value of properties the attorney bought. Investigators said the former lawyer purchased rundown properties and then quickly resold them for as much as eight times their actual value. He had colluded with unscrupulous appraisers and falsified documents to show higher property values and better conditions, and he used them to obtain mortgages worth far more than the properties. Many of the mortgages were resold to wholesale capital management and real estate financing companies. At times the buyers' minor children were named as building contractors so that money could be funneled back to buyers. Several properties obtained as a result of this mortgage fraud scheme went into foreclosure, resulting in significant losses to the lenders.

At the parole board hearing the disbarred attorney was not forthcoming about his crime.

QUESTION: Walk us through this, please. How exactly did you get involved in this elaborate scheme?

ANSWER: It's complicated. I'm not sure I can explain it.

QUESTION: Were you in deep financial trouble? Were you living an extravagant lifestyle? Help me out here. Help me understand what happened.
ANSWER: I guess I got greedy. One thing led to another.

I expected that the disbarred lawyer would acknowledge his sophisticated financial scheme, explain how it unfolded, act remorseful, and share his insights about what had led him to use such poor judgment. I expected that the inmate would share details about turmoil in his personal life—perhaps marital discord or desperate financial circumstances—that led him to do what he did. That did not happen. Instead the inmate simply asked the board to parole him to the federal sentence he faced as a result of other charges connected with this case. No insight. No remorse. I was stunned. This inmate deserved to be punished.

What I found in most cases involving inmates who had once led prominent lives is that they were severely impaired in one way or another. Yes, out-and-out greed accounts for some of their crimes, but more often than not I was staring at some kind of severe impairment that clouded the inmates' judgment or led to distressingly impulsive behavior.

Every profession has its relatively small share of severely impaired practitioners, an even smaller percentage of whom commit crimes. In some cases practitioners' crimes were a direct or indirect result of their psychiatric impairment, as in the case of Ron Dauer, the nurse who shot and killed an acquaintance. In other cases practitioners commit crimes as a result of their serious addiction to drugs, alcohol, gambling, or the Internet. In yet other cases practitioners commit crimes because they are severely burned out in their professional work and have lost their moral compass.

And during parole board hearings these inmates often said that they had little or no insight into the extent of their impairment at the time they committed their crimes. As one former physician expressed it at his parole board hearing, following his conviction for writing phony narcotics prescriptions to support his own drug addiction, "I wish I could have been on the outside of myself looking in at my own behavior. At the time I had no clue. I was so lost in the sea of my addiction that I abandoned all of my ordinary sensibilities. I see that now. Honestly I didn't see it then. None of my peers confronted me, even in a gentle way. I wish they had. Mind you, I'm not blaming them. It's my mistakes that put me here, no one else's. But maybe, just maybe, my colleagues could have held my feet to the fire. We need to do that for each other."

IIIIIIIIIIIIIIIIIIIIIIIIIIIIIIIIIIIIIIIIIIIIIIIIIIIIIIIIIIIIII

Inmates don't have a monopoly on shame. Some of their victims, too, are fraught with shame.

Gerilyn Roenicke, twenty-one, had her golden brown hair tucked into a tight bun. She wore a tailored pantsuit. Not all victims dress up for the occasion of a parole board hearing; many arrive in blue jeans, shorts, and T-shirts. Roenicke seemed to have gone out of her way to look professional.

We greeted her and quickly dove into the horrific details of her case. We knew from the records that Roenicke had been molested by her biological father when she was twelve to fourteen. Her father received an eighteen-year sentence and was now eligible for parole. I knew the basic facts, but Roenicke filled in a number of dreadful details.

This is hard for me to talk about, but I've decided I need to do this. My dad—and it's hard for me to call him that—controlled my life for so long. I am not going to let him do that to me anymore. Coming here is part of my therapy. I need to do this. I need to show him that he can't control me any longer.

It all started soon after my twelfth birthday. For years he gave me back rubs at night when he said goodnight and tucked me into bed. Well, one night my mom was out with a group of friends. My dad came into my room when I was getting into bed. I could smell alcohol on his breath. He leaned over and kissed me and told me how much he loved me. He put his hands down my pajama top and began to fondle me. I froze. I didn't know what to do. I let him touch me, and I did what he told me when he asked me to touch him. I felt like someone else was doing this, not me.

It's really hard for me to talk about what happened many times during the next couple of years. I was confused. I liked the attention my dad was paying to me; it seemed like this was the only time he cared about me.

I can't believe I went along with this for so long and kept this whole thing a secret. But my dad had convinced me that our relationship was real special and that he'd get into big trouble if anyone found out. I didn't want him to get into trouble.

By the time I was fourteen I knew I couldn't continue this. I was so upset. And I was really, really ashamed of myself.

One day at school I broke down during class with my favorite teacher, Mrs. Stewart. Right after class she pulled me aside and asked me what was wrong. I decided to tell her. I trusted Mrs. Stewart; she was so nice to me.

Anyway, Mrs. Stewart told me she had to tell the school principal. I understood that. The principal called DCYF [the state Department of Children, Youth, and Families], and I was moved out of the house that night; fortunately I was able to stay with my aunt Sally, my mom's sister. It was awful. I couldn't sleep, I couldn't eat; I just wanted to die.

I lived with my aunt Sally for about six months, but this ended up being hard because of all the tension in the family. My mom blamed me for what had happened.

That July I got a telephone call from Mrs. Stewart. She knew about everything and asked how I was doing. She then told me something I will never forget. She said she and her husband wanted to adopt me. I couldn't believe it. At first it felt weird, but then I jumped for joy. And that's what happened. Mrs. Stewart and her husband are the people who brought me here. To me, they are now my parents.

I cringed as I listened to Roenicke's testimony. As a parole board member I was filled with anger toward her father. As a father of two daughters, I was filled with profound sadness and deep admiration of this young woman's ability to bounce back. I asked her how she was doing at this point.

I'm actually doing okay. I'm sad about my family situation, but I have so much support from the Stewarts. They have saved my life. And I'm in counseling to help me deal with this. I love my therapist, Jenelle;

she's terrific. It's taken me a while, but I no longer blame myself for what happened.

I'm doing well in school and I'm involved in lots of activities. My favorite is competitive tap dancing. I'm about to head to the regional finals. I just love it.

I asked Roenicke to tell the board about her dance activities. When deeply traumatized victims mention something positive in their lives, I often asked them to share some of the details. I found that these upbeat interludes helped to lighten an otherwise dark, morose conversation about serious crime and victimization. It was wonderful to see victims smile when they talked about the bright spots in their lives.

Roenicke told the board about her rehearsal and competition schedules. She explained that she specializes in a cappella tap dancing—dancing without musical accompaniment. I asked her to tell us about her favorite routine. To my delight she asked whether we would like to see a sample, and for the next few minutes the Rhode Island Parole Board witnessed its first-ever tap dancing performance. Gerilyn Roenicke smiled broadly as she danced.

What a way to conclude an otherwise gloomy meeting, and the parole board gave her a standing ovation. Roenicke had a spring in her step, literally and figuratively. This was a young woman who knew how to bounce back from unspeakable adversity, and she inspired all of us on the board.

||||||||||||||||||||||||||||||||||||||||||||||||||||||||||

I marvel at the ability of some victims and inmates to recover from trauma. Many are crushed by their life circumstances and histories and have difficulty moving beyond them, but an inspiring number manage to rebound and even thrive, even those who have been weighed down by deep shame.

I often wonder what enables some human beings to cope so well in the face of such adversity. Can people learn these skills, or is there something more inherent and elusive?

I don't pretend to know the answer, but the closest I have come to a meaningful, sensible explanation derives from a compelling body of academic work by Salvatore Maddi. When he was a University of

Chicago faculty member, Maddi and his team of researchers were especially interested in studying people who functioned well despite high levels of stress. They hoped that if they could identify the characteristics of those who thrived under stress, they could develop ways to help others to develop those characteristics.

In 1975 Carl Horn, a vice president at Illinois Bell Telephone (IBT), arranged for Maddi and his team of researchers to study IBT employees. They followed 430 supervisors, managers, and executives each year using psychological questionnaires and assessment tools, interviews, performance observations, and medical examinations.

In 1981, following major changes in the telephone industry, including deregulation, IBT downsized from twenty-six thousand employees to just over half that many in one year. Company goals, strategies, job descriptions, and supervisory personnel changed frequently. Maddi and his team were able to continue testing the original study group annually until 1987.

What the researchers found was compelling. Roughly two-thirds of the employees showed significant performance, leadership, and health deficits in the face of the relentless stresses they experienced. Most employees experienced heart attacks, strokes, obesity, poor performance reviews, demotions, depression, anxiety states, burnout, substance abuse, interpersonal conflict, and divorce. However, about one-third of the employees maintained health, happiness, and performance and actually thrived during the upheavals. For them the changes provided new opportunities. Despite experiencing as much disruption as their peers, these hardy people gained promotions in the company, felt renewed enthusiasm, showed little illness, and often even improved their family relationships as a side effect of the upward trajectory in their lives.

What Maddi and his team discovered was that those who thrived embraced several key beliefs that helped them turn adversity to advantage. First, the hardy employees had a distinctly positive attitude and a sense of commitment that led them to strive to be involved in ongoing events rather than feel isolated. This group also had a sense of control that led them to struggle to overcome adversity and try to influence the outcome rather than lapse into passivity and powerlessness. In addition, the hardy group stepped up to the challenge in a way that led them to view stressful changes, whether positive or negative, as opportunities for new learning. This team's work also showed that it is possible to teach people ways to enhance their hardiness. Through training Maddi and his team helped IBT employees develop key attitudes and resources for turning change and adversity into opportunity.[25]

I have also met many victims and inmates who have what can best be described as grit, an indomitable spirit and ability to persevere in the face of daunting circumstances. Grit, according to the pioneering researcher Angela Duckworth, entails working strenuously toward challenges, maintaining effort and interest over years despite failure, adversity, and plateaus in progress.[26] Gerilyn Roenicke has grit. So do many other victims.

Some victims and inmates are truly hardy and courageous, and they have taught me a lot about some human beings' astonishing capacity to bounce back from the most dreadful circumstances life can produce. The very real possibility of hardiness, grit, and courage gives me hope. As C. S. Lewis wrote in *The Screwtape Letters,* "Courage is not simply one of the virtues, but the form of every virtue at the testing point."

5

REDEMPTION AND HOPE

"Hope" is the thing with feathers—
That perches in the soul—
And sings the tune without the words—
And never stops—at all—

—EMILY DICKINSON

I WAS DEVASTATED when Carl Blefary walked into the Medium Security prison's parole board hearing room. He looked at me and smiled tentatively and sheepishly. Blefary was appearing before us as an alleged parole violator. My job was to decide, along with my colleagues, whether to revoke Blefary's parole, require him to serve more time in prison, or release him for additional substance abuse treatment.

Almost exactly a year earlier Blefary had been out of prison and in the audience of a regional continuing education lecture I had delivered at a large addictions conference. During a break in that meeting, Blefary had told me excitedly about his new job working as a drug counselor in an outpatient program. We had met previously at three parole board hearings during Blefary's two earlier prison sentences.

When I talked with Blefary at the conference, I was delighted to hear about his progress, recovery, and new job. I remember thinking to myself, "This is the fruit of the labor; this is why I do this work."

My heart sank fast when I saw Blefary back in prison. This was yet another reminder of a time-honored adage in this line of work: Never get too comfortable. Never assume the battle is over. A colleague once told me, "You never know whether someone we release will reoffend, no matter how promising it looks, until their coffin is lowered into the ground."

My parole board votes were based in part on thorough risk assessments using the latest actuarial, state-of-the-art instruments, but forecasting human behavior, particularly among offenders, is far from an exact science. I like to think that the comprehensive reviews greatly increase the likelihood of a good outcome, but they certainly do not guarantee one.

Toward the beginning of his presentation to the board, Blefary addressed me directly:

> Dr. Reamer, I'm so embarrassed to be sitting in front of you again with this uniform on. I was doing so well. Remember when we saw each other last year at the conference where you spoke? I remember the happy look on your face when I told you how I was doing. You told me how proud you were.
>
> And now look at me. I'm just plain ashamed.

I did not hide my disappointment. I told Blefary I was so sad to see him back in prison. I told him how much potential he had and that I still believed in him. I then asked him to tell the board what had led him back to prison.

> Things was going real good. When I got out of prison last time, you guys sent me to Lincoln House for rehab. That's a good place, and I learned a lot. I have nothing bad to say about them. This is my fault, pure and simple.
>
> What happened is that I completed the program, and I was going to NA [Narcotics Anonymous] meetings, mostly at St. Aloysius Church over on Waltham Street. I was working the program like I was supposed to, reporting to parole, all of that. I also got counseling at the Ocean State Center and did random urines. I had a good job at a barber shop, using what I learned here last time in the barbering program. Really, things was good.
>
> I was doing so well that my counselor at Ocean State encouraged me to apply for a job in their new peer support program. At that point

I was clean and sober for a little more than two years. I went to classes to learn how to help other people who are just starting out in recovery. They even sent me for training at the Rhode Island Addictions Center. That's where I saw you, Dr. Reamer, when you gave one of the lectures.

Anyway, about a month ago my mother died. She took a heart attack real sudden. She was everything to me, the only person who stood by me no matter what. I took it hard; I was crying all the time, irritable, sleeping a ton. It was bad. Well, about a week after that my baby mama, she told me she couldn't handle my moods anymore, and she left with my kid. That's what pushed me over the edge. I couldn't bear the pain. I was overwhelmed. I felt like I lost everything, you know what I mean? I guess you could say I kinda gave up.

I called one of the guys I used to hang with when I was using, just for support, you know what I mean? Well, that was a mistake. I went over to his place, and he offered me a line of coke to help me take my mind off my troubles. I was weak. That's what did it.

Two days later my parole officer hit me with a random urine, and here I am. I can't believe it. I know how to stay clean. I know how to stay sober. And this last time I did it for the longest period ever.

I know people say that relapse is part of recovery. I never thought that would be me, you know what I mean? I know I have to do my time; I messed up. But I'm gonna show you. I'm gonna do this right when I get out.

As sometimes happens, Blefary's parole officer recognized that he had made great progress and had an unfortunate slip. The officer understood that slips, even full relapses, are indeed often part of the recovery process. This is not uncommon among inmates with chronic addiction histories (according to the best available national statistics, approximately 40 to 60 percent of people struggling with addiction will relapse following treatment, percentages that are similar to relapse rates following treatment for type 1 diabetes, asthma, and chronic high blood pressure). Blefary's parole officer recommended to us that Blefary complete a program at the prison designed specifically for this kind of inmate—someone who was doing well overall in the community but relapsed. This program requires parole violators to complete a relatively short program in the prison designed to help them assess what led to the relapse and discuss steps they can take, including skills and community resources they can use, to prevent a recurrence. Upon successful completion of this program, offenders are then released to the community, sometimes to a residential treatment program specializing in addictions and sometimes to an outpatient counseling program. The board may require these offenders to wear a GPS ankle bracelet for a period of time so their parole officer can monitor their whereabouts.

In Blefary's case we agreed to release him contingent upon his successful completion of the prison-based program. We voted unanimously to reparole Blefary to a ninety-day residential program that would provide him with more addictions-related counseling and allow him, after a short period in the program, to seek a part-time job as a landscaper with a former employer who was willing to take him back.

IIIIIIIIIIIIIIIIIIIIIIIIIIIIIIIIIIIIIIIIIIIIIIIIIIIIIIIIIIIIII

In one important respect, being a member of a parole board is somewhat akin to working as a hospital trauma nurse or emergency department physician. At the beginning of each shift you know you are likely to encounter a compelling mix of good and bad news. The emergency department sees inspiring, sometimes miraculous, lifesaving moments.

And then there's the other side: the patients who do not make it.

Serving on a state parole board has a similar, inevitable mix of celebratory and tragic moments. On any given day we were likely to hear inspiring news about the impressive successes of inmates and parolees interspersed with discouraging updates about other parolees' misdeeds, mistakes, and worse. At one extreme are the parolees who violate curfew, fail to report for a mandatory urine screen or counseling appointment, or go beyond the permissible geographic range of the GPS device affixed to their ankle. At the other extreme are the nightmare reports of offenders released from prison who, months or years later, commit rape, child molestation, armed robbery, or murder. Between these two extremes are released offenders who commit less serious crimes, such as shoplifting, marijuana possession, or fraudulent use of a credit card.

The reality is that, despite our best efforts, some offenders will commit new crimes at some point once they leave prison, just as some hospital emergency-department patients will die. The best parole boards can do is make the most informed choices possible about whom to release from prison and to surround these parolees with the deepest, widest supports available. Often what the parolee needs is simply not available in the community because of funding shortages or vocal opposition (for example, when neighborhood residents oppose having a group home nearby). We do what we can to tilt the odds in our favor, and then we hope for the best.

For decades skilled researchers have aggregated and examined data on the characteristics and percentages of offenders who commit new crimes following their release from prison. The numbers, which I will share in a moment, are sobering.

In casual conversation people sometimes ask me questions like, "How is it possible that criminals go to prison, get out, and commit a new crime? What's wrong with these people? Even a three-year-old has the capacity to learn that if he misbehaves and is punished, it's best to not misbehave again."

This is tempting thinking, of course, and I certainly don't blame people for scratching their heads in disbelief. But the odds are stacked against many offenders released from prison. I actually am surprised that so many criminals are able to stay out of trouble once they leave prison. The good news—which is not well known—is that many offenders, in Rhode Island and across the country, cope at least reasonably well once they leave prison, at least well enough to avoid committing new crimes and reincarceration.

I am a serious baseball fan. Years ago I played as a catcher, and like many other students of the game, I appreciate the powerful analogies baseball offers. Here is one of my favorites: Hitting a ninety-mile-an-hour fastball thrown by a top-tier pitcher in the major leagues is extraordinarily difficult. The best hitters in the world—a very small percentage—hit the ball successfully nearly one out of three times, for a career batting average of about .333. That rate of success is good enough to get into the baseball Hall of Fame. But think about what that means: the very best, most proficient, athletes in the sport fail two out of three times.

In some ways recidivism rates in criminal justice are similar. For most former inmates the odds are not good. A staggering percentage of offenders leave prison without having graduated from high school and with learning disabilities, a nonexistent or weak employment history, housing options only in high-risk neighborhoods, trauma histories, addiction and mental health challenges, and weak, un-even, or destructive social networks. The inmate who walks out the front gate with solid educational credentials, strong cognitive skills, a supportive and constructive family, stable mental health, no addic-tion, impressive work history, a solid job that pays well, and afford-able housing in a relatively safe neighborhood is as rare as no-winter-coat weather in Rhode Island in January. It happens, it's delightful, but it sure is unusual.

|||||||||||||||||||||||||||||||||||||||||||||||||||||||||||||||

We know a lot about recidivism—how often it occurs and under what circumstances. What amazes me is how consistent the data are from state to state across the United States and over time. The patterns are quite predictable.

- About two-thirds of released prisoners (including those released on parole and those who complete their sentences without parole) are arrested for a new crime within three years, and three-quarters are arrested within five years. The recidivism rates for offenders released on parole are much lower than for inmates who complete their sentences.
- Within five years of release about four-fifths of property offenders (criminals convicted of burglary, larceny, theft, motor vehicle theft, arson, shoplifting, and vandalism) are arrested for a new crime, com-pared to about three-fourths of drug offenders and slightly less than three-fourths of violent offenders.
- Slightly more than a third of all prisoners who are arrested within five years of release are arrested within the first six months after re-lease, with slightly more than half arrested by the end of the first year.

- About two in five released prisoners are either not arrested or are arrested once in the five years after their release.
- A sixth of released prisoners are responsible for almost half of total arrests that occur in the five-year follow-up period.
- A little more than 10 percent of released prisoners are arrested in a state other than the one that released them during the five-year follow-up period.
- Within five years of release more than four-fifths of inmates who were twenty-four or younger at release are arrested, compared to slightly more than three-fourths of inmates ages twenty-five to thirty-nine and about 70 percent of those aged forty or older.[1]

Of course, not all people who are arrested are guilty of having committed a crime, convicted, and sentenced to prison. Many people who are arrested have their charges dismissed or are found not guilty. Nonetheless, these arrest data are troubling.

Former inmates who commit new crimes or violate parole in other ways do so for widely varying reasons. By and large, even though they have harmed others, offenders are a vulnerable group with staggering challenges that impair their ability to make wise decisions. Many parole violations are the result of parolees' relapse on drugs or alcohol. Some parolees violate conditions of parole because they do not follow through with their community-based psychiatric treatment, fail to take their neuroleptic medication, and get into trouble as a result. Some parolees tire of parole supervision and, in fits of frustration and poor impulse control, cut off their GPS bracelets or fail to return to a residential program after a medical appointment in the community. Some parolees have such intense, complicated ties to their victims of domestic violence that the parolees violate a no-contact order issued by the court. Some parolees feel as if they are in such dire financial straits that they must resort to shoplifting or selling drugs to pay the month's rent or buy food. Some parolees violate parole because they were kicked out of a residential treatment program after bringing contraband into the facility (drugs or a weapon, for example), engaging in sex with another resident, or failing to comply with staffers' instructions. Some parolees violate parole when they decide to have "just one drink" at a party and then test positive when their parole counselor orders a urine screen the following day.[2] The list is nearly endless.

Each month the parole board conducts so-called violation hearings. These are scheduled when there is evidence that offenders who were released on parole have committed a new crime or otherwise violated parole rules. That is what happened to Carl Blefary. All board members are on a rotating on-call schedule during nonbusiness hours to respond to parole officers—sometimes in the middle of the night—who call requesting that we issue a warrant authorizing the detention of parolees who allegedly violated one or more conditions of parole, either by committing a new crime or by violating one of the many technical conditions of parole, such as keeping appointments with the parole officer, reporting to work, and abstaining from use of alcohol and drugs.

- Daphne Watt was released on parole after serving about half of her three-year sentence for shoplifting and fraudulent use of a credit card. At her parole hearing it was abundantly clear that Watt's crimes were associated with her long-standing heroin addiction. She had completed a long-term substance abuse treatment program while in prison. The parole board released Watt to a residential treatment program in the community. About six months after her release Watt was brought back to prison on a detention warrant; her parole officer informed the board that Watt had been noncompliant with several conditions of parole and had been arrested once again for shoplifting during a furlough from her treatment program. At the violation hearing Watt spoke at length about how she had stopped taking her medication for clinical depression—because, she said, the medication caused her to gain significant weight that brought on diabetes and debilitating knee pain. Watt said that when her depression had spiked, she used heroin to cope and then shoplifted to pay for the heroin.

- Edgar Fisher was released on parole after serving nearly fourteen months of his sentence for domestic assault. Fisher had an on-again, off-again relationship with the mother of his children. He was originally sentenced to prison for shoving his partner down the steps of their apartment building in the middle of a heated argument. According to the police report, Fisher was enraged that his partner had cheated on him. About two months after his release from prison, Fisher's parole officer requested a detention warrant after Fisher's victim contacted the officer and said that Fisher had sent her a series of vicious, threatening text messages.

- Julio Powell was paroled after serving two years of his three-year sentence for possessing child pornography that he had downloaded to his computer from the Internet. During his prison stay Powell had participated in the institution's sex offender treatment program and received positive recommendations from program staffers. Upon his release Powell registered as a sex offender, as required by law, and received counseling at a local mental health agency. Six months after his release from prison, the community-based sex-offender counselor contacted Powell's parole officer and informed her that Powell had missed the last three counseling sessions without permission. The parole officer reported that she was not able to locate Powell and asked for a detention warrant.

In fact, most parolees who appeared before the parole board for a violation hearing admitted to the violation and did not contest the key allegations. Some parolees quibbled with certain details—such as the time of day the violation occurred, the volume and nature of the drugs they ingested, or how many counseling appointments they missed—but admitted nonetheless that they violated some parole conditions. Most offered detailed explanations of the difficult circumstances they encountered that led to the violation, and most apologized to the board for letting us down.

Only a relative handful of parolees adamantly denied that they violated parole. They did their best to convince us that the urine screen results are completely false, the marijuana the police found in the car belonged to another passenger, they did not threaten their spouse, or they missed the residential program's curfew only because the bus they were on broke down.

Several years ago it occurred to me that criminal justice professionals, as well as the public at large, focus almost exclusively on the dark side of recidivism, the headline-generating cases in which former inmates commit new and, too often, heinous crimes. I fully understand how news of major crimes grabs people's attention. But what we fail to do is focus intensely on the successful cases, those formerly incarcerated offenders—most of whom have lengthy criminal records—who have managed to turn their lives around. Against all—or, at least—significant odds, these people have figured out how to find and keep a job, sustain a nonviolent relationship, pay the rent and utility bills without resorting to shoplifting or selling drugs, abstain from the use of alcohol and narcotics, and drive a car with a valid license and while sober.

Several years ago I suggested that the parole board organize a statewide conference to feature a cross-section of parolees who have done well for significant periods of postrelease time and have them share their insights about what worked. With minimal effort the event attracted a packed house that included prosecuting and criminal defense attorneys, police officers, judges, prison staffers, parole and probation officers, and mental health and addictions professionals. For several hours these wide-ranging practitioners sat riveted in their seats as they listened to offenders' uplifting tales and insights. It was unprecedented and an important reminder that we need to learn as much about what leads to success as what causes failure. This event provided a healthy antidote to the "nothing works" refrain that everyone hears much more often. Most offenders released by the Rhode Island Parole Board do not come back to prison, and that is worth celebrating.

So what have we learned about what works? Most current thinking about the effectiveness of correctional treatment is based on what is known as meta-analysis. This involves the comprehensive review and assessment of all empirical research on a given subject in an effort to get a sense of the big picture by comparing and contrasting diverse results.

Here is what we have learned based on a wide range of reputable studies, and these findings certainly are consistent with my own professional observations:

- Prison-based programs can be effective in reducing recidivism.
- Programs that help inmates manage their problematic thinking (cognitive distortions) and the impact of their thinking on their behavior

(a therapy known in the trade as cognitive-behavioral treatment) are much more effective than interventions based on principles of punishment. These programs are especially helpful when they are offered in community-based settings.

- Intensive prison-based addictions treatment—which a huge percentage of inmates need—can be quite effective, especially when its design is based on reputable research evidence and combined with follow-up community-based treatment.
- Education, vocational training, and prison labor programs increase positive behavior in prison but have modest effects on reducing recidivism after release from prison.
- High-risk offenders benefit from long and intense supervision and treatment. Providing intensive services to low-risk offenders can have diminishing returns and may increase the likelihood of recidivism when these offenders feel as if they are being treated in a way that is out of proportion to the offenses they committed.[3]

The Rhode Island Parole Board expected inmates to participate in rehabilitation programs that address issues relevant to offenders' lives and the crimes they committed. When I presided at a hearing for an inmate who was serving her fourth sentence and whose crime-filled adulthood had been shaped by her heroin addiction, I wanted her to complete the prison's intensive drug treatment program. When I presided at a hearing for an inmate who had gotten into mountains of trouble because of his involvement in gang activity that included robberies and home invasions, I wanted him to complete the prison's cognitive-behavior program, which focuses on so-called criminal thinking. When I presided at a hearing for an inmate who was serving a lengthy sentence because he had punched, kicked, and stabbed his girlfriend, I wanted him to complete the prison's domestic violence program.

When I began my career in corrections, administrators rarely conducted comprehensive and rigorous reviews of research to determine which rehabilitation models and programs are most effective. For decades U.S. prisons offered programs based on a much less formal, seat-of-the-pants, and leap-of-faith instinct about what "made sense." In many corrections departments today's administrators are much more deliberate and purposeful in their review of best practices research and implementation of evidence-based programs. This is no panacea, but this approach greatly enhances the likelihood of success. Of course, ever-present, and often worsening, budgetary constraints often limit what departments can offer. And, by extension, long waiting lists sometimes mean that inmates may not be able to complete a program that the parole board thinks is an essential element of the offender's reentry plan.

In Rhode Island, as in many other (not all) states, the state department of correction's current program lineup is impressive, although waiting lists can be frustratingly long because of limited funding. In the state's women's prisons inmates can access various programs that address substance abuse, mental health, vocational education, secondary education, parenting, victim impact, anger management, and behavior modification.

In the prison system's Intake Service Center, which houses men, inmates can enroll in the program to gain their high school equivalency diploma and in a substance abuse treatment program. Also, this is the facility that houses parole violators who relapsed on drugs or alcohol and who may be eligible to participate in a relatively short-term program designed to enhance their relapse-prevention skills and quickly return them to the community.

The Minimum Security prison in Rhode Island offers programs related to anger management, overdose prevention and substance abuse, domestic violence, education, and victim impact. The Medium Security facility offers programs related to men's unique trauma issues, substance abuse recovery, anger management, domestic violence, sex offenses, mental health counseling, dangerous driving, parenting, education, and ethical issues. The Maximum Security prison offers a similar range of programs, along with a youthful offender program designed for young inmates who have committed such serious crimes as armed robbery, sexual assault, and murder. The High Security prison offers a narrower range of programs; they include mental health counseling, education, anger management, victim impact, parenting, and criminal thinking.[4]

While the meta-analyses that document the effectiveness of many of these programs are valuable, it is also important to think about successes of offenders who have made great progress in prison and those who have been released from prison on parole and have done well. I have many stories to tell about these folks, tales that give me hope.

One of my favorites involves Felix Bertaina, who was serving a fifteen-year sentence for second-degree murder when I met him at his first parole hearing. His story is both terribly sad and inspiring—a combination that is not uncommon in the prison population. Bertaina was eighteen when he was arrested. His high school grades were solid, and he was a basketball superstar. No one in Bertaina's family had ever attended college. His high school social studies teacher recognized Bertaina's potential and went out of his way to mentor him. Because of his unique combination of academic and athletic prowess, Bertaina was wooed by a handful of top-tier colleges in NCAA Division I. His single mother and siblings were extraordinarily proud and planned to escort Bertaina to his first choice among the suitors, a major southern university.

In mid-August Bertaina and his mother went on a carefully planned shopping spree for dorm room essentials. They pored over maps and charted the route they would take to campus in Bertaina's mom's 1996 Honda Civic, which had more than 100,000 miles on it.

And then, in a single moment, it all fell apart. Three days before Bertaina and his mother were to head south, two of Bertaina's neighborhood friends threw him a going-away party. As teenagers the friends had joined a gang, and one had spent time in the state training school after his arrest on assault charges. But Bertaina had known these guys for years, ever since they played together as young children. The trio were loyal to each other.

Unbeknown to Bertaina, on the night of the party his two friends were in the middle of a feud with members of a rival gang. Two rival gang members showed up at the party uninvited and exchanged heated words with Bertaina's friends. One of the rivals pulled out a handgun. Bertaina grabbed the gun and told the uninvited guests to leave. When they refused, Bertaina impulsively fired what he later claimed was a warning shot. It ricocheted off the refrigerator and nicked one of the guests in her carotid artery; the victim died about half an hour later. Several months later Bertaina was convicted and sentenced to prison.

My first hearing with Bertaina was painful. Based on the detailed records I had reviewed, I was expecting Bertaina to be demoralized and shut down, particularly given the bitter disappointment he had experienced when his exciting college plans simply evaporated. I was pleasantly surprised. Bertaina was thoughtful, articulate, personable, and engaging. Some inmates are overly confident and filled with hubris; Bertaina was not. His quiet confidence seemed quite authentic and humble.

I was particularly struck by his maturity. He answered our questions about his crime in a straightforward, nondefensive way.

QUESTION: I suspect it's painful to think about the night of the crime, but I need to ask about that. What are your thoughts about how you handled things that night?

ANSWER: I've replayed that night in my head a thousand times. Sometimes it seems like a bad dream, actually more like a nightmare. I was so happy and excited. I was with my friends, and I was looking forward to driving south with my mom to start my new life. Everything seemed so perfect.

As soon as I fired the gun, I knew it was a mistake. I'm not someone who walks around carrying [a gun]. I know lots of people from my neighborhood who do, but I've never been one of them. I thought I was on a one-way street out of that neighborhood and about to start a new life. I never thought I'd end up here.

Anyway, as soon as Ana Lopes [the victim] started to bleed, someone there called 911 for rescue. I knew right then and there that I was in trouble. I thought about taking off, but I knew that would be a mistake. I stuck around to face the music.

The cops arrived right after rescue and I told them what happened, that it was an accident. They cuffed me and took me in. I didn't lie about anything.

I had a good lawyer who believed in me. The best she could work out was fifteen years.

QUESTION: If you could rewind the tape and go back to that night, how would you have handled things?

ANSWER: You know, it all happened so fast. I just didn't think. I reacted to a bad situation and made it worse. It's easy to say now, but what I should have done was stay out of the fight entirely. I could have just called the cops. To be honest, though, calling the cops in the middle of a situation like that is hard, 'cause I don't want to be a snitch. But that's what I should have done—or just left. That would have been the smart thing to do. I'm paying a big price for getting involved.

But you know what? I feel kinda funny talking about the big price I've paid. The truth is, my victim—Ana—she's paying the biggest price. She didn't deserve that. Yes, she was living the street life and involved in some bad stuff, but she was young, just like I was. That's no excuse for what happened. At some point, I'll get to go home. Ana won't.

QUESTION: I can see here from your records that you've been in lots of programs and worked hard during your time here. Tell us about that. What have you learned from all this?

ANSWER: It's hard to know where to begin. I've been in prison now for five years. Five very long years. If things hadn't gone wrong, I would have probably graduated from college by now. Who knows, I might be playing professional basketball somewhere; everyone told me I was good enough.

Soon after I got here I decided I wasn't going to let this defeat me. I've faced lots of hardships in my life; this is just another one. And I couldn't let my mom down. I knew I had to show her I'm bigger than this. One of the counselors here, Michelle, gave me some good advice; she said, "Felix, you have a long bid [sentence] to do. You have so much potential. You can either let this beat you down or you can beat it down. This tragedy doesn't have to define you." I've held on to those words ever since.

At first I had a hard time here. I had never been in prison before. As a teenager I was held in jail overnight once when I got picked up with some friends who were selling weed and stuff but nothing like this. I turned eighteen just before all this happened, so I got sentenced as an adult. My biggest problem here was being so young. I'm a big guy, so that helped. A few inmates tried to give me a hard time, especially some guys who hung out with my victim as part of her boyfriend's gang.

One of them actually stole some stuff of mine from the footlocker in my cell. Once I figured out who it was, I knew I had to do something. If I didn't confront him, word would get around that I was an easy mark and soft, and I couldn't have that. The problem was that I'm not a fighter. You can see from my record that I'm not a fighter; I'm not one of these guys who's getting thrown into seg over and over for throwing punches.

But I knew I had to fight this guy. One of the older inmates who was watching out for me taught me what to do. I'm not proud of it, but I used what inmates call a slock; that's when you take the combination lock you're allowed to have for your footlocker, put it in a sock, and use it as a weapon. Believe me, it works.

Anyway, one evening, just before lights out, I let this guy have it right in his face; I hurt him bad. I got thrown into seg, just like I knew I would. That's just the price you have to pay. Believe me, word got around fast; no one messed with me again. And since then I haven't had any serious discipline problems.

As you can see, I've completed every program I'm eligible for. I've done victim's impact, cognitive restructuring, anger management, the nonviolence program, the SCORE [Special Community Outreach Education] program where I talk to high school students, the puppy program, and taken a bunch of community college courses offered in here.

QUESTION: I want to commend you for the way you've spent your time during this sentence. Overall, after that rough start your record has been impressive, and a number of COs [correctional officers] and other people have lots of good things to say about you.

Tell me, where do you see yourself headed from here? At this point, what do you want to do with your life?

ANSWER: You know, when I was about to head to college, I mostly thought about playing basketball. I've always been a good student, but basketball is what got me excited. But I'm not about that anymore. This experience has taught me that I can't take anything for granted. I've grown up in here. I'm more mature, and I have real goals.

I'm almost finished with my associate's degree through the Community College of Rhode Island program in here. When I get out, I want to get my bachelor's degree, maybe in social work. I'm good with kids, and my work in the SCORE program has made me want to try to prevent street violence. I've been talking to Sammy Montinegro from the Street Justice program; he and his people come in here to work with young gang members about how to prevent violence once they're back out. Sammy told me that I have what it takes to work with them once I'm released. They said they were going to write me a job letter. Is that in the file?

QUESTION: Yes, I see it right here. That's great. Good for you.

ANSWER: Yeah, I want to get my degree and do this kind of work. I might even be able to use my basketball skills when I work with these kids, you know, using the basketball court as a way to connect with them, relate with them.

Bertaina then brought up a subject I have never heard a prison inmate broach: the stock market. I couldn't help but smile. "This is a very bright guy," I thought, "someone who really thinks outside the box."

The other thing I want to do when I get out is study finance and investments. I'm fascinated by the stock market and have been teaching myself all about it. I can't use the Internet here, but my mom got me a subscription to the *Wall Street Journal*. I've also read a bunch of books about investments, things like *A Random Walk Down Wall Street* and *The Intelligent Investor*. I've learned all about price/earnings ratios, market cycles, betas, book value, value investing, dollar cost averaging, and all that. I love this stuff and may want to get a part-time job in an investment firm.

Look, I even brought you my spreadsheets for the hypothetical portfolio I've created here. Obviously I can't trade stocks in prison, but I track the companies in my portfolio every day to see how well my stocks are doing. I pretend to buy and sell based on the *Wall Street Journal* data. I'm doing pretty good—up almost 9 percent this year.

And there's one other thing I've learned from this: learning about the history of the stock market has been a powerful lesson for me. Have you ever seen the graph showing the history of the Dow Jones Industrial Average starting, like, in the late 1800s? It's amazing. The curve on the graph moves up and down because of market fluctuations and economic events. But the clear overall trend over time is up. Of course, there's the big crash in the 1930s and a bunch of other big drops along the way.

So, here's what's really cool about this. That's what my life, and life for lots of other inmates, is like. We have these times in our lives when there's a huge crash and things are falling apart left and right. But if we do the right things, like investing in ourselves, the overall trend is up. How about that? I keep a copy of that graph on the wall in my cell to keep me motivated.

I was blown away. Never in my wildest dreams did I ever expect to hear a prison inmate ruminate about the complexity of the stock market and, more important, draw on market trends as a powerful metaphor for cultivating a philosophy of life. I felt as if I was watching a flower blossom in front of my eyes.

At that point Bertaina had served only five years of his fifteen-year sentence. The parole board commended him for his impressive insight, program participation, and nearly spotless disciplinary record. But in good conscience we could not parole him so early in his sentence. After all, his victim had died. We agreed to see him again in eighteen months.

|||||||||||||||||||||||||||||||||||||||||||||||||||||||||||

Prisons are full of despair. When I walked through prison corridors, recreation yards, cell blocks, and visiting rooms, I encountered overwhelming numbers of inmates who grew up and lived in poverty; dropped out of high school; had learning disabilities; struggled to communicate; coped with significant psychiatric disorders; had a history of addiction to drugs, alcohol, or gambling; were victims of physical violence, molestation, and other forms of trauma; had spotty employment histories and few skills; had weak, nonexistent, or toxic relationships with people in the community; would return to high-crime neighborhoods upon leaving prison; and would have difficulty finding stable, affordable, and decent housing. In short, the odds against inmates who leave prison are staggering, and finding glimmers of hope among them often is difficult.

Yet I could not have served on the parole board without a deep sense of hope. Hope is what sustained me. Every morning on hearing days, when I drove to Rhode Island's sprawling prison complex, I took a few minutes to reflect on what was likely to await me. By then I had read the detailed records for the inmates I would meet that day. I knew a great deal about the crimes they had committed, the crimes' impact on victims, the inmates' prison conduct and program participation, their criminal record, and some details of their personal histories.

In some instances I felt despair as I anticipated the inmate's parole hearing. But often I found reason to be hopeful. Some inmates write remarkably insightful letters to the parole board in which they reflect on their bad judgment and behavior, the effects of their crime on the victim, what they have learned during their incarceration, and their wish for genuine redemption. Inmates' files often contain inspiring, upbeat comments from prison staffers who have seen impressive evidence of inmates' maturation and emerging insight. I wished this sort of evidence were more pervasive, but I took what I could get and did my best to enhance the likelihood that inmates would move in the right direction.

My work in prisons, in this chronically grim world, has led me to think a lot about hope—what it means, how one finds it amid dire circumstances, and how one holds on to it. To hope is to want something to happen or be true and to think that it could happen or be true. There is no doubt that I hoped inmates would leave prison, lead upright lives, cope with life's challenges in a constructive way, contribute to the world in which they live, and be content. I know in my bones that this can happen.

Most of my thinking about hope has been influenced by two prominent theories. One, developed by the psychologist Charles Snyder, asserts that hope is a cognitive skill that demonstrates an individual's ability to maintain drive in the pursuit of a goal. According to Snyder, a person's ability to be hopeful depends on two types of thinking: agency thinking and pathway thinking.[5] Agency thinking refers to the person's determination to achieve his goals despite actual or potential obstacles. Pathway thinking refers to the specific ways a person believes she can achieve these personal goals. The role of professionals is to help clients overcome barriers that have prevented them from achieving goals. Ideally practitioners help clients set realistic and relevant personal goals, help them remain hopeful about their ability to achieve the goals, and suggest effective pathways.

In a prison context Snyder's perspective makes a great deal of sense. Of course we want inmates, nearly all of whom have led challenge-filled lives, to identify realistic goals, sustain a determined effort to achieve them, and identify effective pathways toward their achievement. Amen to that.

The persistent problem throughout the criminal justice world is putting in place well-trained staffers who have sufficient time, expertise, and resources to help offenders identify their goals, work with them to enhance their motivation and determination, and arrange for and implement the supportive services necessary to help offenders achieve their goals. The ideal is terrific; the reality is hard to achieve, given a mix of funding constraints and politicians and others who oppose such a comprehensive approach on ideological grounds. Some say, "Criminals don't deserve this kind of public spending. Let them do their time." Or they say, "Our budget simply can't afford this, no matter how appealing this approach is." They reject the premise that failure to provide preventive and rehabilitative services leads to even greater costs to society down the road.

Kaye Herth, a nursing educator, presents the other major theory related to hope that I think about a lot. Herth's work has focused on hope among people who struggle with chronic and terminal illness. She writes about how people cope with bad circumstances, particularly those over which they have little or no control.[6] In some important ways, I think, this parallels many criminals' lives. They may not be able to wave a magic wand and undo the ravages of poverty, mental illness, addiction, childhood trauma, betrayal, brain injury, and so on. But, like patients diagnosed with a nasty type of cancer, offenders may be able to cultivate coping skills that give them hope and help them manage having been dealt a lousy hand.

I have been privileged to meet many offenders who have done just that. Sometimes with the help of counselors and sometimes on their own, they have decided to tackle the demons in their lives with zest. Rather than fighting offers of help and being defensive, hostile, and dismissive, these offenders have the courage and strength to concede that their lives have spun out of control and proclaim that they want this nightmare to end. Their progress may occur in fits and starts, but I have witnessed many offenders who have ultimately succeeded, sometimes far beyond my wildest hopes.

Laura Haney was sentenced to two years in prison following her conviction for possessing and using stolen credit cards. This was Haney's third conviction. The court placed her on probation following the first two convictions, both of which involved illegal possession of narcotics.

A staggering percentage of female inmates are serving time for a drug-related offense.[7] Those with addiction issues often have a history of childhood trauma, especially sexual molestation, that led, directly or indirectly, to their drug use and related crimes. In this respect Haney was typical. When she was twelve, her mother's boyfriend began to molest Laura Haney. She reported that the molestation, including sexual intercourse, lasted for nearly two years before she told her biological father during a weekend visit with him. Haney's father, who had recently reentered Haney's life after serving a lengthy federal prison sentence out of state, called the police, who then notified child welfare officials. The mother's boyfriend was arrested. He was charged with, and convicted of, molesting a child. Coincidentally about six months after I participated in Haney's parole hearing, I participated in a parole hearing for her rapist, who had received a twelve-year sentence.

At her first parole board hearing, which took place eight months into her sentence, Haney had not yet enrolled in a drug treatment program. She admitted to a prison counselor that she had a serious cocaine addiction, which had led to the robbery she committed, but she did not ask to participate in the prison-sponsored addictions program.

QUESTION: I see here that you have been struggling for some time with cocaine. Is that right?

ANSWER: Yes.

QUESTION: As far as I can tell from your records, you haven't enrolled in the drug treatment program. Is that true?

ANSWER: Yup. I figure I'll do it on the street if I need help.

QUESTION: Do you think there's a connection between your drug addiction and the fact that you robbed two women at gunpoint, stole their pocketbooks, and used their credit cards at Walmart?

ANSWER: Yeah, but I've got that under control. Besides, I don't have time to go to the program. I need my job working in the kitchen here. I don't have no one to put money in my account. I need to work.

QUESTION: I can understand that you need to work to get some money, but given your record, I'm really concerned that you will leave here without addressing your addiction and will relapse and commit new crimes. Does that worry you?

ANSWER: No.

Following that hearing the parole board denied Haney's release. The minutes, a copy of which the inmate receives the day after the hearing, show our expression of concern about Haney's limited insight and decision to not enroll in the prison's drug treatment program. We encouraged her to reconsider. We informed Haney that we would meet with her again in six months to review her status.

About two months later Haney wrote a letter to the parole board:

Dear Parole Board:

I will admit that I was really disappointed when I got denied parole when I met with you. I know lots of other women here who got parole and I thought I would get it too.

After I calmed down, I read your minutes and thought about what you said to me at that hearing. I talked to my counselor here, and she helped me see that my crimes are because of my drug use, and my drug use is the way I've been handling my anguish about being molested as a child.

I think you're right that I need to start getting help now. I want you to know that I've signed up for the six-month drug program. I hope to complete it in February. I would like to ask that you postpone my December parole hearing until March, so I can complete the program before I see you.

I want to show you, and myself, that I'm doing the right thing. I now know that this is what I need to do.

We postponed Haney's hearing until the following March, as she requested. Not only did Haney complete the drug program, she did so with flying colors. The clinical director wrote a glowing report.

At the March hearing we voted to release Haney to a residential treatment program that would help her continue her recovery and transition to the community. Haney's two children were in foster care during her prison stay. Child welfare staffers brought the children to the prison weekly to see their mother. The residential treatment program staffers agreed to help Haney work with child welfare officials to regain custody of her children once she completed the intensive treatment program.

Nearly three years later I gave a lecture at a professional conference for addictions professionals. Once again a former parolee—in this instance, Haney—approached me to say hello and update me. Haney told me, quite proudly, that she had done so well in the residential treatment program that she was offered a job there after she had been clean and sober for two years. She had regained custody of her children. Haney reminded me that her disappointing first hearing with the parole board had been a turning point for her. She said that she turned her initial frustration and anger, upon learning that the board had denied her parole, into a transformational moment. During our conversation at the conference, I told Haney that this was transformational not only for her but for me as well. Haney's ability to seize hope gave me hope. Indeed, hope can be contagious.

||||||||||||||||||||||||||||||||||||||||||||||||||||||||||||

Laura Haney's journey is not unusual. Time and time again I saw inmates who were defiant, angry, and defensive at their first, second, and third parole board hearings—and beyond. For many, it takes time to recognize what they need to do. Certainly some understand that the moment they walk through the prison gate and exchange street clothes for an inmate uniform. And a relatively small number never understand.

Some compelling research has helped me understand this common trajectory in a way that gives me hope, even when some inmates have not yet reached a point where they are ready to embark on their personal transformation in a sincere, meaningful way. This research, now a staple in the human services, is known as the "stages-of-change" model, first developed by James Prochaska and Carlo DiClemente in the late 1970s.

Studies of change have found that most people trying to modify their behavior move through a series of stages, whether they are trying to lose weight, stop smoking, monitor their diabetes, maintain sobriety, or stay out of legal trouble. How long a person stays in each stage varies.

The stages are precontemplation, contemplation, preparation, action, and maintenance. People in the precontemplation stage are not even thinking about or interested in making a change. Perhaps they are uninformed or underinformed about the consequences of their behavior, or they are so consumed with other issues in their lives that they have no wherewithal to invest in a serious effort to change. Multiple unsuccessful attempts at change, which often occur among people who end up in prison, can lead to demoralization about one's ability to change. People in the precontemplation stage are not reading, talking, or thinking about their high-risk behaviors. Often this is because they do not have access to programs that are designed to meet their needs.

The second stage is contemplation. During this stage people are thinking about the possibility of changing. They are more aware of the advantages of changing—such as staying out of prison, repairing relationships with family members and partners, and regaining custody of their children—but are also acutely aware of the downsides, such as the intense, prolonged effort and frustration involved in trying and perhaps failing, at least in the short run. This vacillating between the costs and benefits of changing can produce profound, tortuous ambivalence; many people spend years in the contemplation stage.

The next phase is called preparation. Here people feel more ready to take action in the direction of change and are willing to try the challenging steps required to get started. These individuals have a plan of action, such as signing up for and attending the prison-sponsored drug treatment program, consulting a mental health counselor, or reading a self-help book from the prison library.

Action is the stage at which people have made specific overt changes in their lifestyles. For example, for former offenders now living in the community, this might involve avoiding the people, places, and things that led them to drink or gamble. For prison inmates the change might involve avoiding use of illegal drugs and steering clear of known troublemakers.

People in the maintenance stage have made specific changes in their lifestyles and are working hard to prevent relapse. During the maintenance stage people grow increasingly more confident that they can continue their changes. This stage can last months or years, depending on the complexity of the individual's challenges.

Research shows that most people cycle in and out of the stages of change. Relapse, especially among offenders, is common; many professionals consider relapse to be part of the process of change and a stimulus to reengage in the effort with even more commitment.[8] In an ideal world, of course, the process would be more linear and end with true termination, that is, with the problem fully resolved forever. Realistically, however, offenders need to make a plan to avoid relapse as much as possible and, should it occur, resume their efforts to change.

Part of the challenge parole boards face is that many inmates are ambivalent about making serious positive changes in their lives. For various reasons they may not trust professionals who claim to want to help them, sometimes because the inmates have had negative experiences with helping professionals.

Parole board members are not inmates' therapists, of course, but their words can sometimes motivate inmates to move in the right direction. In the best of all possible worlds, parole board members would draw on the evidence-based practice of what mental health professionals refer to as motivational interviewing and incorporate that in hearings. Motivational interviewing techniques, first developed by William Miller and Stephen Rollnick, are used by many mental health clinicians to address clients' ambivalence about making significant, constructive changes in their lives. Motivational interviewing relies on a conversational approach designed to help people

- discover ways to make significant changes in their lives;
- express in their own words their desire for change;
- examine their ambivalence about the change;
- plan for and begin the process of change;
- summon and strengthen their ability to talk about change;
- enhance their confidence in taking action and recognizing that even small, incremental changes are important; and
- strengthen their commitment to change.[9]

The relevance of motivational interviewing to the conversations parole board members have with inmates is obvious. Parole board hearings provide unique opportunities to help inmates acknowledge their ambivalence and explore ways to move in the direction of positive change. Thus hearings can be much more than adversarial encounters that lead to thumbs-up or thumbs-down decisions about releasing inmates from prison. Hearings that acknowledge inmates' ambivalence about change and include honest, supportive conversation about ways they can engage in real change can have a profound impact. Motivational interviewing can work. I have seen it happen.

Forecasting when, if ever, inmates will be ready to commit themselves to making serious positive changes in their lives is difficult. During some hearings I thought an inmate was on the cusp, only to have my hopes dashed when the inmate erupted in anger or made threatening comments. It works the other way, too; at times I met an inmate whose prison record was littered with disciplinary sanctions, spotty program participation, and defiance. And then magic happened: the inmate surprised all of us with his emerging insight, maturation, effort, and determination to change. This process can take time, often lots of it.

Pinpointing what causes some inmates to make the positive pivot is difficult; epiphanies happen for all kinds of reasons. Some inmates decide, after many years of incarceration, to show their families, for the first time, that they can amount to something good. Some inmates want to be a good role model for their children, especially when kids reach an age when they begin to understand that daddy or mommy is in prison for "doing bad things." Some inmates simply grow tired of the strains and stresses of their repetitive cycle from prison to home and back again. Whatever the reasons, I will take them, no matter how elusive.

One of the few joys of being on a parole board comes when the hearing itself provides the impetus for real change. These hearings are an intense moment in time; for however long the hearing lasts, its intensity tends to focus many inmates' minds. While some inmates treat parole hearings as pro forma events in the middle of an otherwise mundane day—particularly when they have little hope of being paroled—others walk into the hearing room in a heightened state of anticipation, awareness, and alertness. They badly want freedom, and the parole board literally holds the key. Sometimes a board member's incisive comment, or carefully constructed question, causes inmates to think in profoundly and fundamentally different ways about their crimes and their lives. "How does being in prison affect your life and your family's life?" "How would you like things to be different?" "What do you think you will lose if you give up gambling?" "Who in your life will support you if you decide to get out of the gang and stop dealing drugs?" "How do you want to live your life when you are released from prison?" "How can we help you get the help you want?" Being treated humanely and fairly by parole board members can motivate inmates who, for the first time in their lives, conclude that people in positions of authority believe in them and truly want them to succeed. Sometimes we can inspire inmates.

||||||||||||||||||||||||||||||||||||||||||||||||||||||||||||

Most of the inmates I have met yearn for forgiveness. They care about what others—especially their victims—think of them. Relatively few inmates are so callous and self-absorbed that they are indifferent to the public's and victims' view of them.

Many inmates seek their own form of redemption. Of course, redemption means different things to different people, but the concept generally implies forgiveness, absolution for past sins or errors, or finding a way to right a wrong. The possibility of redemption is central to the world's major faith traditions. In some forms of Buddhism, for example, redemption is achieved through self-sacrifice and is inherent in the discipline of giving up attachment to desires.

Theravada Buddhism teaches that the extinction of desire—including forms of desire that might lead people to commit crimes to satisfy their wishes for revenge, money, material possessions, or sex—is the prerequisite for salvation. While other religions hold up eternal life as the consequence of redemption, the redemptive goal of Theravada Buddhism is release from any and all forms of craving. While other religions provide assistance to people in their quest for redemption, Theravada Buddhism teaches that in this quest one can rely on no one and on nothing but oneself.

In Christian theology redemption is a key element of salvation, which generally means the deliverance from sin. The word *redeem* means "repurchase" or "buy back." In this sense many offenders try to repurchase or buy back their honor and integrity, perhaps by apologizing to their victims and participating earnestly in rehabilitation programs. In the New Testament *redemption* refers to both deliverance from sin and, ironically, freedom from captivity. Theologically redemption can be achieved through atonement, which is certainly how many inmates view their incarceration.

According to Jewish tradition, *redemption* refers especially to God's redeeming the Israelites from their various exiles. The Hebrew verb *gā'al* means "to regain possession of by payment" or "buy back something that was lost." In the Old Testament the verb *gā'al* has been translated as meaning "to redeem," "ransom," and "do the part of a kinsman." For Jews atonement is a key element of redemption. After the destruction of the ancient temple in Jerusalem and the end of sacrificial practices, the rabbis declared: "Prayer, repentance, and charity avert the evil decree." This is an essential refrain during Judaism's holiest day, Yom Kippur, or the Day of Atonement.

In Islam redemption is achieved through being a Muslim, being of sincere faith, and performing virtuous actions. Muslim sinners need only turn to a merciful God in repentance and carry out other good deeds, such as prayer and charity, for redemption to occur.[10]

Many inmates embrace a faith tradition while incarcerated, especially as they seek redemption. Some claim to have been true believers before their imprisonment and strayed from the path. During parole board hearings some of these inmates speak of their faith and its role in their pursuit of redemption. In this way Alvin Hawkins was typical.

When he met with us, Hawkins was serving a three-year sentence for possession of a gun without a permit. This was not Hawkins's first brush with the law. He previously had served a one-year sentence for possession of cocaine, and a judge had placed him on probation three times for drug possession, shoplifting, possession of a stolen car, and driving without a license. While incarcerated this time, Hawkins had participated in a Bible study group and a faith-based correspondence course. Before his parole hearing Hawkins wrote the board a letter:

> Dear members of the Parole Board:
>
> My name is Alvin Hawkins and I am scheduled to appear before you next month. This is my second parole hearing. I was denied last June because of my criminal record and because you wanted me to complete the alternatives to violence and the drug program.
>
> Since then I did the six-month drug program and am almost finished with the violence program. I hope you will see that I'm a very different person now. I no longer want to live the street life. I'm sick and tired of being sick and tired. I'm getting older and understand that playing around with drugs and guns has gotten me nowhere.
>
> I have been studying with Rev. Pinewell in her Bible study group. She has offered me a bed in her transition program when I get out of prison. The reverend and my Bible study have changed my life. My faith means so much to me. Before I got into trouble I was very active in my church, Tabernacle Faith on Blodgett Avenue. But as you can see from my record, I sinned and lost my way. My addiction has a lot to do with that.
>
> I know God wants me to succeed. I promise you, I won't let you or God down.

Other inmates told the parole board—in writing and in person—about their discovery of faith during their incarceration. Some inmates entered the hearing room clutching their Bible. Some wore their crucifix so it showed outside their uniform shirt; some pulled it out during the hearing to be sure that parole board members saw it.

I have no doubt that many inmates embrace their faith sincerely and earnestly. For some both clergy and theology have helped them regain their footing in life, seek redemption, and find hope. But the faith-based claims of other inmates ring hollow and seem manipulative.

Briana Felts was serving a two-year sentence for receiving stolen goods. At the time of her arrest Felts was part of what is known as an ORC ring—organized retail crime ring—that engaged in carefully orchestrated theft in large retail stores, such as Walmart, Target, Home Depot, Sears, and Lowe's. A sophisticated organized retail crime ring can hit a dozen or more large stores in one day and then resell the stolen goods on eBay or at flea markets or store them in a black market warehouse to sell later.

The leaders of ORC groups often hire and pay off their boosters with money or drugs. The boosters often go into several stores a day to steal specific items on the ring's wish list. The easiest items to steal and resell in large volume are over-the-counter medications, baby formula, and health and beauty products. A common tactic, which is the one Felts used, is to select a low-cost item that has a large box, take the item out of the box, fill the empty box with small, high-cost items (especially cosmetics), and seal the box back up with packing tape also stolen from the store's shelves. Then the booster goes to the cash register, pays the amount for the low-cost item that was removed from the box, and exits the store with a box full of costly goods.

Felts and her cronies also lined shopping bags—known as booster bags—with foil to defeat the electronic alarms often found at the exits of retail stores. One of Felts's other tricks was to grab a large, inexpensive plastic storage container from the store's shelf and fill it with small, high-cost items. She would proceed to the self-checkout lane commonly found in large retail stores (to avoid scrutiny by a cashier), scan the bar code on the plastic container, pay the modest price, and walk out of the store with a large collection of expensive items.

Organized retail crime rings of the kind that recruited Felts are a national problem and cost the retail industry and consumers billions of dollars annually. Briana Felts was a relatively small cog in a huge wheel.

Felts did not limit her prolific shoplifting to these techniques. On the day of her arrest the store's video security equipment recorded Felts as she stuffed cosmetic items and DVDs into the backpack on her five-year-old daughter, who walked around the store holding Felts's hand.

Most, but certainly not all, inmates who have a history of shoplifting also have a history of substance abuse. Typically the shoplifting directly feeds the offender's drug addiction. When I prepared for Felts's parole hearing and read the headlines in her file about her extensive shoplifting, I expected to see detailed reports about her addiction. I guessed wrong. Unlike most shoplifting offenders I encountered, Felts was driven primarily by greed. Felts and her accomplices were part of a sophisticated and well-oiled organized crime ring whose principal aim was to make a lot of money. It really was no more complicated than that.

At her parole hearing Felts was cunning. Within a matter of seconds I had a sense that my colleagues and I were engaged in a verbal chess match. I looked for hints of insight and remorse and came up empty.

QUESTION: Did you plead guilty or go to trial?

ANSWER: I went to trial. My attorney thought we had a pretty good case. She said that the loss prevention people at the store didn't follow procedure when they confronted me. Unfortunately the judge didn't buy it, so here I am.

QUESTION: Did you commit the crime? Were you part of this shoplifting ring that's described in the police report?

ANSWER: Yeah, I guess so. It's actually not that big a ring. Just a handful of people.

QUESTION: Let me ask you this: When people shoplift like this, who, if anyone, gets hurt?

ANSWER: I don't really know.

QUESTION: I'd appreciate it if you would think about this for a couple of minutes. [long silence] So, do you have some thoughts about who gets hurt, if anyone?

ANSWER: I'm not really sure.

QUESTION: Okay, well, I'd like to ask you a different question. When people shoplift, who covers the cost of the stolen goods?

ANSWER: I guess the company does, but they probably have insurance for that.

QUESTION: If the company covers the loss, do you think they adjust their prices to make up for the profit they lost?

ANSWER: Yeah, I suppose.

QUESTION: Do customers pay higher prices when companies lose a lot of money due to shoplifting?

ANSWER: Okay, I see.

QUESTION: And if the store's insurance company covers the loss, does that affect the insurance premium that the store has to pay? Is it like when automobile insurance rates go up after a driver has been in a couple of big accidents? And do stores sometimes increase their prices to help pay for the increased insurance premiums?

ANSWER: I suppose. I hadn't really thought about it this way.

Toward the end of the hearing Felts tugged on the crucifix that hung around her neck and that she pulled out of her green prison uniform. She asked whether she had any chance of getting parole.

QUESTION: Please tell us why you think you are a good candidate for parole. Make a good case for yourself.

ANSWER: I've learned my lesson. I hate being away from my kids. I won't do this again, I promise. I'm going to get a regular job, and I'm going to go to church every week.

QUESTION: Were you going to church on the street before you got arrested?

ANSWER: Every once in awhile. But now I'm going to go regular-like. I go to some services here, unless I have a visit.

QUESTION: What's the name of the church you plan to attend? What's the address?

ANSWER: Uh, I don't really remember. It's that big white church over by Mineral Spring Avenue.

QUESTION: Do you know the name of the priest?

ANSWER: Not really.

I know it is possible that anxiety during the formal parole board hearing had led Felts to come across as less than convincing. It may be that she felt great remorse and shame and simply lacked the cognitive and verbal skill to express herself effectively. However, we could use only the information before us. Felts seemed to lack insight and authenticity.

Too often inmates whose prerelease letters and testimony were filled with God references abandoned their newfound faith once they passed through the prison gates. A parole board colleague once observed, "Some inmates discover God when they find themselves in prison, but once they leave, somehow God stays behind."

|||||||||||||||||||||||||||||||||||||||||||||||||||||||||||||||||

Over the years I have been truly inspired by inmates who have turned their lives around. They were earnest, not cynical. They were disciplined in their hope-filled efforts to lead crime-free lives. They did not want to hurt people, steal from them, or cheat the system ever again. They were bravely resolute and hardy. These inmates had searched their souls and wanted redemption. Peter Slom is a compelling example. He speaks publicly about his transformation from cocaine dealer to prison inmate, rehabilitation program client, and graduate school student in social work, eventually becoming the first ex-felon in Rhode Island to be hired to work as a senior clinician and administrator in a state correctional facility.[11] I presided at Slom's 1992 parole hearing and voted to release him.

Many such inmates and parolees are inspired by the dedicated mentors and professionals who care about them. These were lovely sights for my eyes, which were sometimes sore from years of frustration.

Early one afternoon on a hearing day, an inmate serving a lengthy sentence entered our hearing room accompanied by his attorney, Noah Kilroy. Over the years I met most of the criminal defense attorneys who represent inmates before the board. This attorney, however, was new to me.

After brief introductions Kilroy opened the hearing with a thoughtful, impassioned presentation on his client's behalf—the facts of the case, the nature of the crime, and especially the progress the inmate had made during his prison stay. I was impressed. The attorney's presentation was one of the most thorough, comprehensive, and earnest I had seen.

On my drive to my office that afternoon, I reflected on the day's hearings, as I usually did, and wondered about Kilroy, who stood out. When I got to my office I decided to do a Google search to see what I could find out about him—his legal education, where he had practiced law, and so on. I was stunned to find a 2010 news article in the *Newport Daily News* that reported Kilroy had spent four years in prison on drug charges in his late teens and early twenties—"a six-month sentence at the Adult Correctional Institutions in Cranston for delivery of cocaine, followed by a two-year sentence at the ACI for possession of cocaine with intent to deliver. Finally, he served a two-year sentence in a Florida prison for trafficking in cocaine." The prison term for trafficking woke him up:

> "I burnt the bridge to my parents," he said. "They were completely humiliated. In prison, I had solid reflection time. I thought, 'I'm losing a lot of family and friends.' . . .
>
> "Solitude does something to you," he said. "In your darkest hours, you find clarity about your life."
>
> He remembered reading a book by a psychologist who wrote, "Without knowledge of yourself, you can't have knowledge of anything else, because you have nothing to compare it to."
>
> "You have to dissect yourself," Kilroy said. "Maladapted people think their actions are normal."
>
> He discovered reading at the Lawtey Correctional Institution in Florida. "That became my passion," he said. "I got my G.E.D. when I was at the ACI [Adult Correctional Institution, Rhode Island's state prison system], but I had no real education because I didn't have a desire to learn."
>
> Now, he wanted to learn as much as possible.[12]

After his release he returned to Rhode Island and enrolled in college, majoring in social work. "I wanted to understand the underpinnings of advocacy and social work," he said. "Salve [Salve Regina

University] really challenged my thought. I learned the theoretical framework of advocacy. What I learned in prison, I bounced off these theories. It has strengthened me." After college he worked on a project to restore inmates' voting rights and then did an internship at Rhode Island Legal Services, which provides public defenders to the indigent. It inspired him to attend law school.[13]

Wow. I finished reading this news article online and smiled broadly. Wow.

Kilroy indeed went on to law school. He graduated in 2013 and, one week later, wrote this first-person reflection:

Ten years ago, I was serving time in a Florida prison for drug offenses. At the time, I told a fellow inmate in the prison yard that when I got out I was going to go to college. He laughed at me and said, "Noah, you're crazy." In 2009 I graduated college, and last Friday, I graduated from Roger Williams University School of Law. To that unsuspecting inmate in the prison yard that day, I say, "you were right, but I had to be."

To many, graduation is a time to celebrate one's accomplishments. A graduation or commencement ceremony is similar in significance to a wedding or birth of a child. Graduation is bitter sweet in that it signifies the end of one chapter and the beginning of a new. Looking back on my journey from prison yard to law school grad, I concede that the road was not without obstacles. At times, before I eventually hit my stride, it seemed as though that road wasn't even visible.

Charting a career path after prison can be difficult. For me, I often walked a tightrope between what I was able to do given my criminal past, and what I was capable of doing given my ability. Those first few months after being released from prison were often consumed with a feeling of being unsure of myself. One example was when I initially had thoughts of applying to college. I remember saying to myself, "where is the book to read on applying to college with a criminal record?" To my dismay, there were none (that I knew of). However, in that process I realized that what I was really searching for was not a step-by-step guide for ex-offenders getting into an institution of higher education, but rather, validation that my dreams were realistic and attainable. Therein lies my error.

What I was doing when I was initially released from prison was allowing others to define my reality and limitations. By letting others define what I was capable of, I was inevitably bound by their realities. In essence, it was an imprisoning of the mind. As soon as I learned that, despite my criminal past, I did not need the permission of others to succeed, I began to dream big and dream bold. After getting my Bachelor's degree from Salve Regina University, I quickly applied and was accepted into law school. Now, as a law school grad, I have applied for admission to the Rhode Island Bar to become a lawyer.

When reflecting back on my journey, there was a comment that a friend of mine (with a similar background) once made that sums up my current outlook on charting my goals. When speaking of his own journey from prisoner to lawyer, he profoundly said, "you almost have to have unrealistic goals." In the eyes of many they will be unrealistic. However, in the hearts of the willing, those dreams are very real.

It is my hope that others, whether in a prison yard or otherwise, have the courage to dream beyond their wildest dreams. Know that you are the only person that can define your success. Understand that, despite where you come from, hard work and integrity will always transcend your reality.[14]

||||||||||||||||||||||||||||||||||||||||||||||||||||||||||||

If only Noah Kilroy's story were the norm rather than the exception. Yes, there are lots of other success stories. But far too many post-prison journeys do not work out well, stories that are defined much more by hopelessness than hope.

Alonzo Grich walked into the parole board hearing room shackled around his ankles, handcuffed, and wearing the orange uniform that screams, "I'm doing time in the segregation unit." I greeted him as he angled his body gingerly into his seat. Because of the handcuffs and shackles—known among corrections professionals as jewelry—Grich had some difficulty positioning himself.

I worked hard to treat inmates with respect, even those who were belligerent when they appeared before the board. I think it is professional, and my experience tells me that being respectful with inmates more often than not leads to constructive communication and helps to defuse an otherwise tense situation. Most inmates respond in kind with a greeting, sometimes in a clearly perfunctory way and sometimes with enthusiasm. Grich did neither. Rarely did I encounter inmates who were so morose in demeanor. He seemed to resent being asked to meet with the board, as if it were an intrusion.

Grich was serving a nine-year sentence for armed robbery. (He actually had committed three armed robberies that were lumped together by the prosecutor.) In one case Grich and his girlfriend had called a taxi late one night after going to a drug-saturated party. Grich, who had snorted cocaine earlier in the evening, pulled out a handgun, told the cab driver to pull over, pointed the gun at her, and robbed her of all her cash. In Grich's second case he was arrested in downtown Providence and charged with robbing an out-of-town tourist who was taking a stroll along the river near his hotel one evening. Grich hid under a darkened pedestrian bridge, displayed his gun, and demanded the tourist's wallet and jewelry.

The final case involved Grich's robbery of two university students who were walking back to their dorm from the campus gym. The students were crossing a major street when Grich confronted them. One of the students screamed and ran from the scene. The other student handed her pocketbook to Grich.

Grich's parole board hearing did not go well:

QUESTION: Before we begin talking about the crimes that landed you in prison, can you tell us what got you into segregation?

ANSWER: Nothin' big.

QUESTION: What do you mean by nothing big? What happened?

ANSWER: I don't wanna talk about it.

QUESTION: All right, let's move on. It looks like this is your third prison sentence. You served two other sentences, one for assault and one for stealing a car, right?

ANSWER: I guess so.

QUESTION: You're not sure?

ANSWER: Nah.

QUESTION: You also spent some time at the training school as a juvenile. What was that for?

ANSWER: I don't remember.

QUESTION: I'm surprised you don't remember. Most people remember things like that. How far did you get in school, Mr. Grich?

ANSWER: Ninth.

QUESTION: Can you speak up a bit, please. Did you say ninth grade?

ANSWER: Uh-huh.

QUESTION: Did you drop out of school or were you expelled?

ANSWER: Kicked out.

QUESTION: Can you tell us about the armed robberies? What was going on for you during this time?

ANSWER: Not much.

QUESTION: Were you working?

ANSWER: Nah.

QUESTION: You're twenty-seven, right? Have you ever held a job?

ANSWER: [shakes his head no]

QUESTION: Mr. Grich, do you remember that one of the prison counselors came to see you to prepare for this hearing? It says here that
you refused to cooperate? Is that true?

ANSWER: I guess.

QUESTION: I get the strong feeling you don't want to have this hearing, that you don't want to talk to us. Do you want to be considered
for parole?

At that point Grich stood up, shook his head no, and tried to head
out of the hearing room. Because he was handcuffed behind his back,
he had difficulty opening the door to the hearing room. Grich muttered an obscenity as he tried to grab the doorknob with his cuffed
hands. The parole board administrator helped him negotiate the
door and summoned the correctional officer to escort Grich back to
his cell in the segregation unit.

As Grich shuffled out of the hearing room, I could not help but
think we were dealing with a man who was so discouraged, angry, or
shut down that he could not, or would not, engage with the board on
his own behalf. Was he feral, or was there a lot more going on than
he could bear to let others, especially the parole board, see? Chances
are, I will never know.

Most inmates were quite cooperative when they met with the
board. Some were engaging and loquacious; most were invested

in responding to our questions, even if some of their answers were simplistic. Inmates have a strong incentive to do their very best to make a good impression.

Inmates who were as nonresponsive, sullen, and subtly hostile as Alonzo Grich were rare. But it happened. I worked hard to avoid overreacting in such situations. Sometimes it was not easy. At times I could feel my blood pressure rise in frustration, and sometimes anger, yet I knew deep down that it is usually a mistake to confront the inmate. Heated exchanges are nearly always counterproductive and combustible. I learned that it is best to respond to inmates' bad behavior in as cool and calm a way as is humanly possible. My wife is fond of saying, "Strike when the iron is cold." That is good advice.

My encounter with inmate Stan Witten was especially challenging. He was serving a three-year sentence for possession and distribution of child pornography. Like Alonzo Grich, Witten came to the parole board hearing room from his segregation cell in an orange uniform and in handcuffs and shackles. Witten had been placed in segregation for masturbating when a female correctional officer stood in front of his cell to conduct the evening count. Witten had been incarcerated on six other occasions. In four of those instances Witten was arrested for violating a no-contact order imposed by a judge as a result of domestic violence involving three different women.

The hearing did not get off to a good start and quickly headed downhill from there. Unlike Grich, Witten was voluble from the moment he entered the hearing room. He had difficulty letting parole board members finish asking their questions before responding. Some of his answers turned into rants about how the women in his life, the police, and the courts had mistreated him. I imagined that by the end of the hearing he would add the parole board to his list.

QUESTION: Mr. Witten, what happened that you got sent to segregation?

ANSWER: That CO [correctional officer] has been harassing me since the day I got transferred to Medium Security. I can tell she doesn't like me. She thinks she's real tough. I'd like to see how tough she is on the street without her uniform. If she's gonna disrespect me, I'll disrespect her. That's what happened.

QUESTION: Is it true that you masturbated in front of her?

ANSWER: Yeah.

QUESTION: What do you think about that?

ANSWER: I'm not too proud of it, but I got her pretty good.

QUESTION: Mr. Witten, I'm concerned that the way you handled this situation with the CO is part of a larger pattern of problems you've had in your relationships with women. Do you see a pattern here?

ANSWER: What do you mean?

QUESTION: Well, you've been arrested many times for losing control and hurting women. And you're in segregation because you mistreated a woman CO. That's the pattern I see.

ANSWER: Whatever.

QUESTION: Do you think you have difficulty in your relationships with women? Do you think you have difficulty controlling yourself when you get angry and frustrated?

ANSWER: Listen, I get involved with some real crazy women who are no good for me. I mean, they're just nuts.

QUESTION: Do you think you could have handled these situations any differently so you don't get into trouble?

ANSWER: Man, you weren't there when all this stuff happened. It's not like it looks. You can't always believe what the cops say.

QUESTION: Are you saying that the police reports are false?

ANSWER: Yeah, a lot of it.

QUESTION: So, you're saying you didn't do anything wrong in these situations?

Inmate Witten's speech was becoming increasingly intense and pressured. I was sitting close enough to him to see spittle fly off his pursed lips.

ANSWER: I can see I'm not gonna get no parole! I am very unimpressed with this board and your lack of professionalism. You know what, I don't want no parole!

And at that moment Witten stood up and continued to yell obscenities at the parole board. We summoned a correctional officer to take him back to his segregation cell.

My colleagues and I sat in stunned silence. This kind of inmate behavior was very unusual; rarely did we need to summon a correctional officer to subdue or retrieve an irate inmate. We looked at each other and shook our heads in sadness for Witten. The hearing seemed to trigger him, perhaps because of his earlier trauma; Witten became combative in a situation in which coming across in a conciliatory manner would better serve his interests. I wondered about his psychiatric status and suggested that the board request a formal mental health evaluation.

Two weeks later the board's administrator handed me an envelope with my name handwritten on it. The administrator looked at me and said, "You're not going to believe this. All of the board members got a similar letter from him."

The short letter to the board members was from inmate Witten:

> I want to thank you for seeing me at the hearing last week. Thanks for nothing, that is! I don't deserve to be here. You people don't want to give me a chance. I have no respect for you.
>
> I'll see you when I get out. Be careful.
>
> Stan the Convict Man

Cases like Alonzo Grich's and Stan Witten's often left me feeling hopeless. Both men had significant criminal records, hostile attitudes, terribly weak educational and vocational histories, and tremendous difficulty controlling their behavior. Statistically speaking, their futures looked grim. When hearings with such inmates concluded, I often felt intensely disheartened and pessimistic. That they will get out of prison one day and walk the streets scares me—a lot. And I could do little about it.

When inmates behaved poorly during hearings, my instinct was to speculate about why they behaved the way they did, particularly since clear-thinking inmates would know that it was in their self-interest to behave well before a group of people charged with deciding whether they would serve out their prison sentences or be released before their expiration.

I know there are diverse and complicated reasons why some inmates behaved badly in front of the parole board. Some struggled with such severe psychiatric disorders that they had great difficulty managing their impulses, particularly when they were not medicated properly. Usually because of the steady diet of trauma in their lives, other inmates were so defensive that it was hard for them to acknowledge their guilt and responsibility for their criminal conduct. Still others suffered from cognitive impairment or traumatic brain injury that severely limited their ability to respond coherently to our questions; their frustration might trigger angry, provocative, and rude comments.

Whatever the reasons, I always felt terribly sad when inmates misbehaved in our presence. Such conduct did not bode well for their futures. After all, if they could not control themselves in front of the people who held the virtual keys to the front gate, what was the likelihood they would be able to control themselves once they were back on the streets? Not good.

It is hard for me to write these words. By nature I tend to be an optimist and work hard to find the silver linings in the grimmest of circumstances, perhaps to a fault. I do not like giving up on people. Yet the honest-to-goodness truth is that by the end of a small percentage of parole board hearings, I felt hopeless. And in these relatively rare instances, I always hoped—and then hoped some more—that my instinct was wrong.

|||||||||||||||||||||||||||||||||||||||||||||||||||||||||||||

Three hearings after Stan Witten's case, the board met with inmate Gavin Triandos. Three years earlier Triandos, who was twenty-three years old, had pleaded guilty to breaking into nine different homes. I fully expected to find evidence of an addiction problem, but that was not the case. As Triandos admitted during the hearing, he "simply fell into the wrong crowd, which was into all kinds of bad stuff."

I asked Triandos whether he had thought about the impact of his crimes on his victims. He looked at me with a blank, unresponsive stare. I then told Triandos that I wanted to tell him two stories. The first story involved a family I had met whose home was broken into. The children in the family, ages seven and nine, were so traumatized by the break-in that both now suffered from major anxiety symptoms that they had never experienced before. Both children were in counseling to help them cope. The seven-year-old had great difficulty sleeping in his own bed and nearly every night crawled into his parents' bed for comfort and reassurance. The parents were so concerned about their children's intense fear that they had put their home on the market so they could move to a completely different neighborhood. They hoped that this change of scenery would ease their children's worries.

The second story I told Triandos concerned another family whose home was broken into one afternoon. I told him that on the morning of the break-in, the mother had been released from the hospital after painful cancer surgery. The woman, weakened by cancer, hobbled into her house, clinging to her husband's arm, and was horrified to see that someone had broken into and ransacked their home and had stolen lots of jewelry, electronics, and precious family mementos.

I asked Triandos what he thought about those victims. He responded quietly: "That's awful."

"Well, there's one more thing I would like to share with you," I said. "Those two families are your victims. We met with them this morning. Their lives have been changed forever because of what you did to them."

I stared at Triandos and saw tears trickling down his cheeks. I was greatly relieved to see that he had the ability to empathize. I said nothing more, letting the moment speak for itself.

||||||||||||||||||||||||||||||||||||||||||||||||||||||||

Recently I lectured in India. During my stay in Mumbai and Maharashtra I took time to learn about traditional Hindu teachings. Among them is the classic work known as Vishnu Smriti, a collection of aphorisms on the ancient laws of India. One struck a chord with me, especially as I think about the place of hope in the lives of offenders who are trying to turn things around. In Vishnu Smriti, hope, morals, and hard work are represented by the virtuous man who rides in a chariot drawn by his five senses and directed by his hopeful mind to his wishes; he keeps the chariot on the path of the virtuous and thus is not distracted by wrongs such as wrath, greed, and other vices. That works for me.

Hope is the thing with feathers that perches in the soul.

6

THE PURSUIT OF JUSTICE

Justice, justice shall you pursue.
–DEUTERONOMY 16:20

RON VOLK, an inmate, and his attorney walked out of the room at the conclusion of the parole board hearing. Nearly always, I settled on my vote, without much hesitation, as soon as the hearing ended. Before a hearing, after reviewing all the inmate's records, I had formulated tentative impressions; by the end of a hearing I usually had reached a firmer opinion that I shared with my colleagues as we worked toward consensus.

Not this time. I stood up and paced the room as I tried to organize my thoughts and decide. Within a matter of moments, I found myself vacillating ambidextrously: on the one hand, on the other hand. This was one of the few instances when I had genuine difficulty casting my vote.

At the time of the hearing Volk had served nineteen years of a thirty-year sentence for murder. What made this case unusual was that Volk, who was eighteen when he committed his crime, did not pull the trigger on the gun that killed Dante Porter. Volk's codefendant and former friend, John Ward, had decided to rob a well-known gang member who was an adversary. This sort of intergang beef is not unusual. Ward had talked Volk into driving the car to the scene of the crime. Ward saw Porter reach for a gun and shot him. Volk was convicted as an accomplice.

What made this case so hard for me was that Volk had been a model inmate. Surviving relatives of his victim opposed Volk's release on parole. Yet he had received rave reviews from prison staffers and had enrolled in various rehabilitation and educational programs. Clearly Volk had matured and at his hearing displayed keen insight about his bad decisions nineteen years earlier. My strong sense was that, at age thirty-seven, Volk was not likely to reoffend. This was the kind of case that forced me to confront my deepest understanding of justice.

IIIIIIIIIIIIIIIIIIIIIIIIIIIIIIIIIIIIIIIIIIIIIIIIIIIIIIIIIII

I know it sounds idealistic, but I believe it to be true: my principal duty as a parole board member was to seek justice. I took that responsibility seriously. Yet after all these years I still struggle to understand what justice means.

Every culture has its views of justice, some overlapping and some unique. Perhaps the earliest and best-known formulation appears in Plato's *Republic*, in which Socrates attempts to answer the question, What is justice? To explore this Socrates considers what justice should look like in his utopian city of Kallipolis.

Socrates and Glaucon, Plato's older brother, visit the Piraeus, the harbor of Athens, to attend a festival in honor of the Thracian goddess Bendis. Socrates speaks to Cephalus, a wealthy arms manufacturer, about old age, the benefits of being wealthy, and justice. Socrates argues that one would not claim that it is just to return weapons to a friend who is insane; therefore justice does not always mean being truthful and returning what one owes or has borrowed, as Cephalus claims. Thus at the start of the *Republic* we see that justice is complicated, full of twists.

Socrates offers three arguments in favor of the just life over the unjust life. First, the just human is wise and good, and the unjust human is ignorant and bad. Second, injustice produces internal disharmony, which prevents the person from taking effective actions. And third, the just person lives a happier life than the unjust person, since the just person performs the various functions of the human soul well.

When I presided at parole board hearings, justice meant several things to me. At its core justice involves balancing the sometimes competing goals of protecting the public, imposing fair punishment, honoring victims, and recognizing that inmates who have truly turned their lives around—and worked hard to make amends and gain genuine insight—deserve second chances. Striking the right balance is the hardest part of the job.

Another key component of justice is providing opportunities for offenders to take responsibility for their misdeeds and, when feasible, apologize to victims and give back to the communities they have harmed. Recently both moral philosophers and criminal justice professionals have developed and refined their ideas about restorative justice and ways to promote it. These developments had a major influence on my thinking as a parole board member.

Restorative justice is a victim-centered response to crime that provides opportunities for the victim, offender, their families, and representatives of the community at large to address the harm caused by a crime. The number of formal restorative justice programs has increased dramatically, especially since the early 1980s. Although some forms of restorative justice are not feasible in cases with which the typical parole board deals, several are, and it is important to explore the relevant concepts.

Restorative justice is based on a belief that an important goal of the criminal justice system should be to restore victims—both individual victims and the broader community—who have been harmed or injured by offenders. More specifically restorative justice stresses the importance of

- supporting and assisting crime victims;
- holding offenders directly accountable to the people and communities they have violated;
- restoring the emotional and material losses of victims, to the degree possible;
- providing a range of opportunities for dialogue among interested crime victims, offenders, families, and other supportive people;
- offering offenders opportunities for competency development and reintegration into productive community life; and
- strengthening public safety through community building.

Restorative justice models broadly define *victims* as including individual victims (as in cases of murder, armed robbery, aggravated assault, domestic violence, robbery, arson, rape, and child molestation), organizational victims (as in cases of fraud, destruction of corporate property, or embezzlement of funds), and the broader community (as in cases of destruction of public property or theft of public funds).

The concept of restorative justice has ancient roots and a number of contemporary applications that have intriguing relevance to the goals of parole, given our duty to focus simultaneously on offenders (promoting rehabilitation, accountability, deterrence, punishment, and prevention) and the broader community (promoting public safety and opportunities for offenders to make amends to the community). The term *restorative justice* was probably used for the first time in the late 1970s. Formal programs now operate throughout the world.

Restorative justice is one expression of the broader phenomenon of community justice. The principal goal of community justice is to empower communities and enhance citizens' participation in the administration of justice.

Original notions of restorative justice have their roots in Jewish, Buddhist, Taoist, Greek, Arab, Roman, and Hindu civilizations, among others. Contemporary restorative justice programs have evolved from a primary focus on victim-offender mediation to a much more comprehensive approach that views crime as a rupture in relationships between offenders and victims. The first North American victim-offender mediation program, in Kitchener, Ontario, was established by Mennonite Central Committee workers in 1974. Many of the movement's earliest proponents were members of faith communities who designed and implemented programs in the 1970s and early 1980s. Broader community involvement in restorative justice initiatives started primarily in the 1990s. These developments were an outgrowth of a peacemaking process that has been part of North American aboriginal, First Nation, and Native American (especially Navajo) traditions for centuries, traditions that emphasize the importance of confessing one's wrongs, apologizing, forgiving, and reconciling. Indeed, in recent years the Association of Paroling Authorities International—the international association of parole boards around the globe—has featured ambitious discussions of the ways in which parole boards can promote and facilitate restorative justice.

Most restorative justice initiatives are based on several principal assumptions:

- Crime consists of more than violation of the criminal law and defiance of the authority of government.
- Crime involves disruption in a three-dimensional relationship involving the victim, the offender, and the community.
- Crime harms the victim and the community, and the primary goal should be to restore the victim and the community, repair harms, and rebuild relationships among the victim, the offender, and the community.
- The victim, the community, and the offender should all participate in determining what happens, and the government should surrender its monopoly over responses to crime.
- The disposition should be based primarily on the victim's and the community's needs and not solely on the offender's needs or culpability, the danger the offender presents, or the offender's criminal history.

Restorative justice programs take various forms, the most common of which include victim-offender mediation, conferencing (a process that brings together the victim, offender, and family and friends of both to discuss the impact of the crime), and circles (a long-standing Native American and First Nation practice in which community members meet with the offender to discuss the crime and offer opportunities for reparation, restitution, and community service). Contemporary examples of restorative justice programs include crime repair crews, victim intervention programs, conferencing, victim-offender mediation and discussion, peacemaking circles, victim panels that address offenders, sentencing circles, community reparative boards that offenders appear before, offender competency development programs, victim empathy classes for offenders, victim-directed and citizen-involved community service by the offender, community-based support groups for crime victims, and community-based support groups for offenders.[1]

In-person meetings between prison inmates and victims are relatively rare. Most victims would find it extraordinarily difficult to meet their perpetrator face to face. But in those relatively rare instances when victims and inmates are willing to meet, and have been screened and prepared in advance by skilled professionals, the outcomes can be remarkable. The Community Justice Initiatives Association in British Columbia, Canada, once brought together an incarcerated murderer, his mother, and the victim's mother. Years earlier, as the jury deliberated the defendant's fate at the conclusion of the trial, the two mothers had happened to encounter each other in the hallway outside the courtroom. "We're in this together," the defendant's mother whispered to the victim's mother as they hugged. The victim's mother broke the embrace and said, "I must go. My family will be coming back soon and they won't understand."

Twenty years later the convicted murderer was eligible for parole. The victim's mother attended the hearing. Several months before the parole hearing, a mediator from the Restorative Opportunities Program had helped the inmate communicate with the victim's mother and daughter through a series of letters. The daughter agreed to meet the inmate in advance of the parole hearing; two program staffers filmed the meeting and brought it to the inmate's mother for a private viewing. They also showed it to the victim's mother.

After watching the video, the victim's mother was so moved by the changes she saw in the inmate that she offered to speak on his behalf at his parole hearing. She also asked to meet privately with the inmate and his mother after the hearing. Two Restorative Opportunities mediators helped the victim's mother and the inmate speak openly about the murder and its repercussions. The inmate apologized to the victim's mother for taking her son's life. The victim's mother pushed back her chair, walked around the table, hugged the inmate, and whispered to him, "I forgive you."[2]

In Rhode Island there are multiple manifestations of restorative justice. Occasionally—too rarely, I think—inmates and victims have met, along with a trained facilitator. In one instance the parents of a young murder victim met with an inmate serving a life sentence for a remarkably frank and tear-filled exchange.

In the spirit of restorative justice some inmates enroll in programs whose explicit goal is to examine the ways in which offenders' crimes affect victims. Also, some inmates are mandated to comply with restitution orders that compensate victims. Some inmates speak about their crimes and their impact to members of the public—often high school students—who are brought into the prisons for a couple of hours by restorative justice programs. The program that offers select inmates an opportunity to train dogs to assist people with disabilities is yet another example of restorative justice.

Some years ago I presided at a parole hearing for a prominent banker who was sentenced to prison following his conviction on twenty-six counts of embezzlement, conspiracy, and violation of banking laws. The inmate was the president of a loan and investment company when bank examiners determined that millions of dollars were missing from the institution. The disappearance triggered the collapse of forty-four other credit unions and savings institutions. The public was particularly incensed when the banker fled the state, became a fugitive using a disguise and false name, and ended up living on the lam far from Rhode Island before he was caught.

My parole board colleagues and I decided to release the inmate after he had served ten years of his prison sentence. As part of the parole plan, we required that he participate in a package of restorative justice efforts beyond complying with the standard court order requiring him to make monetary restitution payments. Specifically we required the offender to arrange and deliver a series of lectures to undergraduate and graduate students enrolled in college and university business programs about his unwise choices as a senior banking executive and about ethical decision-making in the business world. Responses to this parolee's lectures were enthusiastic.

On occasion incarcerated offenders have opportunities to provide community service while behind bars, a form of restorative justice that pays back that community. Training service dogs for later use by people with disabilities is a good example. Here is another: Dave Sempsrott, the Missouri inmate with whom I worked as he served his multiple life sentences for murdering his best friend, his best friend's girlfriend, and the girlfriend's four-year-old daughter, wrote to me about how pleased he was to give back to the community he had harmed so badly. Sempsrott had started working in a penitentiary job that recorded audio books for people who are blind. He wrote to me, casually describing his new tasks. Perhaps without realizing it, he slipped in several comments that clearly indicated how pleased he was to have the opportunity to help others: "It feels real good to be able to do something to make someone else's life better. I finally feel like I'm making a contribution."

||||||||||||||||||||||||||||||||||||||||||||||||||||||||||||

Isaiah Bauer appeared before the parole board for the fifth time on his twenty-five-year sentence. From hearing to hearing I felt like I was watching him grow up in prison, which he entered at age eighteen. I knew Bauer's case well, having reviewed his records multiple times and having interviewed him during several earlier parole hearings.

Bauer and his codefendant, Tony Weaver, had been arrested and charged with murder. The two had agreed to rob a local convenience store to get money to buy drugs. Weaver had a compact Beretta handgun tucked in his belt and covered by an oversized sweatshirt. Bauer and Weaver entered the store, Weaver pulled the gun out of his belt, pointed it at the clerk, and demanded that she open the cash drawer and hand over the money. The clerk yelled at the pair to get out of the store, grabbed her own handgun from under the counter, and started chasing after the pair. As Bauer and Weaver began to back away, Weaver shot the clerk and killed her. Weaver was sentenced to life in prison; Bauer received twenty-five years because he was an accomplice in a robbery that led to a murder.

Bauer's early years in prison were rather nondescript, with the exception of several disciplinary problems. He was an unusually young inmate and quite immature. He did not sign up for rehabilitation programs and was placed in segregation several times for fighting and disobeying correctional officers' orders. This is not an unusual pattern for young inmates. Often they lack the maturity and insight to manage their behavior and engage meaningfully in treatment programs.

Also, many young inmates feel vulnerable in prison; they may be picked on, sexually harassed, and assaulted. Many feel the need to put on a tough-guy persona in an effort to signal that they won't be pushed around. These inmates often sound tougher, braver, and more courageous than they actually feel. We first met Bauer after he had served a little more than eight years of his sentence. By then he was twenty-six years old. Bauer's participation in treatment programs was cursory and uneven. He had enrolled in a drug treatment program but was terminated in the fourth week when he was placed in segregation for fighting. He was on the waiting list for a violence prevention program. At this hearing the board denied Bauer's parole request and agreed to see him again in eighteen months. The board recommended that he complete both the drug treatment and violence prevention programs and come to the board with a clean disciplinary record. We also recommended that he enroll in the prison's GED program, since he had dropped out of school in the tenth grade.

At Bauer's second parole hearing the board noted that he had completed the drug treatment program and commended him for that. However, Bauer had not completed the violence prevention program; once again he had failed to complete the program because he had been placed in segregation, this time for failing to comply with a correctional officer's order to stand for the count and for cursing at the officer. Also, Bauer had not yet signed up for the GED program. The board denied his parole and agreed to see him in fifteen months.

At Bauer's third hearing the parole board noted significant progress. Since the preceding hearing Bauer had done so well that he had been invited to participate in the SCORE (Special Community Outreach Education) program run by the Department of Corrections that provides an opportunity for carefully selected inmates to share their stories with groups of teens and young adults from the community and to reflect on the ramifications of the choices these offenders had made that led to prison.[3] This program is yet another form of restorative justice, in which inmates do their best to give back to the community by trying to prevent crime.

I have had the opportunity to sit in on a number of SCORE sessions and have been impressed by the inmates' forthrightness and authenticity. When I sit in on the sessions, I typically scan faces in the audience to assess the level of engagement with the presentations. Unlike many lectures I have attended (and delivered), the inmates' presentations nearly always secure rapt attention from audiences. The inmates' stories are compelling, poignant, sad, instructive, and sometimes uplifting.

I was delighted to hear that prison staffers had invited Bauer to participate in the SCORE program. That provided me with corroborating evidence that he was maturing, actively involved in constructive prison activities and programs, and behaving well. These were good signs.

And Bauer's ratings on the formal risk assessment tool that the prison and parole board use to calculate offender risk had improved dramatically. Like many departments of corrections, Rhode Island's uses what is known as the Level of Service Inventory (LSI-R) to assess inmate risk. This is an example of parole boards' growing use of risk assessment tools based on actuarial tables as one of the many factors the boards consider. Although there are some lingering questions about the predictive validity of these instruments, as well as their sensitivity to cross-cultural differences among inmates, most corrections professionals recognize that these tools provide useful supplemental information.

The LSI-R is a validated risk–need assessment tool that identifies problem areas in an offender's life and predicts his or her risk of recidivism.[4] This detailed instrument assesses offenders across various domains that are known, based on extensive empirical research, to predict an offender's likelihood of returning to prison (criminal history, education/employment, financial circumstances, family/marital status, living accommodations, leisure/recreation patterns, companions, alcohol/drug problems, emotional/personal and criminal attitudes/orientation). Research shows that addressing these areas through rehabilitative programs in prison can ultimately reduce an offender's probability of reincarceration. The LSI-R is completed by trained assessors who conduct interviews with offenders and, when possible, verify the information through external sources.

Bauer had also signed up for the prison's GED program and had passed most of the courses. He reported struggling with the math portion of the GED, a common phenomenon among people who take the test while incarcerated; math seems to be the biggest challenge, by far.

I was impressed by Bauer's progress and blossoming insights and maturity. I asked him about his interest in continuing his SCORE-style presentations once he returned to the community:

ANSWER: I would love to do that. When I first started these presentations, I was incredibly nervous. I'd never spoken in front of any kind of group. I hadn't done well in school and I was pretty shy. I had to force myself to do this. But since the DOC [Department of Corrections] staff was so encouraging, I figured I would try. This is actually the first time I've felt successful at anything, other than committing crimes.

QUESTION: Tell us what you like about doing these presentations.

ANSWER: It's hard to explain. Before doing these sessions, I had never really told my story from the beginning. Every time I tell it, I feel like I learn something new about myself and the bad choices I've made. It can be painful, because I often feel ashamed of what I've done with my life, how I've hurt so many people.

Sometimes I feel a little guilty, like I'm getting more out of this than I give. But I know that the kids we talk to get a lot out of this, or at least most of them do. It feels really good to finally do something positive. If telling my story prevents even one bad crime, I'm happy.

At that point Bauer's attorney handed me a pile of photocopied letters that Bauer had received from teens and young adults who had visited the prison and heard him tell his story. I skimmed through them and was moved by the thoughtful and detailed testimonials. These did not seem like canned or formulaic thank-you notes. Rather, these were real letters full of specific references to Bauer's and other inmates' comments and their impact on the writers.

Bauer also talked about his recent completion of the prison's victims' impact and violence prevention programs. The trained professionals who run the programs help inmates understand the impact that their crimes have on victims. Many inmates who complete the programs report that this is the first time in their lives that they have actively and deliberately empathized with their victims. Many members of the public are shocked to learn that many inmates did not and do not think about victim impact. This is sad but true. A well-conducted victims' impact program can have powerful effects.

||||||||||||||||||||||||||||||||||||||||||||||||||||||||||

Of course, some inmates are not good candidates for restorative justice initiatives, often because they are unable or unwilling to empathize with their victims.

What causes many offenders' inability or unwillingness to empathize with their victims? This is complicated.

Most thoughtful criminal justice and mental health practitioners and scholars refer to a unique, and challenging, class of offenders as psychopaths. More technically these are known as individuals with antisocial personality disorder. Many have trauma histories that exacerbate their inability to empathize and lead them to be consumed with meeting their own needs.

Antisocial personality disorder is characterized by a long-standing pattern of disregard for other people's rights, often crossing the line and violating those rights. It usually begins in childhood or as a teen and continues into their adult lives. Most of the inmates with whom I have worked who meet these criteria were arrested as juveniles. Many were incarcerated in juvenile correctional facilities. As teens many were diagnosed with what mental health professionals call oppositional defiant disorder. Often they have had other undiagnosed or inadequately treated mental health issues such as attention deficit hyperactivity disorder, anxiety, depression, learning disabilities, and so on.[5]

Antisocial personality disorder is often referred to in popular culture as psychopathy or sociopathy. People with this diagnosis typically manifest difficulty empathizing and tend to be callous, cynical, and contemptuous of the feelings, rights, and sufferings of others. They may come across as arrogant and full of overweening self-confidence and hubris. Many also come across as excessively opinionated, self-assured, or cocky. They may display a glib, superficial charm and can be quite voluble and verbally facile; some use technical terms or jargon in order to impress people. Some of these individuals tend to exploit others, particularly in sexual relationships.

According to the American Psychiatric Association's formal diagnostic manual, antisocial personality disorder is diagnosed when a person's pattern of antisocial behavior has occurred since age fifteen (although only adults eighteen years or older can be diagnosed with this disorder) and meets a number of the following criteria:

- failure to conform to social norms with respect to lawful behaviors as indicated by repeatedly performing acts that are grounds for arrest;

- deceitfulness, as indicated by repeated lying, use of aliases, or conning others for personal profit or pleasure;
- impulsivity or failure to plan ahead;
- irritability and aggressiveness, as indicated by repeated physical fights or assaults;
- reckless disregard for the safety of themselves or others;
- consistent irresponsibility, shown by repeated failure to sustain consistent work behavior or honor financial obligations; and
- lack of remorse, as demonstrated by being indifferent to or rationalizing having hurt, mistreated, or stolen from another.[6]

In most important respects this characterization has been around for decades. What is truly fascinating is that in recent years, a group of talented and creative researchers have found compelling evidence that key organic features of many offenders' brain physiology and structure are linked to antisocial personality disorder. This is one of the most important developments in the criminal justice field. This evidence suggests that for some—perhaps many—offenders, their harmful conduct is not simply a matter of unthinking, insensitive, and willfully exploitative choices. Organic brain factors may be key, propelling the behavior. Thus criminal conduct is not always a matter of callous free will. It may be organically driven and a function of complex neurobiology.

Recent research shows that when people with psychopathy imagine others are experiencing pain, brain regions associated with empathy and concern for others do not activate or connect with brain areas involved in emotional processing and decision-making. In one major study researchers investigated the neurological roots of the disorder by examining 121 inmates at a medium security prison in the United States. The inmates were divided into highly psychopathic, moderately psychopathic, and weakly psychopathic groups on the basis of a widely used diagnostic tool.

These researchers scanned the brains of the participants while showing them images depicting physical pain, such as a finger getting caught in a door or a toe caught under a heavy object. The participants were told to imagine the accident was happening to them or to someone else. They were also shown images of neutral objects, such as a hand on a doorknob.

When the highly psychopathic individuals imagined the accidents were happening to them, their brains lit up in the anterior insula, the anterior midcingulate cortex, the somatosensory cortex, and the right amygdala—all areas involved in empathy. The response was quite significant, suggesting psychopathic individuals are sensitive to thoughts of pain.

But when the highly psychopathic inmates imagined the accident was happening to others, their brains failed to light up in the regions associated with empathy. In fact, an area involved in pleasure, the ventral striatum, lit up instead. Furthermore, these individuals showed abnormal connectivity between the insula and the ventromedial prefrontal cortex, an area important for empathetic decision-making.

In contrast the less psychopathic individuals showed more normal brain activation and connectivity in these areas. The patterns of brain activation and connectivity in highly psychopathic individuals suggest that they did not experience empathy when imagining the pain of others and may have taken pleasure in it. Some research has shown that some psychopaths can feel empathy when explicitly asked to, suggesting this ability to understand another person's feelings may be repressed rather than missing entirely in psychopathic individuals.[7]

In my experience one of the major appeals of restorative justice programs is that they can enhance offenders' ability to empathize. Yes, some participants may simply go through the motions, but many offenders are earnest about giving back to or paying back their victims. Often, I found, inmates experience a deep sense of shame about their criminal conduct and appreciate an opportunity to grapple with and expiate this shame. That was certainly the case for Isaiah Bauer.

Some professionals refer to this process more formally as reintegrative shaming. The theory of reintegrative shaming grew out of various Asian policing and educational practices, various regulatory practices for responding to corporate crime in Asia and the West, and a number of Western parenting practices. According to this perspective, which is based in part on classic child development theory regarding the importance of moral reasoning, both laissez-faire parenting that fails to confront and disapprove of children's misconduct *and* punitively authoritarian parenting may produce many delin-quents and, ultimately, adult criminals.[8]

Restorative justice conferences or meetings that focus on reinte-grative shaming invite victims and their supporters (typically, fam-ily members and/or close friends) to meet with the offender and the people who care about and are respected by the offender. This group engages in a discussion about the crime, focusing especially on the feelings and experiences of the people who were harmed. The group brainstorms the ways in which the harm might be repaired and any steps that should be taken to prevent recidivism.

A key feature of the group discussion is the subject of shame, par-ticularly the shame that offenders feel in the eyes of the people they care about and trust the most: family and friends (rather than law en-forcement officials and the media, for example). The concept of rein-tegrative shaming builds on philosophies that have existed for hun-dreds of years, such as those of the Maori, the indigenous people of New Zealand. Maori perspectives on *whanau* (extended family) con-ferences make frequent references to the words for shame (*whakama*) and healing, or embrace. In Maori tradition what is most important is the shame that comes from disappointing one's extended family.

Many scholars believe that the shame that many offenders experi-ence can, if left unresolved, be a destructive emotion that leads of-fenders to attack others, purposely harm themselves physically, avoid people, or withdraw from people who are important in their lives. What restorative justice provides, when it works well, is a process of "constructive conflict" that enables offenders to deal constructively with and confront the shame they experience when they commit seri-ous crimes. In a fascinating assessment of the effects of constructive conflict facilitated by the use of group conferences in New Zealand, researchers found that the minority of offenders who failed to apolo-gize during conferences were three times more likely to reoffend than those who had apologized.[9]

I have met some offenders who committed serious crimes, feel deep shame for their actions, and are willing to admit it, often accom-panied by tears. However, in prison settings inmates may be loathe to admit their shame for fear of showing any sign of weakness that other offenders may exploit to their advantage. Also, some inmates find that dwelling on their terrible crimes is simply too painful emotionally. This was certainly the case for Dave Sempsrott, which he expressed in one of his letters about the night he murdered three people. In responding to a question I posed concerning the extent to which he reflected on his crimes, he wrote:

> Some of my thoughts frighten me. I've always thought of myself as a very easy going person, going out of my way to make others like me. Next thing I realized, I was going to trial for killing three people, one a four-year-old girl. That was a hell of a shock. I've been trying to keep my mind void of anything to do with it, but it doesn't work. It will slip in at any time, and there seems to be nothing I can do to combat it. . . .
>
> I really hate playing the role of killer in here. Unfortunately, it's the only way I can survive. Unless I was to tell everyone how I really feel about murder, they have no way of knowing how I feel. It's enough to make them leery of you. Actually, I'm scared to death in here, but I can't let that show. You know as well as I do what would happen if people knew that. Each day is a danger.

This helped me begin to understand why Dave was never willing to talk to me about the murders he had committed when we met in person in prison. The handwritten letters he sent me for nearly three decades were much safer. His sense of shame felt intolerable to him; he could not bear it.

IIIIIIIIIIIIIIIIIIIIIIIIIIIIIIIIIIIIIIIIIIIIIIIIIIIIIIIIIIIII

One of the most painful, and recurring, scenes in my prison work involved inmates with serious mental illness. These are the inmates with significant histories of schizophrenia, bipolar disorder, and so on, often with previous psychiatric hospitalization. I often wonder whether incarcerating them is just.

Elmore Showalter sat down at the parole board hearing table in the High Security facility. He had what I describe as "the look": a vacant stare, no eye contact, spoke in a wooden manner, and did not smile. I guessed—it turned out I was right—that he was heavily medicated with neuroleptics, antipsychotic medication.

Showalter was serving a six-year sentence for assaulting a man with a knife in downtown Providence. He lived at a shelter for people who are homeless and was considered disabled because of his significant psychiatric challenges. When the social safety net was working, Showalter received counseling and medication from a community mental health center. When the system was not working, Showalter missed appointments, abused alcohol, stopped taking his medication, and had no one to help him access the care he needed. That was when, predictably, his life would spiral out of control. His life resembled a rollercoaster ride with some rather steep twists and turns, peaks and valleys.

About two years earlier, Showalter was not in good psychiatric shape. He had relapsed on alcohol and stopped going to the mental health center for counseling and medication. One evening he was wandering around an urban park where people who live in shelters or on the street sometimes congregate. Showalter encountered a man who, he said, had stolen money from him about a year earlier when both resided at a shelter. Showalter, who had been drinking that evening, confronted the man. The dispute escalated, and the two started punching and wrestling with each other. In court Showalter testified that at the time he was hearing voices telling him to attack his victim.

During the fracas Showalter pulled out a large Swiss army knife and stabbed his victim. When the police arrested Showalter, he was ranting in what the arresting officer described as an "incoherent tirade with lots of mumblings." The police locked Showalter up and, when it became clear that he had serious mental illness, obtained court authorization to transfer him to the state's forensic unit for evaluation and treatment. After his psychiatric symptoms were stabilized, primarily with the help of medication, Showalter was transferred to the prison and held for trial. Despite his attorney's best efforts to get Showalter acquitted based on his serious psychiatric illness and diminished capacity, he was found guilty of felony assault and sentenced to prison.

In what strikes me as a gross injustice, many inmates with serious psychiatric illness that clearly led to their crimes are housed in prisons rather than treated in psychiatric facilities. One commonly heard observation among criminal justice professionals is that deinstitutionalization of psychiatric hospitals, which began in earnest in the 1960s, has led to the overpopulation in today's prisons of people with significant mental illness. What was once celebrated—especially in the 1960s and 1970s—as the much-needed emptying of public psychiatric hospitals, where many patients were abused and warehoused, is now decried because of the lack of truly comprehensive community-based mental health services for many people who need them, usually because of funding constraints. Too many people who are not able to access services decompensate; when their lives fall apart, some commit crimes. Often prison is the placement of last resort.

Deinstitutionalization, a noble ideal, began in the mid-1950s with the widespread introduction of chlorpromazine, commonly known as Thorazine, the first effective antipsychotic medication, and received a major impetus in the mid-1960s with the enactment of the federal Medicaid and Medicare programs, which funded psychiatric services.

Deinstitutionalizing people with severe mental illness qualifies as one of the most significant social movements in American history. In 1955 slightly more than 500,000 patients with severe mental illness were living in the nation's public psychiatric hospitals. By 1994 that population had been reduced to fewer than 100,000 patients, a dramatic decrease, especially considering the significant increase in the U.S. population during this period.[10]

Most of those who were deinstitutionalized from the nation's public psychiatric hospitals had serious mental illness. About half had been diagnosed with schizophrenia. Another 10 to 15 percent had been diagnosed with manic depressive illness and severe depression. An additional 10 to 15 percent had been diagnosed with organic brain diseases—epilepsy, strokes, Alzheimer's disease, and brain damage resulting from trauma. The remaining individuals residing in public psychiatric hospitals had such conditions as mental retardation with psychosis, autism, other psychiatric disorders of childhood, and alcoholism and drug addiction with concurrent brain damage.

While many high-quality community-based mental health programs exist, the magnitude of deinstitutionalization created a crisis by discharging people from public psychiatric hospitals without ensuring that they received the medication and rehabilitation services necessary for them to live successfully in the community. When people with serious mental illness are arrested, charged with crimes, and incarcerated, they often end up in what can only be described as the least hospitable environment imaginable for the constructive treatment of mental illness.

By the early 1980s interest in the problem of incarcerating people with serious mental illness was growing and became the subject of several major studies. Researchers in Chicago used a structured psychiatric interview in meeting with 728 people arrested and jailed and found that 6.4 percent met diagnostic criteria for schizophrenia, mania, or major depression. In Philadelphia researchers interviewed ninety-six randomly selected admissions to the jail and reported that 4.6 percent had schizophrenia or manic depressive illness. Several additional studies show that when inmates are actually interviewed in depth, a higher percentage are found to be seriously mentally ill.[11]

All of us are aware of the steady litany of major news stories suggesting that people with major psychiatric illnesses have committed horrific crimes (although most people with major mental illness do not commit serious crimes). In Aurora, Colorado, James Holmes, who clearly suffers from major mental illness, shot many people in a movie theater on July 12, 2012, killing twelve and wounding seventy. And there are other notorious people with mental illness who committed heinous crimes. David "Son of Sam" Berkowitz murdered six people and wounded others in New York City in 1976–77. John Hinckley attempted to kill President Ronald Reagan in 1981. Jeffrey Dahmer committed the rape, murder, and dismemberment of seventeen men and boys; he ate part of at least one before he was arrested in 1991. Kenneth Bianchi, known along with his cousin Angelo Buono Jr. as the Hillside Stranglers, was tried and convicted in 1979 for the rape and murder of twelve victims. Issei Sagawa killed and ate a Dutch exchange student studying in Japan in 1981. John Wayne Gacy raped and murdered thirty-three men and teenage boys between 1972 and 1978. Charles Whitman climbed the University of Texas tower with an arsenal and shot indiscriminately at people in and around the tower in 1966. Also that year Richard Speck forced his way into a house for student nurses in a Chicago suburb, herded six women into a bedroom, made them lie down, tied them up, and then raped, stabbed, and strangled them one by one. In 1969 Charles Manson and a number of his followers, known as "The Family," drove to the residence of Sharon Tate, the pregnant wife of the film director Roman Polanski, and brutally murdered Tate and several guests. Eric Harris and Dylan Klebold walked into Columbine High School, where they were students, tossed homemade bombs throughout the school, and fired from a large arsenal, killing twelve students and one teacher before committing suicide in 1999. Gary Ridgway, known as the Green River Killer, was caught in 2001 and initially convicted of forty-eight murders and later confessed to nearly twice that number. Dennis Rader, known as the BTK killer (bind, torture, kill), murdered ten people in Kansas in the 1970s through the 1990s before he was caught in 2005. He sent letters describing the details of the killings to police and local news outlets during the period in which the murders took place. The legal proceedings in these cases produced compelling evidence of serious psychiatric disturbance.

The intersection of major mental illness and heinous crime is not a new story. These infamous cases, along with thousands of others that are not well known, should lead us to think long and hard about the harm we cause when prisons become the default option when people with psychiatric illness commit serious crimes. Certainly such dangerous people should not be released into the community. But believing that incarceration, rather than skilled mental health treatment in a secure setting, is the answer is both shortsighted and naive.

||||||||||||||||||||||||||||||||||||||||||||||||||||||||||

One of my major justice-related concerns has to do with the impact of placing misbehaving inmates with major psychiatric problems in long-term segregation, otherwise known as solitary confinement.[12] It is well known that imprisoning people with mental illness may be necessary at times because of the threat they pose, but it often exacerbates their psychiatric symptoms. Placing inmates with mental illness in solitary confinement compounds the problem and often worsens their symptoms and threatening behaviors.

I certainly understand that dangerous inmates who have mental illness cannot circulate in the prison's general population; that poses serious risks to other inmates and increases the likelihood that inmates with psychiatric problems will be harassed and assaulted. These inmates require intensive psychiatric help, not lengthy isolation for punitive purposes.

For most of the twentieth century, prisoners' stays in solitary confinement were relatively short. More recently increasing numbers of inmates are locked in segregation cells for twenty-three hours each day, often in tiny cells with solid steel doors. Many of these inmates live with extensive surveillance and security controls, no ordinary social interaction or natural light, abnormal environmental stimuli, and often only three to five hours a week of so-called recreation—alone in empty, caged enclosures. During one parole board hearing, an inmate told us, "I'm going mad in that cell. I'm not sure how much more of this I can take. I'm talking to myself. I'm hearing things that aren't real. I've never been like this before. Man, it's bad."

In segregation there is little, if any, educational, vocational, or other programs. Segregated inmates are handcuffed and frequently shackled every time they leave their cells. As segregation has become more common, so too have questions about its psychological impact, particularly when an inmate with mental illness has long-term stays in segregation.

I saw inmates who had been placed in segregation in two types of circumstances. Prisons use disciplinary segregation when inmates violate rules. Among the inmates I met, the most common infractions arose from fights with other inmates, disobeying correctional officers' orders and being verbally abusive toward them, possessing contraband such as drugs or weapons, using drugs, engaging in sexual activity with visitors or other inmates, and being in an unauthorized location.

Then there is what is known as administrative segregation. This is used when inmates pose a threat to staffers or other inmates, or when inmates—especially those who have some sort of notoriety—are at risk of being harmed by other inmates.

By now we have solid research evidence documenting the impact that long-term segregation has on a significant number of inmates. Common consequences include anxiety, panic, depression, insomnia, perceptual distortions and hallucinations, obsessions, disorientation, self-harming behaviors, and aggression. Among those inmates with a history of psychosis, exacerbation of psychotic symptoms is not uncommon, including worsening of delusions and hallucinations.

Ironically mental health professionals are often unable to address the psychiatric harm offenders suffer when they are placed in segregation for long periods of time. Mental health services in segregation units are typically limited to psychotropic medication, a mental health professional who stops at the cell front to ask how the prisoner is doing (typically known as mental health rounds), and occasional meetings in private with a clinician. Individual therapy, group therapy, educational, recreational, and other therapeutic interventions are usually not available because of safety risks, insufficient resources, and rules requiring prisoners to remain in their cells. In short, this is a toxic mix and often a recipe for psychiatric disaster.

This issue has come to the courts in cases in which litigants, often in the form of a class-action lawsuit, challenge the segregation of inmates with serious mental illness as unconstitutionally cruel because of the psychological harm it can inflict. Federal courts have issued rulings or accepted settlements that prohibit or sharply curtail the practice. International treaty bodies and human rights experts, including the United Nations Human Rights Committee, the United Nations Committee against Torture, and the United Nations Special Rapporteur on Torture, have concluded that solitary confinement may amount to cruel, inhuman, or degrading treatment in violation of the International Covenant on Civil and Political Rights and the Convention against Torture and other Cruel, Inhuman, and Degrading Treatment or Punishment.

A United Nations expert on torture recently called on all countries to ban the solitary confinement of prisoners except in exceptional circumstances and for as short a time as possible, with an absolute prohibition in the case of juveniles and people with mental disabilities. Juan E. Méndez, the UN Special Rapporteur on torture, told the General Assembly's committee that deals with social, humanitarian and cultural affairs that the practice could amount to torture.

Segregation, isolation, separation, cellular, lockdown, Supermax, the hole, Secure Housing Unit . . . whatever the name, solitary confinement should be banned by States as a punishment or extortion technique. Solitary confinement is a harsh measure which is contrary to rehabilitation, the aim of the penitentiary system. Considering the severe mental pain or suffering solitary confinement may cause, it can amount to torture or cruel, inhuman or degrading treatment or punishment when used as a punishment, during pre-trial detention, indefinitely or for a prolonged period, for persons with mental disabilities or juveniles. In the exceptional circumstances in which its use is legitimate, procedural safeguards must be followed. I urge States to apply a set of guiding principles when using solitary confinement.[13]

||||||||||||||||||||||||||||||||||||||||||||||||||||||||

Brenda Hunter, thirty-seven, was serving a four-year sentence for assault. At age nineteen she was diagnosed with paranoid schizophrenia. Hunter received disability payments because of her mental illness and lived in a group home for people with psychiatric challenges.

When she was thirty-four, Hunter experienced what mental health professionals refer to as decompensation: her symptoms reappeared with significant exacerbation. Hunter became more and more paranoid. One afternoon, while helping a group home staffer make dinner for residents, Hunter began to hear voices. She accused the staffer of poisoning the food. The staffer tried to calm Hunter, to no avail. Hunter grabbed a kitchen knife and stabbed the staffer in her torso. The staffer survived, although she required surgery and was traumatized.

Hunter was sentenced to prison. The prison's psychologist and psychiatrist evaluated her soon after her admission and placed her on medication. About three weeks later Hunter argued with another inmate about use of the day room telephone and assaulted her. Hunter was placed in segregation for thirty days. During her segregation stay, according to the prison's disciplinary reports, Hunter was disciplined for relentless cursing at correctional officers about how they were poisoning her food.

By the time Hunter met with the parole board, she was reasonably stable on medication and had not had any disciplinary problems in months. It was clear to me that Hunter would be better served in a psychiatric program that would help her manage her psychiatric symptoms, provide supportive services, and help her transition to the community. The board voted to parole Hunter to a well-regarded mental health program about six months before the end of her sentence. For me that was justice in action.

The debate about the detrimental impact of segregation often centers on alleged violations of the Eighth Amendment to the U.S. Constitution. In my experience the vast majority of prison staffers, especially correctional officers, treat inmates fairly and with respect and do not abuse them.

However, there are noteworthy exceptions in every prison system, including Rhode Island's. Although I never witnessed severe inmate abuse firsthand, correctional officers have been disciplined and, in several cases, indicted, convicted in criminal court, and, ironically, sentenced to serve time in the very prison in which they once worked. Here is one account from the *Providence (RI) Journal*:

> In a tense, emotionally-charged courtroom, Superior Court Judge Daniel A. Procaccini on Thursday sentenced a former ranking corrections officer to 18 months in prison for assaulting and abusing inmates at the Adult Correctional Institutions.
>
> Gualter Botas, 44, of Johnston, an ex-captain who ran minimum security, apologized to his family, fellow corrections officers, the state and the court for his behavior in 2005 and 2006 that led to his conviction on seven counts of simple assault.
>
> "I look back at that time and wonder who that person was," said Botas, who was composed as he read a prepared statement.
>
> . . . Procaccini shot down a motion to reduce the sentence or have him [Botas] remain at home with an electronic monitoring bracelet on his ankle. . . .
>
> The sentencing ends the criminal case that has been slowly wending its way through the court system for five years. On Aug. 1, 2008, a Superior Court jury found Botas and Kenneth Viveiros, 65, a former ACI lieutenant, guilty of 11 counts of simple assault and battery for striking four inmates. . . .
>
> The trial stretched three weeks and featured 24 witnesses including the four inmates. . . . Two months later, Procaccini rejected motions from Botas and Viveiros who sought new trials, saying the jury had sufficient evidence to find them guilty of assaulting the inmates. He also

recalled the testimony of [someone] who claimed that Botas grabbed his testicles and "pulled down real hard."[14]

Rhode Island prisons are hardly alone with regard to staffers' occasional abuse of inmates.

- A former corrections officer admitted to sexually assaulting five female inmates while working at a Pennsylvania prison between 2002 and 2011. He was sentenced to up to eight years in prison.
- A former correctional officer in the Baltimore City Detention Center was sentenced to more than two years in prison after admitting that she had sexual relationships with two inmates.
- Four former Georgia guards were sentenced in federal court for their part in the beating of inmates in 2010 and subsequent cover-up.
- A former California prison guard was sentenced to more than four years in federal prison for abusing inmates. He shackled two prisoners and took them in a van to the prison's administrative segregation unit. When they arrived, the officer threw the shackled inmates from the van. Because their hands were bound, the inmates were unable to break their falls and suffered injuries.
- Two Oregon jail staffers were sentenced to prison after being convicted of having sex with the same inmate.[15]

This is a mere fraction of the abhorrent instances of prison staffer misconduct and inmate abuse.

Cases involving inmate abuse, inappropriate use of segregation and isolation that exacerbate mental illness symptoms, and unacceptable prison conditions force me to think hard about what justice means and to stare squarely at the prison-based implications of the Eighth Amendment, which prohibits "cruel and unusual punishment." A number of key court cases over the years have established parameters concerning Eighth Amendment violations involving prison inmates. In a line of cases starting with *Estelle v. Gamble* in 1976, the Supreme Court has ruled that inmates' constitutional rights may have been violated if inmates are exposed to unconstitutional conditions that satisfy two key elements. First, inmate plaintiffs must show as an objective matter that they suffered a "deprivation [that was] sufficiently serious." Second, they must show that officials acted with a "sufficiently culpable state of mind," that of "deliberate indifference," which the court has defined as actual awareness of the risk.

On November 9, 1973, J. W. Gamble, an inmate of the Texas Department of Corrections, injured his back while performing a prison work assignment. Although he complained numerous times about his injury and received some pills, the guards accused him of malingering. In January the disciplinary committee placed Gamble in solitary confinement for refusing to work. On February 4, 1974, he asked to see a doctor for chest pains and blackouts. Almost twelve hours later a medical assistant saw him and had him hospitalized.

The next morning, after an electrocardiogram, Gamble was placed on quinidine for treatment of irregular cardiac rhythm and moved to administrative segregation. On February 7, after experiencing pain in his chest, left arm, and back, Gamble asked to see a doctor and was refused. The next day he was refused again. After finally seeing the doctor again on February 9 and being given quinidine, Gamble swore out a complaint that the staff had "subjected him to cruel and unusual punishment in violation of the Eighth Amendment."

In *Estelle v. Gamble* (1976) the court concluded that deliberate indifference to serious medical needs of prisoners constitutes "unnecessary and wanton infliction of pain," whether the indifference is displayed by prison doctors in their response to the prisoner's need or by prison guards who deny or delay access to treatment or interfere with the treatment. The court, however, ruled that "every claim by a prisoner that he has not received adequate medical treatment" does not constitute a violation of the Eighth Amendment. An "inadvertent failure to provide adequate medical care" is not "an unnecessary and wanton infliction of pain" or "repugnant to the conscience of mankind." Only deliberate indifference "can offend 'evolving standards of decency' in violation of the Eighth Amendment." Because Gamble saw medical personnel seventeen times over three months, the court did not find this a violation of the Eighth Amendment, ruling, "A medical decision not to order an X ray or like measures does not represent cruel and unusual punishment."[16]

Over the years the Supreme Court has established several tests to determine whether conditions or actions violate the Eighth Amendment:

- Do the actions or conditions offend concepts of "decency and human dignity and precepts of civilization which Americans profess to possess"?
- Are the actions or conditions "disproportionate to the offense"?
- Does the punishment violate "fundamental standards of good conscience and fairness"?
- Is the punishment unnecessarily cruel?
- Does the punishment go beyond legitimate penal purposes?[17]

When judges sentence people to prison, they place offenders in potentially dangerous conditions while depriving them of the ability to provide for their own care and protection. The state therefore has a duty to protect prisoners from serious physical and psychological harm. This obligation, which amounts to an ongoing duty to provide for prisoners' basic human needs, is described by lawyers as the state's "carceral burden" (the term derives from the Latin for "in prison," *in carcerem*). Prison conditions are considered cruel when the state is indifferent to its obligation, fails to carry this burden, and thereby causes serious harm to prisoners. The carceral burden allows society to remove certain individuals from the community but only on the condition that the state assumes its obligation to meet the basic human needs of the people who are incarcerated and to treat them fairly.

Several other landmark Eighth Amendment cases changed the way prisoners can be held in segregation and isolation. In one of the earliest cases to raise issues about the Eighth Amendment, *Holt v. Sarver* (1971), a U.S. District Court in Arkansas found "solitary confinement or close confinement in isolation units of prisons not unconstitutional per se, but, depending on circumstances, it may violate the Eighth and Fourteenth Amendments." Isolation cells in an Arkansas prison were used for prisoners who broke rules, those who needed protective custody to separate them from other inmates, and those who were general escape or security risks or who were awaiting trial on additional charges. Confinement in isolation cells was not considered "solitary confinement" in the conventional sense of the term.

The U.S. District judge found that "if confinement of that type is to serve any useful purpose, it must be rigorous, uncomfortable, and unpleasant. However, there are limits to the rigor and discomfort of close confinement which a state may not constitutionally exceed." The court found that the confinement of inmates in these isolation cells, which were "overcrowded, dirty, unsanitary, and pervaded by bad odors from toilets, constituted cruel and unusual punishment." The judge also stated that "prolonged confinement" of numbers of men in the same cell under unsanitary, dangerous conditions was "mentally and emotionally traumatic as well as physically uncomfortable. It is hazardous to health. It is degrading and debasing; it offends modern sensibilities, and, in the court's estimation, amounts to cruel and unusual punishment."

In addition, those Arkansas inmates who were not in isolation slept together in barracks where many of the inmates had weapons and attacked each other. While the court recognized that assaults, fights, and killings occurred in all prisons, it found that parts of the state prison system had not taken reasonable precautions. Prisoners should at least be "able to fall asleep at night without fear of having their throats cut before morning, and the state has failed to discharge a constitutional duty in failing to take steps to enable them to do so."

The U.S. Supreme Court reviewed the case in 1978. The chief question before the court was whether more than thirty days in isolation could be considered "cruel and unusual punishment" under the U.S. Constitution. The court affirmed the U.S. District judge's findings and rulings.[18] In another landmark case, *Hutto v. Finney* (1978), the U.S. Supreme Court addressed isolation conditions in prison, again in Arkansas. The state sentenced inmates to punitive isolation in extremely small cells for an indeterminate period, with their status reviewed at the end of each fourteen-day period. While most inmates were released within fourteen days, many remained in those small cells for weeks or months, depending on their attitudes as appraised by prison personnel. Usually the inmates shared a cell with one other inmate, and at times three or four were together, causing them to sleep on the floor. Justice John Paul Stevens wrote the opinion affirming the conclusion of the district court and the appellate court that the Arkansas prison conditions constituted cruel and unusual punishment. In another important case, *Rhodes v. Chapman* (1981), the

Supreme Court ruled that housing prisoners in double cells was not cruel and unusual punishment. The justices maintained that:

> conditions of confinement, as constituting the punishment at issue, must not involve the wanton and unnecessary infliction of pain, nor may they be grossly disproportionate to the severity of the crime warranting imprisonment. But conditions that cannot be said to be cruel and unusual under contemporary standards are not unconstitutional. To the extent such conditions are restrictive and even harsh, they are part of the penalty that criminals pay for their offenses against society.

The court concluded that the Constitution "does not mandate comfortable prisons," and only those "deprivations denying the 'minimal civilized measure of life's necessities'" violate the Eighth Amendment.

In two later cases the Supreme Court held that unpleasant or inadequate prison conditions and poor medical care did not constitute cruel and unusual punishment unless deliberate indifference by the authorities could be demonstrated. The court established this principle in *Wilson v. Seiter* (1991) when it upheld the judgment of a lower court that prisoners "claiming that conditions of confinement constituted cruel and unusual punishment were required to show deliberate indifference on the part of prison officials." Pearly L. Wilson, the petitioner, "alleged overcrowding, excessive noise, insufficient locker storage space, inadequate heating and cooling, improper ventilation, unclean and inadequate restrooms, unsanitary dining facilities and food preparation, and housing with mentally and physically ill inmates" but proved "at best" that the authorities were negligent. The court found that Wilson had insufficient grounds for claiming Eighth Amendment protection.

In *Helling v. McKinney* (1993) the court ruled that a Nevada inmate had the right to bring a court action because he had been assigned to a cell with another prisoner who smoked five packs of cigarettes daily, and he had not been informed of the health hazards that he could incur from secondhand smoke. Quoting its 1989 decision in *DeShaney v. Winnebago County Dept. of Social Services*, the court declared:

When the state takes a person into its custody and holds him there against his will, the Constitution imposes upon it a corresponding duty to assume some responsibility for his safety and general well-being. . . . The rationale for this principle is simple enough: when the state by the affirmative exercise of its power so restrains an individual's liberty that it renders him unable to care for himself, and, at the same time fails to provide for his basic human needs—e.g., food, clothing, shelter, medical care, and reasonable safety—it transgresses the substantive limits on state action set by the Eighth Amendment.

The justices asserted that prison administrators could not

ignore a condition of confinement that is sure or very likely to cause serious illness and needless suffering the next week or month or year. In *Hutto v. Finney* (437 U.S. 678, 1978) we noted that inmates in punitive isolation were crowded into cells and that some of them had infectious maladies such as hepatitis and venereal disease. This was one of the prison conditions for which the Eighth Amendment required a remedy, even though it was not alleged that the likely harm would occur immediately and even though the possible infection might not affect all of those exposed. . . . Nor can we hold that prison officials may be deliberately indifferent to the exposure of inmates to a serious, communicable disease on the ground that the complaining inmate shows no serious current symptoms.

With specific respect to cases involving abuse of inmates by correctional officers, in *Whitley v. Albers* (1986) the Supreme Court ruled that guards, during prison disturbances or riots, must balance the need "to maintain or restore discipline" through force against the risk of injury to inmates. Those situations require prison officials "to act quickly and decisively" and allow guards and administrators leeway in their actions. In *Whitley* a prisoner was shot in the knee during an attempt to rescue a hostage. The court found that the injury suffered by the prisoner was not cruel and unusual punishment under the circumstances.

In another case involving correctional officers' treatment of inmates, *Hudson v. McMillian* (1991), Keith Hudson, an inmate at the state penitentiary in Angola, Louisiana, argued with Jack McMillian, a guard. McMillian placed the inmate in handcuffs and shackles to take him to the administrative lockdown area. One guard "punched Hudson in the mouth, eyes, chest, and stomach," while another guard "held the inmate in place and kicked and punched him from behind." During the beating Arthur Mezo, the supervising officer on duty, looked on and warned the two guards "not to have too much fun." Hudson sued, accusing the guards of cruel and unusual punishment.

A magistrate found that the guards used "force when there was no need to do so," and the supervisor allowed their conduct, thus violating the Eighth Amendment. The Court of Appeals for the Fifth Circuit, however, reversed the decision, ruling that inmates claiming use of excessive force in violation of the Eighth Amendment must prove (1) significant injury; (2) resulting "directly and only from the use of force that was clearly excessive to the need"; (3) the excessiveness of which was objectively unreasonable; and (4) that the action constituted an unnecessary and wanton infliction of pain." The Court of Appeals agreed that the use of force was unreasonable and was a clearly excessive and unnecessary infliction of pain. However, the Court of Appeals found against Hudson because his injuries were "minor" and "required no medical attention." *Hudson v. McMillian* reached the U.S. Supreme Court, which held that the use of excessive physical force against a prisoner may constitute cruel and unusual punishment even though the inmate does not suffer serious injury.[19]

No one wants to be sentenced to prison. For people who need to be imprisoned—to protect the public and to serve justice—we have a fundamental duty to ensure that their conditions of incarceration are free of abuse and discrimination. We must continue to hold prisons to the high, and essential, standard established by the Eighth Amendment to the U.S. Constitution. These protections must be more than an ideal—they must be reality as well.

‖‖‖

Perhaps the most compelling, overarching issue concerning prison-based justice is the overwhelming rate at which the United States incarcerates offenders, especially when compared with other nations. And we cannot ignore compelling evidence of racial and ethnic disparities in our incarceration rates.

People often ask me whether my parole board votes were influenced by prison overcrowding, that is, whether I ever voted to release an inmate in order to reduce the prison's daily census and related expenses. My unequivocal answer is no. During my tenure on the board, I never received even the slightest form of pressure from an administrator or politician to address prison overcrowding through parole board votes. Not once. Further, I always felt obligated to make my decisions based on each case's merits, independent of census or budgetary concerns. That said, my votes did not take place in a hermetically sealed container. I thought about the broad context in which parole board decisions occur. The sum total of the board's votes does have census and budgetary consequences.

Here is the context I considered: Since 2002 the United States has had the highest incarceration rate in the world. The rate of incarceration for industrialized countries comparable to the United States hovers around 100 prisoners per 100,000 residents. In stark contrast the U.S. rate is about 700 prisoners per 100,000 residents. Most reputable studies estimate that the U.S. rate of incarceration is five to ten times higher than the rates in western Europe and other democracies.

Put simply, the United States puts people in prison for crimes that many other nations do not, mostly drug-related offenses, and keeps people in prison much longer. Yet the best available evidence indicates that these long sentences have had at best a marginal impact on crime reduction. And the consequences of incarceration reverberate across generations. Nearly three million American children have a parent in prison or jail. Growing up with an incarcerated parent can negatively affect childhood development. As but one example of the ramifications, research shows that children with fathers who have been incarcerated are nearly six times more likely to be expelled or suspended from school. It is well known among seasoned professionals that children of incarcerated parents often develop serious emotional and behavioral problems that are linked to the trauma of losing a parent to prison.

In its recent groundbreaking study of incarceration in the United States, the highly regarded National Research Council found that after decades of stability from the 1920s to the early 1970s, the rate of incarceration in the United States more than quadrupled, starting in the mid-1970s. The U.S. prison population is the largest in the world. Nearly 25 percent of the world's prisoners currently are held in U.S. prisons, although the United States accounts for about 5 percent of the world's population.

High rates of incarceration in the United States are a direct by-product of policy, ideology, and politics. These include police decisions to emphasize street-level arrests of drug dealers and the decisions of prosecutors and judges to deal more harshly with criminals.

The increase in U.S. incarceration rates since the mid-1970s is preponderantly the result of increases in both the likelihood of imprisonment and lengths of prison sentences, especially since 1990. And these increases are a product of the proliferation in nearly every state and in the federal system of laws and guidelines mandating lengthy prison sentences for drug and violent crimes and repeat offenses, as well as the enactment in more than half the states and in the federal system of three-strikes-and-you're-out and truth-in-sentencing laws. Significantly in 2015 the U.S. Justice Department released roughly six thousand inmates from federal prisons—the largest one-time release of federal prisoners in U.S. history—as part of an effort to ease overcrowding and reduce the harsh penalties given to nonviolent drug dealers in the 1980s and 1990s. Some states, most notably California, have also taken aggressive steps to reduce prison overcrowding. In 2009 a federal court ordered the state to reduce its overcrowded prison population. In 2014 California voters approved Proposition 47, a ballot measure that reclassified low-level property and drug offenses from felonies to misdemeanors. This law has led to drastic reductions in California's prison population.[20]

|||||||||||||||||||||||||||||||||||||||||||||||||||||||||||||

No discussion of social justice issues facing parole boards can ignore the racial and ethnic makeup of inmates. Racial disparities in incarceration rates are glaring. Those who are incarcerated in U.S. prisons come largely from the most disadvantaged segments of the population. They comprise mainly minority men younger than forty who are poorly educated and struggling with drug and alcohol addiction, mental and physical illness, and a lack of job preparation or experience.[21]

Mandatory prison sentences, intensified enforcement of drug laws, and long sentences have contributed not only to overall high rates of incarceration but also to extraordinary rates of incarceration in black and Latino communities in particular. Intensified enforcement of drug laws subjected blacks, more than whites, to new mandatory minimum sentences—despite evidence that blacks have lower levels of drug use and do not deal drugs at higher levels than whites. Blacks have long been more likely than whites to be arrested for crimes involving violence. Three-strikes and truth-in-sentencing laws have likely increased sentences and time served for blacks more than whites.

Although racial and ethnic disparities in incarceration are large, differences by age, sex, and education are even larger. The combined effects of racial and education disparities have produced extraordinarily high incarceration rates among young minority men with little schooling. Although most inmates are relatively young, the prison population has aged significantly as time served in prison has increased. As a result most departments of corrections are scrambling to put in place effective ways to manage a high-need, high-cost geriatric inmate population.

Incarceration rates have increased more rapidly for females than for males, especially since the early 1970s. In 1972 the prison and jail incarceration rate for men was estimated to be twenty-four times higher than that for women. By 2010 men's incarceration rate was about eleven times higher. Thus the incarceration rate for women has risen twice as rapidly as men's in the period of growing incarceration rates. The racial disparity in incarceration for women is similar to that of men. That is, a black woman is more likely than a white woman to serve time for the same offense.[22]

Many state prisons and the Federal Bureau of Prisons now operate at or above 100 percent of their capacity. With overcrowding, cells designed for a single inmate often house two and sometimes three people. Research suggests that overcrowding, particularly when it persists at high levels, is associated with a range health and behavioral problems and an increased risk of suicide. It is well known that the risk of suicide among prison inmates is much higher than in the general population.

Incarceration is also strongly correlated with negative social and economic outcomes for former prisoners and their families. I have seen evidence of this among many parolees. Men with a criminal record often experience reduced earnings and employment after prison; many employers are reluctant to hire ex-cons. Fathers' incarceration and family hardship, including housing insecurity and behavioral problems in children, are strongly related. Ambitious prisoner reentry programs, which work hard to help offenders make a good transition to the community once they leave prison, face daunting challenges.

Among the most compelling questions for us to consider, particularly in relation to the role of parole, is whether incarceration works. We know that many former inmates return to prison. The recidivism rate among parolees is much lower than for offenders who complete their sentences without early supervised release, but any recidivism rate higher than zero is more than we want.

A large body of research has studied the effects of incarceration and other criminal penalties on crime. Much of this research examines the belief that incarceration reduces crime through incapacitation and deterrence. But the accumulating corpus of rigorous research on the impact of incarceration suggests that long prison sentences have minimal impact and that shorter sentences do have a material deterrent effect on a crime-prone population. Sometimes less is more.

Much research on the effects of incarceration on future crime attempts to measure reductions in crime that might result from deterrence and incapacitation. Research on deterrence suggests that would-be offenders are deterred more by the risk of being caught than by the severity of the penalty they would face if arrested and convicted. High rates of incarceration may have reduced crime rates through incapacitation (locking up people who might otherwise commit crimes), although there is no strong consensus on the magnitude of this effect. And because offending declines markedly with age, the incapacitation effect of long sentences is likely to be small.

Many studies have attempted to estimate the combined incapacitation and deterrence effects of incarceration on crime. Most studies estimate the crime-reducing effect of incarceration to be small, and some report that the size of the effect diminishes with the length of incarceration. Overall, studies support the conclusion that the growth in incarceration rates reduced crime, but the magnitude of the crime reduction remains highly uncertain, and the evidence suggests it was unlikely to have been large.

In sum, the National Research Council's ambitious, painstaking, and comprehensive review and analysis of the nature and impact of incarceration in the United States reached the following compelling conclusions:

- The growth in incarceration rates in the United States since the mid-1970s is historically and internationally unprecedented.
- The unprecedented rise in incarceration rates can be attributed to an increasingly punitive political climate surrounding criminal justice policy during a period of increasing crime and rapid social change. This provided the context for a series of policy choices—across all branches and levels of government—that significantly increased sentence lengths, required prison time for minor offenses, and intensified punishment for drug crimes.
- The increase in incarceration may have caused a decrease in crime, but the magnitude is highly uncertain and the results of most studies suggest it was unlikely to have been large.
- The incremental deterrent effect of greater use of lengthy prison sentences is modest at best. Because recidivism rates decline markedly with age, unless lengthy prison sentences specifically target especially busy or extremely dangerous offenders, such sentences are an inefficient approach to preventing crime by incapacitation.
- The change in penal policy since the mid-1970s may have had a wide range of unwanted social costs, and the magnitude of crime reduction benefits is highly uncertain.
- People who live in poor and minority communities have always had substantially higher rates of incarceration than other groups. As a consequence the effects of harsh penal policies since the mid-1970s

have fallen most heavily on blacks and Hispanics, especially the poorest.

- Given the small crime prevention effects of long prison sentences and the potentially high financial, social, and human costs of incarceration, federal and state policy makers should revise current criminal justice policies to significantly reduce the rate of incarceration in the United States. In particular, they should reexamine policies regarding mandatory minimum sentences and long sentences. Policy makers should also take steps to improve the experience of incarcerated men and women and reduce unnecessary harm to their families and their communities.[23]

Following rigorous analysis of incarceration trends and their by-products, the scholars and practitioners assembled by the National Research Council concluded that incarceration decisions should be guided by four central principles. These make considerable sense to me and were certainly relevant to my parole decisions:

- *Proportionality: Criminal offenses should carry sentences in proportion to their seriousness.* As a parole board member, my principal task was to determine what portion of inmates' sentences they should serve. My judgments, as required by law and based on my own sensibilities, were based on the severity of the inmate's offense, victim impact, previous criminal record, insight with regard to the factors that led to the crime and criminal career, participation in rehabilitation programs, prison conduct, and release plan (home and job). Wrapped around my consideration of these important factors was my sense of what is fair in the truest sense of the term, given the crime for which the inmate was serving time. My goal, always, was proportionate justice.
- *Parsimony: The period of confinement should be sufficient but not greater than necessary to achieve the goals of sentencing policy.* I fully understand that people who commit serious crimes need to be imprisoned, both to protect the public and to convey the important message that people who harm others must face consequences. That said, consistent with the goal of proportionate justice, as a

parole board member I did my best to gauge the extent to which inmates needed to be kept in prison in order to accomplish these central goals. My votes were the result of my best efforts to weigh diverse, sometimes competing, factors related to victim impact and the simultaneous goals of punishment, rehabilitation, deterrence, and protecting the public.

- *Citizenship: The conditions and consequences of imprisonment should not be so severe or lasting as to violate one's fundamental status as a member of society.* With few exceptions—those offenders who are sentenced to life without the possibility of parole and inmates who die while incarcerated—every sentenced inmate will return to the community. They become our neighbors, the people with whom we stand in line at the supermarket, the stranger we barely notice while crossing a city street, the person pumping gas right next to us at the service station, our landscaper or roofer, and the employee who serves us food in the local restaurant. Most citizens have little clue about the vast numbers of former inmates and people on post-prison probation or parole who cross our paths every single day. Selfishly I want these individuals to behave well when they are in the community, and I firmly believe that the likelihood increases when they feel part of, and invested in, the community. The more that former inmates feel ostracized, scorned, vilified, stigmatized, and ridiculed, the greater the chances that they will go underground, withdraw, and isolate themselves, and that, I believe, greatly increases their alienation from the community and exacerbates the likelihood that they will reoffend. After all, people who feel no positive connection with their neighbors may be much less likely to empathize and consider the impact of their crime on victims.

Thinking more magnanimously, I want to live in a world where people have a sense of community engagement and shared purpose. I did what I could, through the recommendations I offered as part of an offender's parole conditions, to help former inmates reconnect with the world when they left prison and to feel invested in the commonweal and our shared quality of life. I want former inmates to care about the news; which politicians are running for office; the quality of neighborhood parks, schools, and streets; and crime rates. I want former inmates to be willing to shovel snow for a disabled neighbor and to drive a car only when they have a valid license and are not under the influence of substances. For this to happen, former inmates need to feel valued as part of the community, not like pariahs.

I certainly understand that some former inmates' crimes are so heinous and egregious that average citizens want to keep their distance. That is understandable. But wholesale ostracizing of former inmates, without any consideration of the earnest steps many have taken to atone and reform, is both counterproductive and shortsighted. Enhancing former inmates' civic engagement to the greatest extent possible is in our own self-interest—and the right thing to do.

- *Social justice: Prisons should be instruments of justice, and as such their collective effect should be to promote and not undermine society's aspirations for a fair distribution of rights, resources, and opportunities.* Parole board members' decisions do not occur in a vacuum. Yes, their principal duty is to make decisions case by case, examine the lives of individual inmates one at a time, and treat them fairly. That is what I consider to be justice at the retail level. But, for me, making decisions about parole also means being mindful of justice issues at the wholesale level. I did what I could to ensure that my decisions were sound and principled in a way that strengthens the broader social fabric and were not tinged with racism, social class bias, or any other form of discrimination.

This sentiment is echoed in one of my favorite passages in the Torah: "You shall commit no injustice in judgment; you shall not favor a poor person or respect a great man; you shall judge your fellow with righteousness" (Leviticus 19:14). For me this is the epitome of fairness and justice.

Prisons are responsible for the most vulnerable people on the planet, regardless of the severity of their crimes. I take seriously the adage that a society will be judged by how it treats its most vulnerable members, some of whom are dangerous and unappealing. Affording inmates genuine due process and fairness is not an empty cliché. At the end of every hearing day I sought to feel confident that I had administered justice, which is far more challenging than simply getting through the day's lengthy calendar. Indeed, it is hard work filled with uncertainty and all the vagaries that come with human judgment.

||||||||||||||||||||||||||||||||||||||||||||||||||||||||

Years ago I read a compelling essay by the famed philosopher of science Karl Popper entitled *Of Clouds and Clocks: An Approach to the Problem of Rationality and the Freedom of Man*. I thought about this essay often during parole board hearings. Popper's thesis is elegant: Making predictions is extraordinarily difficult. The metaphor of clocks and clouds describes the two ends of the spectrum. Clocks represent the predictable and orderly. Clouds represent the unpredictable, disorderly, amorphous, and irregular.

My clouds are intended to represent physical systems which, like gases, are highly irregular, disorderly, and more or less unpredictable. I shall assume that we have before us a schema or arrangement in which a very disturbed or disorderly cloud is placed on the left. On the other extreme of our arrangement, on its right, we may place a very reliable pendulum clock, a precision clock, intended to represent physical systems which are regular, orderly, and highly predictable in their behavior.

According to what I may call the commonsense view of things, some natural phenomena, such as the weather, or the coming and going of clouds, are hard to predict: we speak of the "vagaries of the weather." On the other hand, we speak of "clockwork precision" if we wish to describe a highly regular and predictable phenomenon.[24]

In my dreams, as a parole board member I had the ability to forecast offenders' future behavior with clock-like precision. Alas, during my waking hours I knew better; making such forecasts is much more cloud-like.

Being responsible for decisions about the fate and freedom of other human beings is daunting. During my career I have made tens of thousands of such decisions. I tried hard to make sound and principled judgments. Whether I got all of them right is hard to know, especially since I do not know how to assess what constitutes the right decision in every case. I know that I never wanted to vote to release an inmate who should not have been released because the inmate was dangerous to the community; at the same time I did not want to continue incarcerating an inmate who deserved parole and whose supervised release might decrease the likelihood of recidivism. This is a delicate balance, and every inmate I faced deserved to have me make my decisions with a deep sense of humility and fairness.

I did not work in a perfect system. Heaven knows, much about the criminal justice system needs both minor and major surgery to enhance its effectiveness and fairness. Parole boards encounter inmates at the end of what is typically a protracted series of steps in the criminal justice process, steps that are sometimes accompanied by injustices, abuses, disparities, and discrimination, none of which is acceptable.

The good news is that over the years, legions of principled, earnest, and dedicated professionals have tried their best to make things better; during my career I have seen major progress firsthand, albeit not enough. I am hopeful that we are moving in the right direction. As Martin Luther King Jr. said, "The arc of the moral universe is long, but it bends towards justice." I want that to be true.

Aristotle had many wise insights concerning justice. One is that determining justice is inherently hard and often defies precision. In his *Nicomachean Ethics* Aristotle wrote, "The mark of an educated man and a proof of his culture is that in every subject he looks for only so much precision as its nature permits."

Aristotle believed that justice consists of giving people what they deserve and that a just society is one that enables human beings to realize their highest nature and to live the good life. That sounds right to me, and that was what I aimed for every time I came face to face with an inmate who wanted more than anything to be released from prison. Aristotle also said this, and I tried to keep it in mind every step of the way: "In justice is all virtues found in sum."

NOTES

1. GETTING STARTED

1. State law required the parole board to conduct a hearing if it was the inmate's first parole hearing, even if the inmate was in segregation at the time and therefore ineligible for parole. After the first hearing the board had discretion to hold or cancel a hearing and sometimes allowed inmates to present their case, despite their segregation, in anticipation of their eventual release from prison. Often the board used this opportunity to tell the inmate what the board wanted the inmate to accomplish (completing certain programs, for example) before the next parole hearing.
2. For a broad overview of parole, including its history, see H. Abadinsky, *Probation and Parole: Theory and Practice* (Upper Saddle River, NJ: Prentice Hall, 2015).
3. For the appellate court decision in Dave Sempsrott's case (the only opinion in the case that has been published), see State of Missouri v. Sempsrott, 587 S.W.2d 630 (1979), http://law.justia.com/cases/missouri/court-of -appeals/1979/40292-0.html.
4. *Sempsrott*, 587 S.W.2d 630.
5. The phenomenon of substance-induced psychosis is discussed in S. Mathias, D. Lubman, and L. Hides, "Substance-induced Psychosis," *Journal of Clinical Psychiatry* 69 (2008): 358–67.
6. "Letters to the Editor," *Time,* October 4, 1982, 6.
7. The moral philosopher Gerald Dworkin compiled a collection of classic perspectives on free will and determinism in *Determinism, Free Will, and Moral Responsibility* (Englewood Cliffs, NJ: Prentice Hall, 1970).

8. P. de Laplace, *A Philosophical Essay on Probabilities* (London: Chapman & Hall, 1901).

9. John Hospers's comments appear in "What Means This Freedom?" in *Free Will and Determinism*, ed. B. Berofsky (New York: Harper and Row, 1966), 40.

10. Immanuel Kant's views on punishment can be found in his classic work *Die Metaphysik der Sitten* (*Metaphysics of Morals*), published in 1797.

11. Tolstoy's comments appear in A. Kenney, "Freedom, Spontaneity, and Indifference," in *Essays on Freedom of Action*, ed. Ted Honderich (London: Routledge & Kegan Paul, 1973), 89.

2. GOODNESS AND EVIL

1. For discussions of the concept of evil, see S. Baron-Cohen, *The Science of Evil: On Empathy and the Origins of Cruelty* (New York: Basic Books, 2011); M. Heinberg, *Retribution: Evil for Evil in Ethics, Law, and Literature* (Philadelphia: Temple University Press, 1990); D. Koehn, *The Nature of Evil* (New York: Palgrave Macmillan, 2005); and L. Russell, *Evil: A Philosophical Investigation* (New York: Oxford University Press, 2014).

2. For a discussion of the concepts of type I and type II errors, see N. Weiss, *Introductory Statistics*, 10th ed. (Old Tappan, NJ: Pearson, 2015).

3. Philip Hallie, *Lest Innocent Blood Be Shed: The Story of the Village of Le Chambon and How Goodness Happened There* (New York: Harper & Row, 1979), 3–4.

4. Ibid., 11.

5. I discuss my views about the causes of crime in F. Reamer, *Criminal Lessons: Case Studies and Commentary on Crime and Justice* (New York: Columbia University Press, 2003), and *Heinous Crime: Cases, Causes, and Consequences* (New York: Columbia University Press, 2005).

6. C. Erickson, *The Science of Addiction: From Neurobiology to Treatment* (New York: W. W. Norton, 2007).

7. C. Sarteschi, "Mentally Ill Offenders Involved with the U.S. Criminal Justice System: A Synthesis," *SAGE Open*, July 16, 2013, http://sgo.sagepub.com/content/3/3/2158244013497029; D. James and L. Glaze, *Mental Health Problems of Prison and Jail Inmates*, Bureau of Justice Statistics Special Report, September 2006, http://www.bjs.gov/content/pub/pdf/mhppji.pdf.

3. ON BEING A VICTIM

1. Several publications describe the impact of crime on victims: R. Davis, A. Lurigio, and S. Herman, eds., *Victims of Crime*, 4th ed. (Thousand Oaks, CA: Sage, 2013); S. Herman, *Parallel Justice for Victims of Crime* (Washington, DC: National Center for Victims of Crime, 2010); E. Hickey, *Serial Murderers and*

Their Victims, 6th ed. (Belmont, CA: Wadsworth, 2013); and A. Karmen, *Crime Victims: An Introduction to Victimology* (Belmont, CA: Wadsworth, 2013).

2. Karmen, *Crime Victims*.

3. The decision may be found at 410 U.S. 614 (1973).

4. L. Herrington et al., *President's Task Force on Victims of Crime: Final Report*, December 1982, http://www.ovc.gov/publications/presdntstskforcrprt/welcome .html.

5. See Payne v. Tennessee, 501 U.S. 808 (1991).

6. For an overview of diverse perspectives on the nature of forgiveness, see C. Griswold, *Forgiveness: A Philosophical Exploration* (Cambridge: Cambridge University Press, 2007), and M. McCullough, K. Pargament, and C. Thoresen, eds., *Forgiveness: Theory, Research, and Practice* (New York: Guilford, 2000).

7. A good general source on forgiveness is R. Helmick and R. Petersen, eds., *Reconciliation: Religion, Public Policy, and Conflict Transformation* (Radnor, PA: Templeton Foundation Press, 2001).

8. The various costs associated with crime are discussed in M. Cohen, ed., *The Costs of Crime and Justice* (New York: Routledge, 2005), and J. Roman, T. Dunworth, and K. Marsh, eds., *Cost-Benefit Analysis and Crime Control* (Washington, DC: Urban Institute Press, 2010).

4. PUNISHMENT, RETRIBUTION, AND SHAME

1. The concept of deterrence in criminal justice is discussed in D. M. Kennedy's *Deterrence and Crime Prevention: Reconsidering the Prospect of Sanction* (New York: Routledge, 2009).

2. Discussion of the concept of retribution can be found in M. Moore, "The Moral Worth of Retribution," in *Punishment and Rehabilitation*, ed. J. Murphy, 3rd ed., 94–130 (Belmont, CA: Wadsworth, 1995), and A. von Hirsch, "Penal Theories," in *The Handbook of Crime and Punishment*, ed. M. Tonry, 659–82 (New York: Oxford University Press, 1998).

3. Diverse views of the role of punishment are available in P. Bean, *Punishment: A Philosophical and Criminological Inquiry* (New York: John Wiley, 1982); G. Ezorsky, ed., *Philosophical Perspectives on Punishment* (Albany: State University of New York Press, 1972); H. Hart, *Punishment and Responsibility: Essays in the Philosophy of Law* (New York: Oxford University Press, 1968); and M. Tunick, *Punishment: Theory and Practice* (Berkeley: University of California Press, 1992).

4. M. Roth discusses the history of crime and punishment, including the law of talion, in *An Eye for an Eye: A Global History of Crime and Punishment* (London: Reaktion, 2014).

5. These excerpts are from Exodus 21:22–25, Deuteronomy 19:16–21, and Leviticus 24:17–21.

6. The passage may be found at Qur'an 5:45.

7. M. Alexander discusses the role of race in criminal justice and, especially, incarceration in *The New Jim Crow: Mass Incarceration in the Age of Colorblindness* (New York: New Press, 2012). J. Travis, B. Western, and S. Redburn, eds., *The Growth of Incarceration in the United States: Exploring Causes and Consequences* (Washington, DC: National Academies Press, 2014), includes a detailed analysis of incarceration trends and racial correlates. M. Mauer's *The Changing Racial Dynamics of Women's Incarceration* (Washington, DC: Sentencing Project, 2013) examines racial disparities in women's incarceration rates.

8. Office of Justice Programs, "Racial Profiling and Traffic Stops," National Institute of Justice, January 10, 2013, http://www.nij.gov/topics/law-enforcement/legitimacy/pages/traffic-stops.aspx; J. MacDonald, J. Arkes, N. Nicosia, and R. Pacula, "Decomposing Racial Disparities in Prison and Drug Treatment Commitments for Criminal Offenders in California," *Journal of Legal Studies* 43 (2014): 155–87; Alexander, *New Jim Crow,* 197.

9. C. Spohn summarizes debates about sentencing guidelines, trends, and reforms in *How Do Judges Decide? The Search for Fairness and Justice in Punishment,* 2nd ed. (Thousand Oaks, CA: Sage, 2009).

10. For the act see 18 U.S.C. §§ 3551–3626 and 28 U.S.C. §§ 991–98.

11. C. Kidialis, "Police: Man Linked to Child Death Had Abandoned Pregnant Teen, Toddler," *Las Vegas Review-Journal,* April 8, 2015, http://www.reviewjournal.com/news/las-vegas/police-man-linked-child-death-had-abandoned-pregnant-teen-toddler.

12. For this discussion I am indebted to discussions of the death penalty in R. Baird and S. Rosenbaum, eds., *Punishment and the Death Penalty: The Current Debate* (Prometheus, 1995); H. Bedeau and P. Cassell, eds., *Debating the Death Penalty: Should America Have Capital Punishment? The Experts from Both Sides Make Their Case* (New York: Oxford University Press, 2004); R. Hood and C. Hoyle, *The Death Penalty: A Worldwide Perspective,* 5th ed. (New York: Oxford University Press, 2015); R. Paternoster, *Capital Punishment in America* (New York: Lexington, 1991); and S. Turow, *Ultimate Punishment: A Lawyer's Reflections on Dealing with the Death Penalty* (New York: Picador, 2003).

13. U.S. v. Jackson, 390 U.S. 570 (1968); Witherspoon v. Illinois, 391 U.S. 510 (1968).

14. Furman v. Georgia, 408 U.S. 238 (1972).

15. Exodus 21:12–17, 23–25, 28–29.

16. Exodus 22:18–20.

17. Leviticus 20:2, 10–16, 27.

18. Thorsten Sellin's classic discussion appears in his work *The Death Penalty* (Philadelphia: American Law Institute, 1959).

19. Discussions of the deterrence value of the death penalty appear in W. Bailey and R. Peterson, "Capital Punishment, Homicide, and Deterrence: An

Assessment of the Evidence and Extension to Female Homicide," in *Homicide: A Sourcebook of Social Research,* ed. M. Smith and M. Zahn, 257–76 (Thousand Oaks, CA: Sage, 1999); I. Ehrlich, "The Deterrent Effect of Capital Punishment: A Question of Life and Death," *American Economic Review* 65 (1975): 397–417; L. Klein, B. Forst, and V. Filatov, "The Deterrent Effect of Capital Punishment: An Assessment of the Estimates," in *Deterrence and Incapacitation: Estimating the Effects of Criminal Sanctions on Crime Rates,* ed. A. Blumstein, J. Cohen, and D. Nagin, 336–60 (Washington, DC: National Academy of Sciences, 1978); R. Peterson and W. Bailey, "Murder and Capital Punishment in the Evolving Context of the Post-*Furman* Era," *Social Forces* 66 (1988): 774–807; F. Zimring and G. Hawkins, *Capital Punishment and the American Agenda* (New York: Cambridge University Press, 1986).

20. Discussion of discrimination in death sentences appears in W. Bowers and G. Pierce, "Arbitrariness and Discrimination Under Post-*Furman* Capital Statutes," *Crime & Delinquency* 26 (1980): 563–632; M. Radelet, L. Hugo, and A. Bedeau, *In Spite of Innocence: Erroneous Convictions in Capital Cases* (Boston: Northeastern University Press, 1992); and S. Gross and R. Mauro, "Patterns of Death: An Analysis of Racial Disparities in Capital Sentencing and Homicide Investigation," *Stanford Law Review* 37 (1984): 27–153. See also S. Arkin, "Discrimination and Arbitrariness in Capital Punishment: An Analysis of Post-*Furman* Cases in Dade County Florida, 1973–1976," *Stanford Law Review* 33 (1980): 75–101; D. Baldus, C. Pulaski, and G. Woodworth, *Equal Justice and the Death Penalty* (Boston: Northeastern University Press, 1990); W. Bowers, "The Pervasiveness of Arbitrariness and Discrimination Under Post-*Furman* Capital Statutes," *Journal of Criminal Law and Criminology* 74 (1983): 1067–1100.

21. Information about the Innocence Project is available at http://www .cardozo.yu.edu/innocenceproject. Information about the Center on Wrongful Convictions is available at http://www.law.northwestern.edu /legalclinic/wrongfulconvictions/. Data from the Death Penalty Information Center are available at http://www.deathpenaltyinfo.org/.

22. See U.S. Department of Justice, Office of Public Affairs, "Detroit Area Doctor Sentenced to 45 Years in Prison for Providing Medically Unnecessary Chemotherapy to Patients," July 10, 2015, http://www.justice .gov/opa/pr/detroit-area-doctor-sentenced-45-years-prison-providing -medically-unnecessary-chemotherapy, and Robert Allen, "Cancer Doctor Sentenced to 45 Years for 'Horrific' Fraud," reprinted from *Detroit Free Press* in *USA Today,* July 11, 2015, http://www.usatoday.com/story/news /nation/2015/07/10/cancer-doctor-sentenced-years-horrific-fraud/29996107/.

23. Cases involving police misconduct include A. Baker and J. McGinty, "NYPD Confidential," *New York Times,* March 26, 2010, http://www.nytimes .com/2010/03/28/nyregion/28iab.html?hp&_r=1; U.S. Department of Justice, "Former Memphis Police Officer Sentenced for Civil Rights Violations,"

September 13, 2007, http://www.justice.gov/archive/opa/pr/2007/Septem
ber/07_crt_715.html; C. Arnold, "Steven Rios Seeks New Trial for 2004
Murder of MU Student," *Columbia Missourian,* April 9, 2011, http://www
.columbiamissourian.com/news/local/steven-rios-seeks-new-trial-for
-murder-of-mu-student/article_1cea6d2d-1eec-5f83-9883-ab198ab52d81
.html; N. Flake, "Ex-CPD Officer Tindall Convicted of Bank Robbery," *Cou-
rier* (Houston), March 11, 2010, http://www.yourhoustonnews.com/courier
/news/ex-cpd-officer-tindall-convicted-of-bank-robbery/article_f9d126fa
-5e11-5037-ba0e-c7ef781d0532.html; M. Kent, "Former Chickasaw Police
Officer Convicted of Raping Stepdaughter Found Dead," *Press-Register*
(Montgomery, AL), February 25, 2010, http://blog.al.com/live/2010/02/former
_chickasaw_police_office_1.html. See also K. Flynn, "Police Officer Facing
Disciplinary Charges Commits Suicide," *New York Times,* September 25,
1999, http://www.nytimes.com/1999/09/25/nyregion/police-officer-facing
-disciplinary-charges-commits-suicide.html?pagewanted=1; T. Haydon,
"Former Woodbridge Cop Convicted a Third Time for Sex Assault," *NJ
Advance Media,* September 14, 2012, http://www.nj.com/middlesex/index
.ssf/2012/09/former_woodbridge_cop_convicte.html; L. Keene, "205-Year
Term for Former West Sac Cop," *Davis (CA) Enterprise,* April 6, 2014, http://
www.davisenterprise.com/local-news/crime-fire-courts/205-year-prison
-term-for-former-west-sac-cop/; I. MacDougall, "Providence Detective Sentenced in Police Drug Case," *Telegram & Gazette* (Worcester, MA), February 18, 2011, http://www.telegram.com/article/20110218/NEWS/102180494;
J. Treaster, "Convicted Police Officer Receives a Sentence of at Least 11
Years," *New York Times,* July 12, 1994, http://www.nytimes.com/1994/07/12
/us/convicted-police-officer-receives-a-sentence-of-at-least-11-years.html
?pagewanted=1.

24. M. McKinney, "RI Supreme Court Upholds Officer's Rape Conviction,"
Providence (RI) Journal, June 27, 2013, http://www.providencejournal.com
/article/20130627/News/306279886; A. Milkovits, "Former North Providence
Police Chief Heads Back to Jail," *Providence Journal,* July 7, 2015, http://
www.providencejournal.com/article/20150707/NEWS/150709511; A. Milkovits, "Ex-Pawtucket Cop Sentenced to Prison in Assault, Attempted Stran-
gulation of Girlfriend," *Providence Journal,* November 19, 2014, http://www
.providencejournal.com/article/20141119/NEWS/311199932; K. Mulvaney,
"Ex-North Providence Police Sgt. Ciresi Seeks Early Release," *Providence
Journal,* May 12, 2014, http://www.providencejournal.com/article/20140512
/News/305129980.

25. Salvatore Maddi's work on hardiness is summarized in *Hardiness: Turning
Stressful Circumstances into Resilient Growth* (New York: Springer, 2013).

26. A. Duckworth, *Grit: The Power of Passion and Perseverance* (New York: Scrib-
ner, 2016).

5. REDEMPTION AND HOPE

1. Compelling recidivism data are presented in a U.S. Department of Justice study, M. Durose, A. Cooper, and H. Snyder, *Recidivism of Prisoners Released in 30 States in 2005: Patterns from 2005 to 2010,* April 2014, http://www.bjs .gov/index.cfm?ty=pbdetail&iid=4986. See also E. Latessa, S. Listwan, and D. Koetzle, *What Works (and Doesn't) in Reducing Recidivism* (Waltham, MA: Anderson, 2014).

2. Joan Petersilia provides an informative overview of reentry challenges faced by inmates released on parole in *When Prisoners Come Home: Parole and Prisoner Reentry* (New York: Oxford University Press, 2003).

3. The effectiveness of prison-based programs is discussed in D. Andrews et al., "Does Correctional Treatment Work? A Psychologically Informed Meta-analysis," *Criminology* 28 (1990): 369–404; D. Antonowicz and R. Ross, "Essential Components of Successful Rehabilitation Programs for Offenders," *International Journal of Offender Therapy* 38 (1994): 97–104; F. Cullen and P. Gendreau, "The Effectiveness of Correctional Rehabilitation: Reconsidering the 'Nothing Works' Debate," in *The American Prison: Issues in Research and Policy,* ed. L. Goodstein and D. MacKenzie, 23–44 (New York: Plenum, 1989); G. Gaes, "Correctional Treatment," in *The Handbook of Crime and Punishment,* ed. M. Tonry, 712–38 (New York: Oxford University Press, 1998); P. Gendreau and R. Ross, "Revivification of Rehabilitation: Evidence from the 1980s," *Justice Quarterly* 4 (1987): 349–407; S. Hodgins and R. Muller-Isberner, eds., *Violence, Crime, and Mentally Disordered Offenders: Concepts and Methods for Effective Treatment and Prevention* (Chichester, UK: Wiley, 2000); F. Loesel, "Effective Correctional Programming: What Empirical Research Tells and What It Doesn't," *Forum on Corrections Research* 8 (1996): 33–37; J. McGuire, ed., *What Works? Reducing Reoffending* (Chichester, UK: Wiley, 1995); and T. Palmer, *The Re-Emergence of Correctional Intervention* (Newbury Park, CA: Sage, 1992).

4. The names of Rhode Island's prisons are a bit misleading. Its Maximum Security prison is less secure than its High Security prison because the Maximum Security facility is much older. The state corrections department opted to retain the name of the latter prison after the newer High Security prison was built.

5. C. Snyder summarizes his ideas about hope in *The Psychology of Hope: You Can Get There from Here* (New York: Free Press, 1994).

6. Kaye Herth's ideas about hope appear in C. Farran, K. Herth, and J. Popovich, *Hope and Hopelessness: Critical Clinical Constructs* (Thousand Oaks, CA: Sage, 1995).

7. Common challenges faced by female offenders are discussed in M. Cheney-Lind and L. Pasko, *The Female Offender: Girls, Women, and Crime,* 3rd ed. (Thousand Oaks, CA: Sage, 2013).

8. A good book about the stages-of-change model is J. Prochaska, J. Norcross, and C. DiClemente, *Changing for Good: A Revolutionary Six-Stage Program for Overcoming Bad Habits and Moving Your Life Positively Forward* (New York: HarperCollins, 2006).

9. W. Miller and S. Rollnick provide a comprehensive overview of motivational interviewing in *Motivational Interviewing: Helping People Change* (New York: Guilford, 2013).

10. J. Bowker, *World Religions: The Great Faiths Explored and Explained* (London: DK Publishing, 2006).

11. A. Provan, "There's More to Justice Than Prison," *Providence (RI) Phoenix,* April 15–21, 2005, http://www.providencephoenix.com/features/top/multi /documents/04613701.asp.

12. S. Flynn, "Changing Sides: Former Law Breaker Will Study to Be a Lawyer," *Newport Daily News,* April 3–4, 2010, http://opendoorsri.org/node/575.

13. Ibid.

14. Noah Kilroy, "A Letter from Noah Kilroy," May 20, 2013, Transcending Through Education Foundation, https://transcendingthrougheducation .wordpress.com/2013/05/20/a-long-way-from-prison-noah-kilroy-graduates -rwu-school-of-law/.

6. THE PURSUIT OF JUSTICE

1. Useful overviews of restorative justice appear in J. Braithwaite, "Restorative Justice," in *The Handbook of Crime and Punishment,* ed. M. Tonry, 323–44 (New York: Oxford University Press, 1998); J. Braithwaite, *Restorative Justice and Responsive Regulation* (New York: Oxford University Press, 2002); L. Kurki, "Restorative and Community Justice in the United States," in *Crime and Justice: A Review of the Research,* ed. M. Tonry, 235–303 (Chicago: University of Chicago Press, 2000); M. Umbreit and M. Armour, *Restorative Justice Dialogue: An Essential Guide for Research and Practice* (New York: Springer, 2011); D. Van Ness and K. Strong, *Restoring Justice: An Introduction to Restorative Justice,* 5th ed. (New York: Routledge, 2015); and K. van Wormer and L. Walker, eds., *Restorative Justice Today: Practical Applications* (Thousand Oaks, CA: Sage, 2013).

2. Letter by Supriya Deas, which appeared in M. Tamminga, "Dona Cadman to Speak Alongside Mother of Her Son's Killer," *Langley (BC) Times,* October 24, 2012, and was incorporated in the 2013 annual report of the Victim Offender Mediation program sponsored by the Community Justice Initiatives Association in British Columbia, Canada, http://www.cjibc.org /vomp_stories.

3. For information about SCORE see its flyer at http://www.doc.ri.gov /documents/media/S.C.O.R.E.%20Program%20Brochure%20-%20web.pdf.

4. For information about the Level of Service Inventory—Revised, see D. Andrews and J. Bonta, "LSI-R: Level of Service Inventory—Revised," product overview, Multi-Health Systems, Inc., http://www.mhs.com/product .aspx?gr=saf&id=overview&prod=lsi-r.

5. J. Paris provides a succinct overview of antisocial personality disorder in *A Concise Guide to Personality Disorders* (Washington, DC: American Psychological Association, 2015).

6. American Psychiatric Association, *Diagnostic and Statistical Manual of Mental Disorders (DSM-5)*, 5th ed. (Washington, DC: American Psychiatric Association, 2013).

7. For discussions of evidence that antisocial personality disorder may have an organic, biological base, see T. Lewis, "Blame the Brain: Why Psychopaths Lack Empathy," *livescience*, September 24, 2013, http://www.live science.com/39904-why-psychopaths-lack-empathy.html. See also J. Decety, C. Chen, C. Harenski, and K. Kiehl, "An fMRI Study of Affective Perspective Taking in Individuals with Psychopathy: Imagining Another in Pain Does Not Evoke Empathy," *Frontiers in Human Neuroscience*, September 24, 2013, http://journal.frontiersin.org/article/10.3389/fnhum.2013.00489/full.

8. J. Braithwaite discusses the concept of reintegrative shaming in *Restorative Justice and Responsive Regulation* (New York: Oxford University Press, 2002).

9. Braithwaite, *Restorative Justice and Responsive Regulation*.

10. G. Paulson provides a comprehensive overview of the deinstitutionalization movement in *Closing the Asylums: Causes and Consequences of the Deinstitutionalization Movement* (Jefferson, NC: McFarland, 2012). Also see E. Torrey, *Out of the Shadows: Confronting America's Mental Illness Crisis* (New York: John Wiley, 1997).

11. Data on inmates with major mental illness can be found in P. Ditton, *Mental Health and Treatment of Inmates and Probationers* (Washington, DC: Department of Justice, Bureau of Justice Statistics, 1999); D. James and L. Glaze, *Mental Health Problems of Prison and Jail Inmates* (Washington, DC: Department of Justice, Bureau of Justice Statistics, 2006); K. Kim, M. Becker-Cohen, and M. Serakos, *The Processing and Treatment of Mentally Ill Persons in the Criminal Justice System: A Scan of Practice and Background Analysis* (Washington, DC: Urban Institute, 2015); and H. Steadman, S. Fabisiak, J. Dvoskin, and E. Holohean, "A Survey of Mental Disability Among State Prison Inmates," *Hospital and Community Psychiatry* 38 (1989): 1086–90.

12. The impact of solitary confinement on inmates' mental health is explored in H. Andersen et al., "A Longitudinal Study of Prisoners on Remand: Repeated Measures of Psychopathology in the Initial Phase of Solitary Versus Nonsolitary Confinement," *International Journal of Law and Psychiatry* 26 (2003): 165–77; J. Coid et al., "Psychiatric Morbidity in Prisoners and Solitary Cellular Confinement, I: Disciplinary Segregation," *Journal of Forensic Psychiatry and Psychology*, 14 (2003): 298–319; C. Haney, "Mental Health Issues

in Long-Term Solitary and Supermax Confinement," *Crime & Delinquency* 49 (2003): 124–56; F. Kaba et al., "Solitary Confinement and Risk of Self-Harm Among Jail Inmates," *American Journal of Public Health* 104 (2014): 442–47; D. Lovell, "Patterns of Disturbed Behavior in a Supermax Prison," *Criminal Justice and Behavior* 35 (2008): 985–1004; J. Metzner and J. Fellner, "Solitary Confinement and Mental Illness and U.S. Prisons," *Journal of the American Academy of Psychiatry and the Law* 38 (2010): 104–8; J. Pizarro and V. Stenius, "Supermax Prisons: Their Rise, Current Practices, and Effect on Inmates," *Prison Journal* 84 (2004): 248–64; J. Roberts and R. Gebotys, "Prisoners of Isolation: Research on the Effectiveness of Prison Segregation," *Canadian Journal of Criminology and Criminal Justice* 43 (2001): 85–98; and P. Smith, "The Effects of Solitary Confinement on Prison Inmates: A Brief History and Review of the Literature," *Crime and Justice* 34 (2006): 441–528.

13. "Solitary Confinement Should Be Banned in Most Cases, UN Expert Says," UN News Center, October 18, 2011, https://www.un.org/apps/news/story .asp?NewsID=40097.

14. W. Malinowski, "Emotions Boil Over as Former R.I. Corrections Officer Botas Sentenced to Prison for Inmate Assaults," *Providence Journal,* July 19, 2013, http://www.providencejournal.com/breaking-news/content/20130718 -emotions-boil-over-as-former-r.i.-corrections-officer-botas-sentenced-to -prison-for-inmate-assaults.ece.

15. See S. Lange, "Former Corrections Officer Sent to Prison," *WNEP News,* September 18, 2015, http://wnep.com/2015/09/18/former-corrections-officer -sent-to-prison/; C. Campbell, "Two Corrections Officers Sentenced in BGF Jail Conspiracy," *Baltimore Sun,* March 12, 2015, http://www.baltimoresun .com/news/maryland/crime/blog/bs-md-ci-corrections-officers-sentenced -20150312-story.html; S. Visser, "Former Georgia Prison Guards Get Sentences of Their Own," *Atlanta Journal-Constitution,* December 4, 2014, http:// www.ajc.com/news/news/state-regional-govt-politics/former-georgia -prison-guards-get-sentences-of-thei/njLtJ/; W. Bigham, "Chino Prison Guard Sentenced to Prison in Inmate Assaults," *Daily Bulletin* (Inland Valley, CA), June 7, 2010, http://www.dailybulletin.com/general-news/20100 607/chino-prison-guard-sentenced-to-prison-in-inmate-assaults; E. Smith, "Brett Robinson, Jail Worker Who Had Sex with Inmate, Gets 3 Years in Prison," *(Portland) Oregonian,* June 2, 2015, http://www.oregonlive.com /hillsboro/index.ssf/2015/06/brett_robinson_jail_worker_who.html.

16. Estelle v. Gamble, 429 U.S. 97 (1976).

17. S. Dolovich, "Cruelty, Prison Conditions, and the Eighth Amendment," *New York University Law Review* 84 (2009): 881–979.

18. Holt v. Sarver, 300 F. Supp. 825 (E.D. Ark., 1969); 309 F. Supp 362 (1970), aff'd. 442 F.2d 304 (8th Cir. 1974).

19. Hutto v. Finney, 437 U.S. 678 (1978); Rhodes v. Chapman, 452 U.S. 337 (1981); Wilson v. Seiter, 501 U.S. 294 (1991); Helling v. McKinney, 509 U.S. 25 (1993);

Whitley v. Albers, 475 U.S. 312 (1986); and Hudson v. McMillian, 503 U.S. 1 (1991). See also Farmer v. Brennan, 511 U.S. 825 (1994). Dolovich provides a comprehensive overview of Eighth Amendment violations of inmates' rights in "Cruelty, Prison Conditions, and the Eighth Amendment."

20. The National Research Council study can be found in J. Travis, B. Western, and S. Redburn, eds., *The Growth of Incarceration in the United States: Exploring Causes and Consequences* (Washington, DC: National Academies Press, 2014); it provides an in-depth overview of incarceration rates and trends. The U.S. Justice Department's efforts to reduce the federal prison population are discussed in S. Horwitz, "Justice Department Set to Free 6,000 Prisoners, Largest One-Time Release," *Washington Post,* October 6, 2015, https://www.washingtonpost.com/world/national-security/justice-depart ment-about-to-free-6000-prisoners-largest-one-time-release/2015/10/06 /961f4c9a-6ba2-11e5-aa5b-f78a98956699_story.html. On the reduction of California's prison population, see S. Moore, "Court Orders California to Cut Prison Population," *New York Times,* February 9, 2009, http://www.nytimes .com/2009/02/10/us/10prison.html?_r=0, and M. Gutierrez, "California Prisons Have Released 2,700 Inmates Under Prop. 47," *San Francisco Chronicle,* March 6, 2015, http://www.sfgate.com/crime/article/California-prisons -have-released-2-700-inmates-6117826.php.

21. Travis, Western, and Redburn, *Growth of Incarceration in the United States.*

22. Ibid.

23. Ibid.

24. Karl Popper, *Of Clouds and Clocks: An Approach to the Problem of Rationality and the Freedom of Man* (St. Louis: Washington University, 1966), 207–8.